Europe's Experimental Union

Rethinking integration

Brigid Laffan, Rory O'Donnell and Michael Smith

London and New York

First published 2000
by Routledge
11 New Fetter Lane, London EC4P 4EE

Simultaneously published in the USA and Canada
by Routledge
29 West 35th Street, New York, NY 10001

Routledge is an imprint of the Taylor & Francis Group

Typeset in Baskerville by Keystroke, Jacaranda Lodge, Wolverhampton
Printed and bound in Great Britain by Biddles Ltd, Guildford and King's Lynn

British Library Cataloguing in Publication Data
A catalogue record for this book is available from the British Library

Library of Congress Cataloging in Publication Data
Laffan, Brigid.
    Europe's experimental union: rethinking integration / Brigid
Laffan, Rory O'Donnell, and Michael Smith.
    Includes bibliographical references.
    1. European Union. 2. Europe – Economic integration.
I. O'Donnell, Rory. II. Smith, Michael. III. Title.
JN30.L34   1999
341.242′2 – dc21
99–22357

ISBN 0 415 10260 X (hbk)
ISBN 0 415 10261 8 (pbk)

Contents

Conclusions   187

9 A new model of internationalisation   189

Tables

Preface

This volume was written for fellow analysts of integration but it became surprisingly topical as Europe's political leaders began to grapple with the nature and purpose of the Union in the light of enlargement, the single currency and political and popular disenchantment with the existing structures and practices. In this volume, we attempt to capture the characteristics of the European Union as an economic and political order, given its growing salience in the European and global environment.

The volume arose from a desire to bring a multidisciplinary approach to bear on the Union and to go beyond the sterile 'either/or' debates on the nature of integration. All three authors agreed on the historical contingency of integration, on the ties and tensions that animate the development of the Union and on the need to explore the re-configuration of territory, identity and function in Europe. The volume grapples with the 'betweenness' of the Union and its role in an unsettled Europe. We delve into the distinctiveness of the Union and its mode of governance in search of ways of analysing it and in search of categories to express its distinctiveness. The dual perspective of strength/weakness – arising from the examination of the Union in terms of traditional international organisation and classical statehood – runs through the volume. It leads us to the conclusion that the Union is not evolving towards a federal superstate but is an arena of deep economic integration governed by a prismatic polity characterised by innovation, experimentation, pragmatism, decentralisation and delegation. The system operates on the basis of embedding the national in the European and the European in the national rather than the zero-sum language of supercession characteristic of classical federalism or state sovereignty. In the years ahead the EU faces the triple challenge of implementing the single currency project, enlarging to its east and south and democratising its internationalised governance structures. As the EU approaches these challenges, it is imperative that analysts of integration guard against misconceived theoretical positions and the interpretative pitfalls that face us all in grappling with the dynamics of European integration.

The book evolved through a series of dialogues among the authors about the framework and its application to different aspects of the Union. A considerable amount of time was spent arguing about terminology and the conceptual vocabulary necessary for the task of characterising the Union. We all enjoyed the conversations, which took place on two continents and in different EU states, and which produced this book. We all found the interdisciplinary focus challenging but immensely rewarding. It will be a bonus if our approach in this volume contributes to the understanding of governance in the Union, a debate that is not just of academic interest, but has a bearing on how the system consolidates over the next thirty years. There is still much to play for.

Brigid Laffan
Rory O'Donnell
Michael Smith
Dublin and Loughborough, June 1999

Acknowledgements

We would like to thank Susan Neilson and Jennifer Brown for their expert work on the manuscript. We are grateful also to our editor at Routledge, Victoria Smith, for her patience and support. Finally, a special thanks to Paul Gillespie, foreign editor of the *Irish Times*, whose subtle analysis of the EU was a corrective against misconceived theoretical positions.

Abbreviations

CAP	Common Agricultural Policy
CE	Communauté Européenne
CEC	Council of the European Community
CEN	European Committee for Standardisation
CENELEC	European Committee for Electrotechnical Standardisation
CFSP	Common Foreign and Security Policy
CMEA	Council for Mutual Economic Assistance
COMETT	Community Action Programme for Education and Training for Technology
COREPER	Committee of Permanent Representatives
COSAC	Conference of European Affairs Committees
CSCE	Conference on Security and Cooperation in Europe
CSF	Community Support Framework
CSU	Bavarian Christian Social Union
DG	Directorate-General
DM	Deutschmark
EC	European Community
ECB	European Central Bank
ECJ	European Court of Justice
ECOFIN	Economic and Finance Council of Ministers
EEA	European Economic Area
EEC	European Economic Community
EFTA	European Free Trade Area
EMEA	European Agency for the Evaluation of Medicinal Products
EMS	European Monetary System
EMU	Economic and Monetary Union
EP	European Parliament
EPC	European Political Cooperation
ERASMUS	European Community Action Scheme for the Mobility of University Students
ERDF	European Regional Development Fund
ERM	Exchange Rate Mechanism
ESF	European Social Fund

ETUC	European Trade Union Confederation
EU	European Union
FDI	foreign direct investment
GATT	General Agreement on Tariffs and Trade
GDP	gross domestic product
GSM	Global System for Mobile Communications
HDTV	high definition television
ICP	inter-university cooperation programme
IGC	intergovernmental conference
ILO	International Labour Organisation
ISO	International Standards Organisation
IPE	international political economy
JHA	Justice and Home Affairs
LINGUA	Promotion of the Teaching and Learning of Foreign Languages in the EU
MAAs	mergers, acquisitions and alliances
NAFTA	North American Free Trade Area
NATO	North Atlantic Treaty Organisation
NTB	non-tariff barriers
OECD	Organisation for Economic Cooperation and Development
OSCE	Organisation for Security and Cooperation in Europe
PETRA	Partnership between Education and Training
QMV	qualified majority voting
R&D	research and development
SEA	Single European Act
SEM	Single European Market
SME	Small and Medium Sized Enterprises
SMP	Single Market Programme
SPD	German Social Democratic Party
TENs	Trans-European Networks
TEU	Treaty on European Union
UK	United Kingdom
UN	United Nations
UNICE	Union of Industrial and Employers' Confederation of Europe
US	United States
USSR	Union of Soviet Socialist Republics
WEU	Western European Union
WTO	World Trade Organisation

Introduction

1 Unsettled Europe

Introduction

The starting point of the analysis in this book is the perception that changes in economic regulation, in mechanisms of governance and in the wider European order, have set in train complex and interconnected processes of institutional adaptation and regime change in Europe since the late 1980s. Such changes have been radical and, in many cases, disconcerting, not least because they have had major implications for the myriad west European institutions that mushroomed in the post-Second World War period. Gone are the shared assumptions and comfortable certainties of a divided Europe, a divided Germany, bloc confrontation and a neatly delineated western Europe. Absorbed with a demanding internal agenda, but with no realistic prospect of insulating itself from broader change, the EU has had to raise its sights to the needs of its continental environment. Events since 1989 also remind us that diversity, division and conflict have characterised the European order for much of its past, and that the dynamics of European integration are interwoven with the wider dynamics of continental and global change. 'Europe' has thus become a powerful and contested value in political discourse about the future continental order, and 'European integration' has shared in this unsettling analytical and policy milieu. We are thus confronted not only with an unsettled Europe, but also with unsettled questions of concepts and analysis.

Unsettled Europe

In the early 1980s, institutional paralysis, the effects of recession, a divergence of economic policies and a contentious budgetary debate, prevented the European Community from confronting a series of pressing issues and problems. There appeared to be little or no collective purpose among member states about the 'internal' development of the Community, and at the same time there were often peremptory challenges from the outside world, for example through the assertive policies of Reaganism and the tensions of the 'New Cold War'. Yet, even while scholars of integration were alluding to 'Eurosclerosis', to stagnation and to the possible disintegration of the EC, political and economic forces were gathering, which would, by the mid-1980s, lead to a revival in the fortunes of the EC and a resurgence of formal integration among the member states. Significantly, these new or revived forces brought together the political economy of integration, the changing politics of Europe and changes in the mechanisms of governance; they also created close links between the European Community processes and those of the wider Europe, through the uncertainties of the post-Cold War world and the possibility of enlargement, whilst they also engaged with the broader development of the international political economy and the coexisting trends towards regionalisation and globalisation.

In the area of political economy, the key development during the late 1980s was the programme for completion of the Single European Market (SEM), also known as the '1992' programme. But this programme was not simply one of market integration; it also encompassed a wide-ranging legislative agenda, and it undeniably contributed to a perception that the EC would muster increasing political influence. The late 1980s thus saw a move, largely inspired by the SEM, from 'Eurosclerosis' to 'Europhoria'. The perception that significant movement or progress was impossible, was replaced in many quarters by a feeling that almost anything was possible. Both perceptions, of course, were inaccurate: more progress was possible in the early 1980s than might have been expected, and less was possible after the late 1980s than might have been hoped.

One objective of the 1992 programme was also to enhance the competitiveness of the west European economies by strengthening market integration in goods, services, capital and the free movement of labour. At one level, this was a response to perceptions of European frailties in the light of global competition, particularly from the United States and Japan; thus, the progress of the SEM was again linked to perceptions of the EC's potential global role. At another level, the breadth and depth of internal market regulation led to a Europeanisation of public policy in important areas, with the result that few fields of domestic policy in EU member states are today without a European dimension, however limited and circumscribed. European regulation has thus seeped into the nooks and crannies of the state, and has acted as a catalyst in wide-ranging restructuring both of the economic and of the political contexts. One important consequence of this process was the mobilisation of a growing range of political and economic actors with the aim of influencing policy at the European level.

Alongside the 1992 programme went an intensive process of constitution-building, which has changed the decision-rules governing the Union and has greatly expanded its policy remit. The member states have convened six intergovernmental conferences (IGCs) on treaty reform since the decision to establish the European Coal and Steel Community in 1950, but four of these have taken place since 1985. This points to the unprecedented nature of the current wave of treaty change in the Union. This period of treaty-making has altered the institutional dynamics of the Union's policy process, added new principles which govern the policy process, and greatly expanded the policy remit of the Union. The cumulative process of reform and task-expansion brought the Union into core areas of state activity – monetary policy, foreign and security policy, justice and home affairs. Not surprisingly, this series of encroachments has led to considerable if patchy resistance on the part of national authorities, unsettled by the EU's new assertiveness. Constitution building in the Union, which has developed in a contested and incremental manner, has thus led to a highly fragmented, procedurally complex, heavily bargained system of public policy-making.

This, however, has not been a simple linear process of advance in European integration. The robustness of the EU was severely tested in 1992 when the Danish electorate voted against the Treaty of European Union (TEU) and the Exchange Rate Mechanism (ERM) collapsed; these two events produced a crisis of confidence that led many to question the legitimacy of the 'European project', and some to argue for the renationalisation of certain policy areas. National parliaments and national courts have become ever more sensitive to changes in the Union's reach and have demanded increasing involvement in the EU as it has touched areas of policy defined as vital national interests. This is part of a broader debate about how internationalised governance structures can be rendered accountable and legitimate (Dunn 1993; Dahl 1994).

The intensification of formal integration among the member states of the European Union is taking place against the backdrop of a profound transformation of the wider continent. The Soviet Union's retreat from empire ended the Cold War and its artificial division of Europe between east and west. The two parts of Europe are beginning the slow and tortuous process of overcoming the legacy of communism and division (Smith 1996a). Historic links between east and west are being reformed; *Mitteleuropa* is once again not just an 'imagined space' but has geographical, cultural and political meaning. Central Europe forms a transition zone, or 'middle zone' both geographically and culturally between the western political tradition and the one which evolved in Russia (Wandycz 1992; Schôpflin 1993). The former communist states, having found the freedom to determine their own futures, are refashioning their economies, and their political and legal systems. Forty years of communist rule and command economy left them with an outmoded industrial fabric, a pattern of trade oriented towards the Soviet Union and extensive ecological damage. Perhaps more damaging still was the destruction of civil society, the erosion of autonomous associations outside state control (Schôpflin 1993, p. 226). This accentuates the difficulty of establishing western-style liberal democracies with a clear commitment to universal rights and the rule of law.

For the west, and especially western Europe, the transformation of eastern Europe raises questions about the western model of integration, Europe's boundaries and European identity (Smith 1996a; Wallace 1997). Significantly, the enhanced status of the EU became linked in the early 1990s with the pressure for an end to division in Europe, through demands for enlargement to the east. The prospect of an eastern enlargement introduces additional pressures – constitutional, political and economic – to the Union's edifice, and may require profound changes in the integration model used so far to propel the Union. At the same time, enlargement to the east is linked to the increased weight of Germany in the European order in the wake of unification, and to the role a united Germany might play (Bulmer *et al.* 1996; Katzenstein 1997).

Profound change in Europe, both east and west, must be seen against a backdrop of increasing internationalisation, both in the political and in the economic domain. The international system is characterised by increasing interconnections and interdependence, which is driven by capital flows, technology, investment patterns, growing linkages between societies and more rapid dissemination of ideas. The acceleration of internationalisation in the 1990s has profound implications for political and economic order at the international, regional and national levels. It affects the reach of political agency and the relationship between public and private power. European integration has always implied a model of internationalisation but this is now challenged by a context of globalisation in which increased transnational integration and market/production structures arguably go beyond the forms of continental integration on which earlier European integration was based.

Europe is thus in the throes of change in its political order and economic system. The shifting dynamic of European integration outlined in this chapter has contributed to making the European Union a more meaningful economic and political space for its member states, their regions, external powers and economic actors both inside and outside the Union. A growing number of writers refer to a process of 'Europeanisation', which serves to 'make Europe a more significant political community and thereby European boundaries more relevant politically' (Ladrech 1994; Olsen 1995, p. 21; Tarrow 1995). The resurgence of formal integration and the collapse of the post-war order have disturbed and will continue to disturb economic structures and political arrangements both within and between the states of Europe. Questions of 'how much Europe', 'what kind of Europe', 'which Europe' are part of the national and European agendas of different states and their peoples. It is in this sense that we are confronted with a still unsettled Europe.

Unsettled analysis

Systemic transformation of the kind that has occurred in Europe during the 1990s provides opportunities for the analyst because 'Crises pry open the political scene, throwing traditional relationships into flux. Groups, institutions, and individuals are torn loose from their moorings, their assumptions their loyalties, their "cognitive road maps". Circumstances become less certain, and their solutions less obvious' (Gourevitch 1984, p. 99). At the same time, the types of change described above are unsettling for the analyst, since they demand new approaches and an awareness of the linkages between change in different but intersecting domains. It is thus not surprising that the 1990s have seen a sustained search for new approaches to the analysis both of the EU and of the new Europe.

The relaunching and refashioning of the integration project has been accompanied by a relaunching of enquiry into integration. The changing dynamics of European integration and its greater salience for political order have proved a major incentive to scholars in search of theoretical explanations of the process of European integration. Research on integration experienced a 'doldrums era' in the 1970s and 1980s when American social scientists lost interest in the phenomenon after the pathbreaking work of Haas, Lindberg, Schmitter and others (Caporaso and Keeler 1993); whether this stagnation was also true in European scholarship is a matter of debate. It is clear, though, that the pace and scope of change in Europe after the late 1980s, which took the scholarly community by surprise, raised a number of unresolved analytical issues about the dynamics of integration and re-opened the conceptual debate about European integration. On the one hand, the ambiguous and indeterminate nature of the Union continues to puzzle while at the same time acting as an incentive to scholarly engagement. On the other hand, the analysis of integration is no longer the preserve of a limited number of 'integration specialists' and Brussels watchers. Lawyers, political scientists and economists can no longer analyse a national system or a particular sector without some familiarity with the European Union. Similarly, the close linkages between events in the EU and the broader world political or economic systems mean that it cannot be treated as a sealed universe. As a result, there is a renewed incentive to bring together analysis from such intersecting areas as comparative politics, public policy, international relations and international political economy. The analytical challenge is of more than academic relevance, since it may have a bearing on the political, economic, cultural and institutional problems that confront the Union, and on substantive areas of negotiation or policy-making such as those connected with enlargement.

The burgeoning literature on European integration and on Europe more generally in the 1990s consequently differs in some important respects from earlier writing on integration. The new literature is characterised by a desire to go beyond disciplinary boundaries, by the use of new conceptual tools in the traditional disciplines and by a broadening of the range of disciplines analysing European integration. Hamm argues that 'Europe' is a challenge to the social sciences, that 'the European process is far too complex and has too many theoretical and practical implications as to be analysable adequately from a unidisciplinary perspective . . . the perspective must be holistic and the approach problem-oriented' (Hamm 1992, p. 15). As implied by the arguments in the previous section, many of the unsettled questions about European integration and about its location in the wider Europe lie at the borderline between different disciplines. Whilst the European integration process has traditionally attracted the attention of lawyers, economists and political scientists, its renaissance and its linkages with profound processes of change in Europe have increased the incentives for others to become involved. Thus, for example, one commentator has argued that

> it is impossible to talk of matters like the deregulation of European markets, taxation policy, federalism, common military organisation and nationalism without an understanding of the formation and organisation of the societies which will face changes in all these areas.
>
> (Bailey 1992, p. 3)

Likewise, scholars working in sociology and cultural studies have become aware of 'the symbolic boundaries and material borders which separate and unite, and their relationships with the facts and fancies of the EC' (Wilson and Smith 1993, p. 5) and of the forces that can lead Europeans to 'redefine their histories and cultural traditions, re-evaluate the importance and futures of their cities and regions, re-explore their attitudes towards race, ethnicity and nationality' (Wilson and Smith 1993). Insights drawn from sociology, anthropology and cultural studies provide a useful corrective to traditional economic, legal and political analyses of European integration, but at the same time they inevitably raise further unsettling questions, either about the nature of 'Europe' or about the role of the European integration project.

The approach adopted in this volume

The empirical and analytical shifts outlined above lead directly to the approach adopted here. Our first step is to explore the context within which the European integration project has unfolded during the 1990s. Ironically, this involves to some extent 'taking the emphasis off integration', in order to establish the context within which European integration is evolving. It also involves 'taking the emphasis off integration theory': in other words, we are concerned to establish the disciplinary approaches that can feed into and inform an analysis of the unresolved empirical and analytical questions posed above. The approach derives from the observation that most political, social and economic agents in Europe pursue a wide range of political, social, economic and cultural projects, not the project of European integration *per se*. A remarkable feature of the European integration project is the manner in which it has been grafted on to other projects such as peace, national rehabilitation, modernisation, liberalisation, deregulation and fiscal consolidation. There is also a European project in its own right, the proponents of which set out to alter and restructure relations between states and societies in Europe, and which grows out of the broader concern for legitimacy and citizenship in the post-Cold War era. It is the relation of these projects and practices to European integration that we wish to understand.

In exploring these intersecting projects, processes and approaches, we are guided by four analytic assumptions.

- First, we recognise the contingent nature of the integration process. Much of the observed European integration process may be contingent on the material, political and intellectual circumstances in which integration happens to take place. The trend line in the integration project is highly contingent on developments in the member states and in the wider international system.
- Second, we accept that integration need not be unidirectional. This contrasts with a view – common among economists and modernisation theorists in other disciplines – that integration is a one-way process reflecting the evolution from isolated and traditional economies and societies to internationally

engaged economies and, eventually, globalisation. Progress or regress of integration may be a residual in the play of much larger forces.

- Third, we recognise that there is an interaction between an 'inside-out' set of political and economic processes rooted in national societies or in European institutions, and an 'outside-in' set of processes emanating from the world political and economic arenas. It is precisely the fluidity and complexity of these interactions that creates central questions about the policy process and policy outcomes.
- Fourth, we recognise the need to analyse developments in the system over time: in other words to take account of the historical backdrop to developments in the 1990s and to use these as a means to evaluate the nature and extent of change and challenge.

Our approach in general can thus be described in terms not unlike those used by Peter Gourevitch in discussing the linkages between domestic and international forces:

> The international system is not only a consequence of domestic politics and structures but a cause of them. Economic relations and military pressures constrain an entire range of domestic behaviours, from policy decisions to political forms. International relations and domestic politics are therefore so interrelated that they should be analysed simultaneously, as wholes.
>
> (Gourevitch 1978, p. 911)

Whereas Gourevitch is concerned with tracing the impact of the international system on domestic politics and policy choices, the task here is to construct a framework for analysing the interplay of international, EU and national forces. A holistic approach to the study of integration requires this because the European Union is an arena of politics and a single market embedded in the wider international system.

In developing our argument, we make use of two particular conceptual devices. First, we identify the issues arising from the interaction of *territory, identity and function*. Whereas these factors are traditionally associated with the development of the nation state, we contend that, in the unsettled Europe of the late 1990s, they are more than simple categories: rather, they are expressions of problems that demand investigation, and their interaction is part of the fluid political and economic context with which we are confronted. A key argument in this volume is thus that the relationships between territory, identity and function are being redefined and reconfigured in contemporary Europe.

Our second conceptual focus is on *ties and tensions in the integration process*. Alongside the complex interaction of territory, identity and function, we identify four key areas in which the process of EU and wider European integration has thrown up particular contradictions: first, the tension between a union of states and a market; second, the tension between the polity and problem-solving arena; third, the tension between EU policy-making and multilevel policy-making; and finally, the tension between the EU universe and its global environment. In each of these areas, the process of integration is precisely the factor that creates or exacerbates the tensions and contradictions.

Our conceptual framework thus has three central elements: recognition of interconnectedness and contingency; awareness of complex relationships between territory, identity and function; and sensitivity to the ties and tensions emerging from the process of integration itself. These will form implicit organising devices for the treatment in Chapters 2–8, and will be the explicit focus of our argument in Chapter 9, where we propose a 'European model of internationalisation' as a means of evaluating changes in the late 1990s.

Part 1

Contexts

Part 1 of this volume establishes, in two ways, the broad framework approaches that mould and shape the European Union. First, it explores the concepts that have characterised debates in key areas of analysis. Second, it relates these concepts and approaches to the nature of change in Europe, and the challenges this has generated for the European Union. In doing so, it refers particularly to the first two elements in our framework for analysis: the recognition of inter-connectedness and contingency in processes of integration, and the importance of territory, identity and function.

Chapter 2 explores the changing nature of states and nations in contemporary Europe. Given the centrality of the nation state to political and economic order in Europe, any exploration of challenges to the EU must rest on an appreciation of just what the European nation state is becoming at the end of the twentieth century. Are nation states 'hollowing out' or are they adapting and adjusting to new pressures? How do we deal with issues of identity that may be seen as strengthening, transcending or subverting the nation state? Undoubtedly, many of the pressures on individual states emanate from changes in world politics and in the international political economy, and these are analysed in Chapters 3 and 4. In both of these contexts, the questioning of territory, identity and function takes place at the global level, but also in the context of a changing Europe, with highly significant implications for the status and functioning of the EU. Thus, in Chapter 3, we are concerned with the challenges posed by shifting definitions of statehood, power and institutions in world politics, and in Chapter 4, with the contrary tendencies towards regionalisation and globalisation as they have penetrated and been expressed by the EU.

2 European states and nations

Introduction

A central feature of the development of the European state system has been its malleability, adaptability and fluidity. The absolute monarchies of the eighteenth century were transformed into the industrial and national states of the nineteenth century, and into the welfare states of the twentieth century. Threats of hegemony and domination either by individual states or by coalitions were countered by balance of power politics and the development of diplomatic constraints, albeit with limitations and often considerable costs, as in the First and Second World Wars. The Cold War (see Chapter 3) can be seen as representing an interruption of a process that would have encompassed the whole of the continent, and the ending of the Cold War as posing the challenge of resuming such a process. In order to explore the impact of European integration on Europe's political and economic order, and to analyse the governance structures that are emerging in the European Union, it is thus necessary to have an understanding of changes to the form, functions and normative context of the state in Europe. What is the European nation state in the process of becoming at the end of the twentieth century? Just what is contained in the complex interrelationships of state, polity, economy and society at national level? These questions raise important issues about the intersection and interaction between change in the EU and at the level of the nation state, given the intimate links between the European integration process and the changing fortunes of European statehood.

The objective of this chapter is to analyse the changing nature of the state in the context of the three dimensions of statehood outlined in Chapter 1. Europe's nation states evolved on the basis of a relative congruence between bounded *territory* within which sovereignty was exercised, a collective *identity* arising from the dominance of nationalism and a set of *functions* – internal and external security, economic governance, the fostering of a social consensus and the maintenance of balance between different levels of government. It is the link between bounded territory, identity both in terms of politics and culture, and the array of functions performed by states that renders the nation state a resilient and powerful social organisation. According to Taylor, 'The real mark of this power is that it has become hard to imagine a world that is not parcelled up into separate national sovereignties. States as nation-states appear to be almost natural entities beyond the realm of political discourse' (Taylor 1993, p. 5). Yet states have had to respond to the growing interconnectedness and interdependence between states and societies and to changes in the balance between public and private power (see Chapters 3 and 4). The challenge of interdependence is particularly acute in Europe because of the density of states and peoples in a relatively small geographic area.

This chapter proceeds by dealing with three central sets of issues: first, controversies about the role of the nation state and, in particular, those centred around issues of territory, identity and function; second, the challenges to states and nations created by changes in political and economic conditions during the contemporary era; and finally, the specific issues crystallised by the reconfiguration of states and nations in the context of the EU.

Controversies about the nation state

There is considerable scholarly debate and contention about the challenges facing the contemporary nation state and about the changing nature of statehood in Europe, and this debate is focused in particular by the two processes at the core of our argument: the ending of the Cold War and the evolution of European integration. The literature is replete with references to state retreat, government overload, and crisis in western Europe, and with discussion of the challenges facing new or newly-independent states in central and eastern Europe. It is not the purpose here to give a detailed account of the major controversies. Rather, it is our purpose to identify major trends before turning to an analysis of the links between identity, territory and function in contemporary Europe.

The continuing centrality of nation states is asserted trenchantly by many authors, who point to the depth and breadth of the institutions they have spawned and to the 'infrastructural power' they express (Krasner 1988). The encompassing nature of the nation state is also emphasised by Mann when he argues that 'The modern nation state remains a uniquely intense conception of sovereignty. Militarism, communications, infrastructure, economic, social and familial regulation, and intense feelings of national community attachment have been fused into a single caging institution' (Mann 1993, p. 118).

Yet there are other scholars who would argue strongly against the image of the state as a 'single caging institution'. They point to more porous borders and to perforated sovereignty, to the possibility of 'prismatic' patterns of political authority scattering allegiances and dispersing them not only at the national but also at the subnational and the supranational level, and to multiple loyalties. Some scholars argue that the state is being 'hollowed out', undermined from above and below, whereas others point to its adaptability, persistence and resilience (Rockman 1990; Hirst and Thompson 1992; Mann 1993; Muller and Wright 1994; Dunn 1995). Whether these factors promote the retreat of the state, its 'hollowing out', diversification or redefinition are central themes in all contemporary writings about the state.

Controversy about the contemporary role of the state is bound up with debates about the relationship between European integration and statehood in such a way that it has given rise to one of the most sustained debates about statehood and its future. From the outset, there has been considerable scholarly dispute about the consequences of integration for the autonomy and form of the nation state, generating very different interpretations of the relationship between integration and statehood. Integration is viewed by some as leading to a transnational polity that compromises the sovereignty of its members and which will, in the end, take over all of their essential functions. From this perspective, integration transcends the nation state in a process akin to classical state-building; the likely outcome in terms of political order is the establishment of a European federation of one kind or another. Others depict the Union as a creature of its member states, an intergovernmental organisation that has strengthened, not weakened the authority of the west European state. Such state-centric analysis sees integration as an instrument of national polities, with member states retaining firm control and oversight over the transfer of sovereignty and competence to the Union level. From one perspective the state is rescued and strengthened, from another the state is undermined and subordinated (Milward 1992; Moravcsik 1994; Marks *et al.* 1996a).

Much of the literature on the European Union tends to focus on the state as an agent or actor in the Union's intense bargaining system; thus, even if the state is not superseded by a European super-state, it is thoroughly absorbed in what appears to be an irreversible process of constraint and bargaining. While this approach has considerable relevance, it overlooks the extent to which the so-called national interest and state preferences are moulded by the continuing vitality of the state in economic governance, in the provision of public goods and in mediating with social forces. Nor should we neglect the state as a normative order, a sphere of justice, where notions of the common good and solidarity still hold sway. If states remain the primary political communities in Europe, this has important implications for the feasibility of democratic and legitimate EU governance (see Chapter 5). Nor should it be forgotten that the EU in this context is not – or not yet – 'Europe'; many European states in the late 1990s are influenced by the EU, attracted by it, but not engaged to the degree experienced by its longer-standing members. This brings us to an assessment of the interaction between identity, territory and function in contemporary Europe. Are these separating out again after centuries of converging, and how does this challenge or reinforce the role of the EU?

Territory

Territoriality and borders are intrinsically linked to the emergence of internal and external sovereignty as the defining characteristics of statehood. Internal sovereignty emanates from the presence of a supreme political authority within a defined territory with the monopoly over the legal means of coercion. This connotes the right to make laws, and to enforce such laws with force if necessary.

The focus of sovereignty, originally vested in the Monarch, became vested in the people with the development of modern constitutions and mass politics. Territorial sovereignty was transformed into popular sovereignty, the territorial state into the nation state. As will be argued in Chapter 3, the link between territory and sovereignty fundamentally moulded developments in the international system and in ideas of international order. External sovereignty brought with it the legitimacy conferred by international recognition and the right to participate in the international system, whilst the norms of international politics privileged state sovereignty. Although sovereignty remains a powerful image, both in domestic and in international politics, it has been subject to erosion, transfer and pooling – processes in which the European integration project has been deeply implicated, and where effects can be seen for legal, political and popular sovereignty (MacCormick 1993; Christiansen 1994).

The European Union has substantial but different effects on the exercise of legal and political sovereignty, although there is a general sense in which both the EU political and legal orders render sovereignty divisible. The EC was created by law, in the shape of the founding treaties, its institutions are bound by law and in turn the EC is a source of law (Temple Lang 1996, p. 125). The main principles of Community law as developed by the European Court of Justice establish an authoritative legal order – in some people's eyes, a form of constitution – that is independent of, although not separate from, national legal systems. In a number of judgments, the Court referred to the treaties as a 'constitutional charter' and to the fact that 'the Community Treaties established a new legal order for the benefit of which the States had limited their sovereign rights' (quoted in Obradovic 1993, p. 8). According to Temple Lang,

> Each member state now has two, interlocking constitutions: its national constitution and the Community constitution, which it shares with the other member states. Member states' legislative, executive and judicial powers under their national constitutions can be exercised only within the framework and limits imposed by Community law.
>
> (Temple Lang 1996, p. 126)

The impact of the Union on political sovereignty is less clear-cut. The Union's political order represents a pooling of sovereignty by the member states, although it could be argued that decision-rules, such as qualified majority voting and co-decision with the European Parliament, represent a significant dilution of the political authority of the member states. When a state is out-voted in the Council of Ministers, it is participating in a law making process that it can neither limit nor control. National governments and administrations are tied into an extensive and intensive process of collaborative policy-making that weakens the boundary between domestic and external issues. EU membership has special effects on national governments and administrations and has disturbed relations between different levels of government within states. Political integration, particularly its institutional dimension, is based on the premise that the member state governments can̄ only govern in conjunction with other states; this alters not just the content of domestic politics and regulation but the very processes and potential of domestic regulation. In other words, it alters the exercise of political authority in western Europe in a significant way.

The development of the Union as an increasingly integrated economic space with extensive social exchange has also altered the nature of national borders as systems of inclusion and exclusion. Cross-border cooperation financed by the European Regional Development Fund (ERDF) has added a new dimension to space in the Union by transforming borders into borderlands with considerable institution building at this level. The internal market programme altered the role of internal Community borders, placed renewed emphasis on the external borders of the Union as a whole and highlighted the need for large-scale cross-border developments in infrastructure, known as the Trans-European Networks (TENS). Cooperation on Justice and Home Affairs (JHA) involves collective action concerning the Union's external borders, asylum, visas and international crime. Although such areas are extremely sensitive both politically and legally (and will become even more sensitive with the projected extension of the EU into central and eastern Europe), the Union is increasingly drawn into seeking collective responses to what were once the defining functions of borders as boundary creating and maintaining mechanisms. This brings us to changes in the bonding capacity of states.

Identity: nationalism and regionalism

A central element in the liberal democratic notion of sovereignty is popular sovereignty, which implies that states are political communities. Whereas European integration has transformed legal sovereignty and re-moulded political or state sovereignty as discussed above, it has had only a limited impact on popular sovereignty. This characteristic of the Union is highlighted by Habermas when he argues that 'democratic processes have hitherto only functioned within national borders. So far, the political public sphere is fragmented into national units' (Habermas 1991). The development of European integration has thus created a disjuncture, analysed in more detail in Chapter 5, between legal sovereignty, which has been transferred; state sovereignty, which is increasingly pooled; and popular sovereignty, which remains largely national. Such a process has occurred in some degree in all modern states (see Chapter 3) but, as in other cases, the EU focuses the problem with particular sharpness.

Nationalism, as the sole criterion for legitimate government, became embedded after the French revolution, and in important respects popular sovereignty and nationalism went hand in hand. The essence of the national idea was that each nation should possess its own state, and that it should be permitted to use politics to construct its own economic, social and spiritual life in accordance with its own 'national genius' (Garvin 1990). During the nineteenth and early twentieth centuries the nationality principle became so pervasive that seemingly no state could survive without it (Llobera 1993, p. 65). There was a gradual fusing of the state and nation into the modern nation state; in some cases nations made states, whereas in others powerful states forged nations. If nations are 'imagined communities' to use Anderson's oft-quoted phrase, the fusion of cultural and political identity with state power endowed states with a powerful presence in social, economic and political life (Anderson 1991, pp. 5–7).

This did not mean that the imprint of nationalism was uniform or one-dimensional. For example, Smith distinguishes between 'primordial' and 'instrumental' elements of nationalism (Smith 1983). The first sees nationalism as a reflection of some underlying structure, while the second sees it not as an end itself but as a means of acquiring and legitimating political power. In terms of the discussion here, it is important to note the key role played by conceptions of 'citizenship, common values and traditions among the population based on shared myths of origin and memories' (Smith 1991, pp. 8–12). The emphasis on citizenship and legal equality, which is bestowed by states, is part of the legacy of the Enlightenment. On the other hand, this concept of national identity has a primordial ring to it as myths and shared memories tend to draw on older, pre-modern ethnic ties. This conforms to an important distinction between the civic and ethnic dimension of nationalism.

How does this focus on nationalism help us to evaluate the European integration project? The continuing existence of European nations has received less serious attention than the persistence and power of European states, despite the fact that an antipathy towards the excesses of nationalism was part of the founding ideology of the European Union. The integration project was promoted and conceived as a means of overcoming the irrational and dangerous character of nationalism, which had contributed to two world wars and the rise of fascism. According to Weiler, supranationality in the Union

> is not meant to eliminate the national state but to create a regime which seeks to tame the national interest with a new discipline. The idyllic is a state of affairs which eliminates the excesses of nationalism. The challenge is to control, at a societal level, the uncontrolled reflexes of national interest in the international sphere.
>
> (Weiler 1993, p. 10)

Taming nationalism thus remains central to the discourse on European integration. Just before President Mitterrand of France left office in 1995, in his final address to the European Parliament, he concluded with the observation that

> my generation has almost competed its work; it is carrying out its last public acts . . . It is therefore vital for us to pass on our experience. What I am asking you to do is almost impossible, because it means overcoming our past. And yet, if we fail to overcome our past, let there be no mistake about what will follow: ladies and gentlemen, nationalism means war.
>
> (EP Plenary, 17 January 1995)

What is the national component of contemporary European government and how does it relate to European integration? In order to assess the link between nationalism and European integration, it is useful to distinguish between official nationalism, political nationalism and cultural nationalism (Breuilly 1985). For our purposes, the relationship between official and political nationalism is particularly important.

Official nationalism

Official nationalism in the form of government strategies has accommodated and even embraced the European project in nearly all member states, but for multiple reasons. Integration is seen as serving many state interests, both material and normative, and participation in the European project is often portrayed as intrinsic to the national projects of different member states, be they to do with economic modernisation or political status (Laffan 1996b). For the defeated in the Second World War, European integration after 1945 offered an attractive framework for the emergence of a new external state identity. For the less developed states in western Europe, the European project could be and was portrayed as an affirmation of their national projects which would make these poorer parts of Europe more like core Europe. In addition, for Greece, Spain and Portugal, European integration offered the additional advantage of securing democracy. Each of these justifications, suitably adapted, can be seen during the 1990s in the appeal of the integration project to new and newly-independent states in central and eastern Europe.

The European project does not, however, offer all of its member states an enhancement of their external state identity and their place in the world. It is striking that Denmark, Sweden and the UK, three states whose sense of national identity could not easily be enhanced by the European project, have found it most difficult to adjust to the political dimension of integration, whilst the Norwegians and the Swiss in various ways have rejected the opportunity for fuller integration. Whatever the material reasons for seeking membership, European integration did not, it seems, offer a home for their external state identities.

Political nationalism

It can powerfully be argued that European integration has contributed to taking the sting out of nationalism in western Europe. The experience of the Second World War, as already noted, weakened national myths in many states and gave national political elites an incentive to practice new strategies of statecraft. A number of writers assert that, as a result, there has been a gradual but none the less historical decline in the salience of nationalism in western Europe; thus, Inglehart argues that 'The feeling that the nation state incarnated a supreme political value, as the haven and sole defence of a unique way of life, has largely vanished in contemporary Western Europe' (Inglehart 1990, p. 412). Dogan concurs with this finding when he concludes that many west Europeans express a limited national pride, are not fully confident in their country's army, are unwilling to fight for their country, and have increasing trust in other west Europeans (Dogan 1994).

However, in western Europe there are still many people who define their own and other people's identity in exclusive, closed terms, according to which the very existence of alien people and practices is offensive and a threat to identity. At the same time, those subscribing to a closed exclusive identity are likely to be hostile to European integration. Right wing conservative forces, which have regained an electoral presence in western Europe since the late 1980s, are opposed to the deepening of European integration. Jean-Marie Le Pen and his National Front campaigned against the TEU in the French referendum of 1992 and Jorg Haider was the main leader of the 'no' camp in the Austrian referendum on EU membership during the autumn of 1994. During the French referendum campaign, Le Pen argued strongly against the granting of citizenship rights in the TEU; for him, foreigners who remain in France for short periods could not develop a love of and a commitment to the *patrie*, and to its specific culture and history (Holm 1992, p. 12). Hence, they should not get the political right to vote in municipal elections as promised by the TEU. On the other hand, President Mitterrand argued that the extension of limited citizenship rights was part of France's universalist tradition.

There are echoes of this nationalist discourse in many other member states. Indeed, analysis of voting patterns in the TEU referendums gives some support to the view that the integration project itself may contribute to the revival of political nationalism, as people react against the growing cosmopolitanism of European society and the reduction of barriers implicit in the 1992 programme. It has been suggested that in many European states there may be a 'semieducated and resentful under-class which defiantly takes as its symbols the national flags abandoned by the elites' (quoted in Robbins 1989, p. 385). In France, Denmark and Ireland, support for the TEU tended to come from those who were more highly educated and better paid. The business elite, senior officials and the self-employed were more likely to vote yes. For these people, Europe is a cosmopolitan social space within which they move regularly. In France, the majority of employees and blue-collar workers voted 'no', and in the first Danish referendum two-thirds of unskilled workers voted 'no'. Opponents of integration tend to come from those sections of society for whom the national state is their major protector and a major source of employment, and who harbour a justifiable fear that integration may weaken the redistributive capacity of the nation state. It is possible that such a revival of political nationalism could lead to a backlash against European integration, fostering demands for 'national closure' and a weakening of the web of interdependence (Haas 1990). Whether or not such a backlash occurs, it is clear that the rhetoric of nationalism can still be called upon as a resource in opposing European integration.

Europe's new regionalism

In contrast to the strategies of resistance generated by political nationalism, it appears that European integration can act as a resource for groups trapped inside existing national states. Any assessment of the contemporary west European state must thus address the growth of a new regionalism, examining its economic, political and cultural sources and the purposes it serves for different regional and state actors. The term 'region' is itself problematic; it may simply refer to a sub-unit of government, or it can encompass a historic cultural boundary. It is clear, however, that the new regionalism has an important economic component, reflecting governments' search for new strategies of intervention, and that it also links with the new salience of territorial politics in many states; there are processes of federalisation, regionalisation and decentralisation developing in many EU member states and, since the 1960s, these have been accompanied by a resurgence of regional political and cultural movements. Identities that had been submerged within states have thus been 'rediscovered'. The re-ordering of central, regional and local power has sometimes occurred in response to government 'overload' and pressures for more political participation from below, and has at many points intersected with new regional cultural movements. For these reasons, it is necessary to give consideration to the 'new regionalism' in any attempt to derive new conceptualisations of the contemporary state and integration.

At their most extreme, proponents of regionalism would like to see the disintegration of Europe's historical states and their replacement by older ethnic/linguistic regions. A 'Europe of the Regions' would, by implication, be more democratic, efficient and economically dynamic, according to its proponents in Europe's strong regions. On the other hand, the European Commission advocates and supports a far less radical form of regionalism. A central feature of the 1988 reform of the structural funds was its emphasis on partnership between the EU, national, regional and local governments; for regional and local authorities, the availability of EU funding offers an incentive and a means to exert pressure on and perhaps circumvent unhelpful national governments. The TEU formally institutionalised the regional dimension with the establishment of the Committee of the Regions as a consultative body. The representatives of the German *Länder*, the Belgian regions, the Spanish *Communidades*, Lombardy, Scotland and the French regions are determined to use this institutional toehold to become more important players in the integration project.

Function

States perform a myriad of tasks within their domestic jurisdictions, notably, economic governance, the establishment of distributional coalitions, the provision of welfare and other public goods and the maintenance of balance between different levels of government. This is not, though, to suggest that states operate with complete autonomy: the relationship between the public power and the private sphere at the domestic level responds to shifts in politics, economics, and societal problems, whilst states are constrained in how they adjust to domestic challenges by the international political economy (see Chapter 4). Since the Second World War, European nation states have undergone important changes to form and function, beginning with the emergence of a strongly interventionist state in the immediate post-war period. The breadth and depth of state intervention was threatened by the end of the golden period of economic growth in the 1970s, and by the growth of distributional conflicts which undermined the post-war settlement, whilst adaptation was shaped by changes in the balance of political forces at national level and the increasing pressures of internationalisation. It is within this context that we should analyse the changing pressures on the functions of the nation state, and relate them to the ways in which state functions have been subjected to new strains during the 1990s.

An interventionist state bolstered by social democratic norms

Between 1948 and the end of the 1960s, west European states, apart from the authoritarian states of the Mediterranean (Spain, Portugal and, in varying measure, Greece), evolved a model of economy, society and polity that brought relative prosperity and economic security to a large majority of people. This period was characterised by an interventionist style of economic governance that rested on social democratic norms in politics, and on a broad consensus about the running of the economy. The model was moulded by the shadows of the past, notably, the Depression of the 1930s and the Second World War. Politicians in most west European states, apart from the UK and the neutrals, felt an acute sense of vulnerability as they faced the immense tasks of political and economic reconstruction, and the age-old problem of security. The experience of fascism, the perceived Soviet threat, and the solidarity engendered by the Second World War led political leaders to reconstruct democratic politics on a broader and sounder footing than before. The search for consensus led, in many cases, to a new class compromise with workers and farmers to temper the all or nothing battles of the Depression (Milward 1992). Electoral politics was characterised by considerable stability with little change in the electoral strength of political parties from election to election or from generation to generation (Rose and Urwin 1970, p. 295). Political struggle and distributional conflicts were, to a large extent, tamed, at least if compared with the past.

The interventionist European state, both in terms of economic governance and welfare, was promoted and sustained by a set of political alignments that favoured a new social contract. Social democracy, characterised by a search for consensus between competing interests, set the tone of politics (Dahrendorf 1986, p. 221). This does not imply that social democratic parties dominated European governments after the war; apart from Scandinavia, the pattern was very mixed. Rather, there was what Duverger describes as 'contagion' from the left as 'demands from the left are taken up by other parties and the political ground shifts leftwards' (quoted in Korpi 1989, p. 313). Continental Christian democracy, in particular, embraced the notion of an active social state. After the war, parties on the right accepted economic planning and an expanded welfare state, viewing an active state as part of the tide of history that could not be reversed (Lemke and Marks 1992). In turn, Europe's social democratic parties became reformist in character, shedding their radical socialist past.

The boundaries of post-war politics were characterised by a very specific view of the proper role for the state and state power. As David Held has argued, this view encapsulated:

> a commitment to social and economic reform; an overriding respect for the constitutional state and representative government; and a desire to encourage individuals' pursuit of their interests while maintaining policies in the national or public interest. Underpinning these concerns was a conception of the state as the most suitable means for the promotion of 'the good' of both the individual and the collective.
>
> (Held 1987, p. 221)

This concept of the state legitimised 'big government': although the expanding role of the public economy can be traced to the nineteenth century, in western Europe during the 1950s and 1960s, the state/society line shifted decisively in favour of public power. Public expenditure as a proportion of GDP for the EC Twelve grew from 31.8 per cent in 1960 to 40 per cent in 1974 and 47 per cent in 1988. These figures were significantly higher than those found in the US and Japan (Tsoukalis 1991, p. 28). Other indicators, such as levels of public employment, welfare provision or the power of the state to extract taxes, all pointed to the growth of government in western Europe after the war. Although partly a response to the logic of industrialisation and the increasing complexity of society, the growth of government was embedded in a value system that favoured the use of public power to solve societal problems.

The economic system was characterised by a relatively stable 'regime of accumulation', which produced a golden period of economic growth with average growth rates of approximately 4.4 per cent per annum up to the late 1960s. Growth was translated into additional employment opportunities and higher standards of living. An era of affluence was fostered with per capita income growth of 4.5 per cent a year after 1950 compared with 1 per cent a year between 1800 and 1950 (Williams 1987, p. 27). Governments developed a capacity to 'manage' the national economy. Macroeconomic management was accompanied by a variety of other interventions in industrial policy, the provision of public infrastructure, education and labour market policy. The tentacles of the state extended into the market by means of regulation, taxation, welfare provision, and public expenditure.

Economic governance was accompanied by a growing social state. Although the European welfare state has its origins in the late nineteenth century with the development of poor laws and social insurance, it was not until after the Second World War that welfare provisions were gradually made universal. The idea of national solidarity and social citizenship became the core principles of social security, and a central feature, in turn, of the 'European model' (Flora and Heidenheimer 1982, p. 52). During the 1980s and 1990s, however, both the economic and the political components of this model came under increasing pressure, and this shift is central to the ways in which European states and nations have approached the post-Cold War era.

New challenges to the 'European model'

Having established the central features of what might be described as the 'European model' of statehood, and also related it to the persistence of both national and subnational identities, it is important to evaluate the ways in which, during the past twenty years, new pressures have been exerted on the political and economic 'bargains' that lie at the root of the post-Second World War consensus. These can be explored in two main areas: the bursting of the economic 'bubble' and its accompanying political processes. The analysis reflects what we argued in Chapter 1: that a sense of historical change and development is vital to an understanding of the ways in which the 1990s have posed new challenges, and that the progress of integration is not something to be taken for granted.

Economics when the bubble bursts

Growth and prosperity, during the 'golden age', was promoted by trade liberalisation, monetary stability, the diffusion of US technology throughout the industrialised world, and the availability of an abundant supply of cheap labour. These conditions, which contributed to a 'virtuous circle', began to weaken towards the end of the 1960s, placing severe strain on Europe's system of economic governance and on the consensual tone of politics. Between 1968 and 1973, social democratic values reached their zenith in Europe and the future of the post-war interventionist state seemed assured. Yet in the years since the oil crisis of the mid-1970s, it has become commonplace to talk of a crisis of the state, of 'ungovernability', of 'government overload', of a crisis of legitimacy and of social democracy. In the 1980s there was 'a major change in the dominant macro-economic paradigm from Keynesianism to monetarism and neo-liberalism, from *dirigisme* to market-driven solutions, from fiscal expansionism to restraint, from mercantilism to free trade' (Muller and Wright 1994, p. 2). The post-war polity lost its economic 'anchor', and the philosophical underpinnings of an active state were undermined.

Economic performance in western Europe began to deteriorate towards the end of the 1960s. A combination of internal and external factors contributed to the economic slowdown. In many European states, there was a marked increase in labour militancy. The gradual drying up of surplus labour from agriculture enhanced trade union power. A wave of industrial unrest spread throughout Europe between 1967 and 1970. Workers demanded improvements in working conditions, protection from dismissal, co-determination within companies and better social services. This led to an 'explosion of wages' which put pressure on profits and investment (Boltho 1982, p. 26). In the international political economy, the Vietnam War generated strong inflationary pressures and a weakening of the US economy (see Chapter 4). The dollar came under pressure in 1970–71, which led to the breakdown of the Bretton Woods system in August 1971. This marked the effective end of a system of fixed exchange rates. Since then the compatibility of flexible exchange rates and market integration has been a recurring issue in European integration and has influenced recurrent attempts at monetary cooperation in the Union (see Chapter 6).

Buffeted by monetary turbulence and rising wage costs, the west European economies were badly prepared for the massive supply-side shock of the first (1973/4) and second (1979/80) energy crises. The severity of the shock plunged the west European economies into recession and fuelled strong inflationary pressures. The recessions were characterised by low growth, rising unemployment and high levels of inflation. Between 1973 and 1980, average growth rates were 2.3 per cent, in contrast to 4.6 per cent between 1960 and 1973. Employment was particularly badly hit; total employment in the EC declined by 3 million between 1973 and 1980 and overall unemployment increased fivefold. Marginal groups such as young people, migrants, the disabled and women found it increasingly difficult to break into the jobs market. Because wage levels remained relatively impervious to rising unemployment, Europe experienced persistently high inflation. Growing expenditure on income maintenance increased public expenditure while unemployment affected the revenue base of national budgets. Public finances in many states went unchecked with the result that, by 1989, only five OECD countries were in surplus (Oxley and Martin 1991, p. 147). Although all west European states experienced the dislocation of the oil crisis there was a marked variation in growth rates, levels of inflation and the extent of unemployment across the Community. Divergence of economic performance became an added source of strain within the EC.

Governments responded to the 1973/4 recession with traditional cyclical policies and an expansion of labour market policies – notably, direct job creation, wage subsidies, a reduction of working time, and job sharing. Government subsidies to declining industries grew as politicians attempted to manage the tension between economic adjustment and social costs. Despite subsidies, millions of jobs were lost in textiles, clothing, footwear, shipbuilding, coal and steel. Whole regions, among the most industrialised parts of Europe, became industrial wastelands as competitive pressures were felt in Europe's traditional industries. The style of regulation characteristic of the 'golden age' persisted, however; economic policy was largely determined by the domestic policy process and the distribution of power within national politics (Mjøset 1992, p. 329), and most governments assumed that there would be a return to sustained growth.

As the 1980s progressed, it became clear that there were a number of structural changes taking place in the world economy that undermined the existing 'mode of regulation' and challenged domestic policy processes, making it unlikely that the 'European model' could easily be restored and growth resumed (see Chapter 4).

As these changes are still working their way through the system, it is difficult to arrive at a firm perspective on the shape of the emerging 'mode of regulation'. However, it is necessary to establish the contours of change because these developments have a major bearing on economic governance at EU level and in the member states. Various interpretations of these changes have been offered in recent years. These include the idea that we are moving from 'organised' to 'disorganised capitalism', the idea that the industrialised world is at a 'new industrial divide' between Fordist mass production, which needed large numbers of relatively unskilled labour, and 'flexible specialisation', which requires highly skilled workers but fewer of them. Consequently, industry represents a declining proportion of employment in all west European economies and many low skilled jobs are either redundant or have shifted to low cost producers. The decline of manufacturing has been accompanied by an expansion of the services sector, which creates both highly skilled employment and many 'junk jobs'.

Alongside these 'domestic' explanations of the new challenges, the argument that we have moved from a system of national markets with international competition to a genuinely globalised economic system is increasingly advanced (see Chapter 4). Undoubtedly, many of the traditional levers of economic policy-making lost their effectiveness during the 1980s. Macroeconomic policies became restrictive as expansionary fiscal and monetary policies were eschewed; containing or reducing public expenditure was a major feature of efforts to bring deficits under control. Moreover, policies shifted towards supply-side interventions such as training, science and technology, measures to support small and medium-sized firms and infrastructure. As noted above, these policies were most effective if delivered in a decentralised manner; hence the growing importance of regional intervention. Through these policies, governments sought to accommodate their economies to the shift from mass production to flexible specialisation. In this context, it is possible to interpret the EU's internal market programme both as a response to the declining competitive position of western Europe in the world economy and as an additional source of competitive pressures in the national economies (see Chapter 6).

As the 1980s progressed, the fight against inflation and the search for stable money predominated over the goal of full employment and the search for growth – a substantial shift from the consensus that had prevailed up to the late 1970s. The European Monetary System (EMS) was the anchor for restrictive monetary policies on west European states as they sought to squeeze inflation out of their economies, at the cost of accepting German policy priorities (see Chapter 7). Deregulation of financial markets had a major impact on the relationship between capital, labour and the state: the power of organised labour, which had been in the ascendant in the post-war European state, was weakened in the 1980s, whilst the pressure for competitiveness and the social consequences of economic restructuring raised serious dilemmas for the European welfare state.

From the beginning of the 1980s onwards, a shift in economic policy and in the system of regulation took shape. With the end of the 'golden age', neo-liberal ideas, which called the post-war consensus on economic management and 'big government' into question, gained currency. The interventionist state was portrayed as bloated, inefficient, a cause of, rather than a solution to, societal problems. The neo-liberal critique highlighted the apparently malign effects of 'big government': the 'crowding out' of the private sector and private initiative, and the paralysis of market forces. Arguments that the reach of public power had extended beyond its grasp began to exert a powerful hold on political discourse, and the traditional social democratic commitment to an 'active state' became an electoral liability, particularly in the UK. Socialism in western Europe lost its monopoly over 'the discourse of dissent' (Lemke and Marks 1992, p. 10).

The elections of Ronald Reagan as US President and of Margaret Thatcher as UK Prime Minister gave such neo-liberal ideas a powerful political platform. Mrs Thatcher's policies broke with the consensual norms of post-war politics and set out decisively to weaken the power of organised labour in the UK, representing the most extreme form of neo-liberalism in western Europe. Significantly, but with inexorable logic, the policies of successive British Conservative governments promoted a vision of the European Union and the goals of European integration that proved highly influential during the 1980s; the European integration project was represented not only as a threat to vital national interests, but also to the free play of market forces. The international manifestation of Thatcherism was the promotion of market integration as a vast deregulated economic space. Mrs Thatcher's September 1988 speech to the College of Europe in Bruges has often been cited as the purest expression of such a position, permeated as it was by her view 'we haven't worked all those years to free Britain from the paralysis of socialism to see it creep through the back door of central control and bureaucracy in Brussels' (Thatcher 1988). The Thatcher vision of Europe jostled for supremacy with other visions, notably those promoted by Jacques Delors, that sought to preserve the values of social stability and consensus during the 1980s. Although Thatcher presented her policies with ideological commitment and rhetorical relish, neo-liberal policies took hold even where social democratic governments were in power.

Politics when the bubble bursts

A number of distinct trends can be observed in European politics since the end of the 'golden period of growth'. Just as the European economies began to display some of the problems that would plague them in the 1970s, the famed post-war political stability began to falter. The protests of May 1968, centred in France but affecting many other west European countries, came to symbolise the breakdown of the post-war consensus and provided a challenge to the prevailing ethos of growth. The 'spirit of '68', underlined by massive student unrest and the rise of new movements under the broad title of the New Left, was about further redistribution, democratisation of institutions, and greater participation in all aspects of society. According to Dahrendorf, 'after a time of quantitative economic advances one looked for qualitative social change. People began to seek a better life and not just more of the same thing' (Dahrendorf 1986, p. 13). Social democratic parties were being asked to look beyond managed growth towards a more radical redistribution of economic power (Padgett and Paterson 1991, p. 40). The legacy of 1968 may be found in the proliferation of new social movements, notably the greens, women's groups, the anti-nuclear movement, human rights and community groups, all of whom exerted considerable influence on public-policy and created new avenues for politics during the 1980s. A number of key values, notably, quality of life, individual self-realisation, peace, conservation and human rights, underlay the new politics. In contrast to conventional forms of politics, the new movements tended to rely on informal structures, networks, and non-bureaucratic organisations. Social movements are less territorially bound than conventional political parties, seeking alternative forms of political activity and additional political channels of influence. As such, they represent a key part of the reconfiguration of European states and nations during the 1990s, but their influence stems from the 1970s and 1980s.

Notwithstanding moves towards more associative forms of democracy, electoral competition between parties has remained central to government formation. During the 1980s there was a discernible shift to the right in west European politics, although not in all states. In 1979, the British Conservative Party regained power from Labour. In 1981/2, social democrats were displaced from coalition governments in Belgium, the Netherlands and Denmark, the SPD lost power in Germany and the Austrian Social Democratic Party lost its majority. In contrast, socialist parties gained power in France (President Mitterrand in 1981), Spain and Greece. North European social democracy appeared to suffer from electoral set-backs whereas the performance of socialist parties in the Mediterranean states was impressive. The latter can be explained by the role socialist parties played in consolidating democracy, by President Mitterrand's success in overcoming the fragmentation of the French left and by their absence from power during the hard times of the 1970s. Yet in office, the left-wing governments were forced by the major structural forces we have described to pursue relatively liberal economic strategies.

At the same time as the limits to autonomy were being felt by governments of the left, extreme right-wing parties, neo-fascist in tone, regained an electoral presence in many west European states. The Republikaner Party in Germany, the French Front National, the Flemish Vlaams Blok, the Norwegian Progress Party and the Austrian Freedom Party made electoral gains. Right-wing parties gained an important electoral presence in many cities in Europe with large migrant populations, coupling calls for strict controls on immigration and immigrants with an appeal to the glories of the past and displaying a nostalgia for a model of economy and polity based exclusively on the nation state. An exclusive 'closed' view of both national and European identity is proffered by these parties, and it is not surprising that they have also been in the forefront of opposition to further European integration (see above).

A re-configuration of the nation state?

This chapter has put forward an analysis of the contemporary nation state in Europe from the perspective of territory, identity and function. The analysis leads to the conclusion that the congruence between bounded territory, identity and function is being eroded, and that European integration is part of that erosion. European states are no longer as sharply bounded, purposeful and highly centralised as they once were (Tilly 1975). Societies, economies and polities are 'no longer contained in a container' to borrow a phrase from the French regional economist, Perroux. The pillars of the Westphalian state system – sovereignty rooted in bounded territory, legitimated by the bonding capacity of a collective national identity – are being undermined in contemporary Europe. It is not just that territory, identity and function are separating out after centuries of converging, but that each of these dimensions of the nation state is undergoing a transformation.

The internationalisation of technology, capital, markets and firms has had a major impact on the capacity for economic governance, a core function of states in the post-war period, and the traditional levers of economic policy have lost their effectiveness in large and small countries. National industrial policy is undermined by the importance of international markets and technology transfers, whilst other fields such as the environment require, by definition, a collective response. Proponents of the 'hollowing out' thesis go further, arguing that internationalisation undermines the capacity of national governments to sustain social consensus with redistributive and fiscal policies. In other words, the state's role in economic governance and in social provision is being undermined. There is impressive empirical evidence to support the view that the ending of the golden period of economic growth and the intensification of internationalisation in the global economy have altered the relationship between states and markets and between public and private power.

During the 1980s and 1990s, all European states have thus had to search for new strategies aimed at maintaining the competitiveness of their economies, and all have faced tax and regulatory competition which constrained their choices in fiscal policy and public provision. Although considerable cross-national and sectoral variations persist, strategies adopted by states have included privatisation of public utilities and publicly owned commercial enterprises, particularly in the internationally traded sectors, deregulation or re-regulation at the European level, processes of deconcentration, changes in labour market laws, and public/private partnerships. States are undergoing changes both to their form and function which represent a reduction in decisiveness, capacity and autonomy. States have a weaker steering capacity. Contemporary governance requires them to engage in more bargained, negotiated forms of policy-making with different levels of government and private actors.

Apart from the United Kingdom, however, where the Conservative Party, in power from 1979 to 1997, set out to undermine the desirability and legitimacy of important elements of public provision and the trade union movement, the commitment to social peace and consensus remains strong in western Europe. Neo-liberal ideas have dented but not fundamentally undermined the political commitment of parties of the centre left and centre right to the European social model. The Delors paper on 'Growth, Competitiveness and Employment', the Commission's paper on social policy and the inclusion of an employment chapter in the June 1997 Treaty of Amsterdam, are part of an ongoing search for European strategies to deliver both efficiency and equity. In this context, it is at least arguable that the 'state functions' of regulation and social provision are alive and well, but not always provided through the national state authorities characteristic of the classic 'European model'.

No less than form and function, there is a re-configuration of territory and borders in contemporary Europe. The territory of each member state is increasingly embedded in a wider economic and social space that alters the role of national borders as systems of inclusion and exclusion. Europe's borders – lines on the map – have become more permeable and fuzzy with the development of collaborative strategies for combating crime and fraud. The Schengen Agreement on free movement, incorporated into the Treaty of Amsterdam, makes provision for the free flow of people in the Union, and also for mechanisms to deal with the public order and regulatory implications of such processes. Cooperation on justice and home affairs and market integration have fostered a 'new territoriality' in Europe which does not demand national state policing; rather, it embeds national territories in a wider European territoriality. Each member state is expected to patrol its national borders, not only in their own interests but in the interests of their partners as well.

Europe's new regionalism also affects territorial politics within states. The increasing importance of the regional government in economic management leads central governments to cooperate with lower tier government and private actors, with central governments sacrificing autonomy in order to achieve public-policy goals through decentralisation and partnership. Central government autonomy is further weakened by the growth of transnational ties and the search for representation in the decision-making arenas of the EU. The existence of the Union in this context provides opportunities to subnational actors to build networks with their counterparts in other states as they can pursue horizontal as well as vertical lines of communication and influence. By doing so, the EU reshapes the 'political opportunity structure' in and between its member states. In those member states where separatist forces question the authority of the state, European integration can provide a framework for the working out of nationalist/separatist politics.

The transformation of the salience of bounded territory and the change to the form and function of states is bound up with questions of identity. Nationalism has produced one of the most powerful and emotive forms of collective identity in the world, but national identities are no longer as solid or as distinct as they once were. It is increasingly problematic for many European states and the EU to determine 'who belongs' and who does not. Conflicts about citizenship laws and about the concept of European citizenship are central to issues of inclusion and exclusion. Questions of identity are raised by immigration, the new regionalism, a greater emphasis on personal life style, electronic communication, and the large scale dissemination of consumer products. Greater mobility for work and leisure allows for multiple identities and the development of varieties of citizenship that go beyond the state. It would be foolhardy, however, to argue that the EU represents a post-nationalist environment. Rather, the EU has contributed to the spread of liberal nationalism in Europe. A revival of political nationalism using the symbols and rhetoric of traditional nationalism can, however, act as a strong countervailing force to political and constitutional development in the EU.

The analysis in this chapter does not therefore lead us to accept a hard version of the 'hollowing out' thesis. Although persuasive in some respects, the notion that the state is being 'hollowed out' must be qualified in a number of important respects. There is still a lot left in the nation state. State agents remain the primary guarantors of internal security, albeit with closer external collaboration within their territories. National legal systems continue to have a major presence in all aspects of national life by defining rights and duties for citizens, by regulation and arbitration. National citizenship continues to bestow many tangible rights and benefits. The nation state is the primary arena for interpersonal solidarity in Europe because of the continuing significance of the welfare state. States continue to represent the primary political communities within which democratic norms, processes and practices are exercised. Even in the economic sphere, where the 'hollowing out' thesis is most convincing, national governments remain crucial for economic performance, particularly in relation to supply side policies of innovation, education, labour markets and infrastructure which influence corporate investment strategies. The fiscal muscle of the state remains powerful. National governments, in many European states, foster the creation of distributional coalitions and wage bargaining.

Notwithstanding the growing interconnectedness of states and societies in the contemporary world system, 'adaptation' and 'redefinition' or 'reconfiguration' rather than 'hollowing out' best captures the processes we have described. The substance of state policy, the processes of policy-making, and even the form of state institutions are adapting to European integration and wider internationalisation. At the same time, personal, group and national identities are reshaped but not entirely recreated by the interaction of needs, demands and institutions at several different levels, including that of the reconfigured state.

Conclusions

This chapter has put forward a number of perspectives on the evolution of the contemporary nation state in Europe. We have explored the changing contours of the nation state in Europe because of the symbiotic relationship between statehood and European integration. Integration intersects and interacts with changes in the form and function of the member states and with shifts in their societies and polities. In the post-war period we observed the parallel growth of 'big government' and an active state, with growing collective governance between states in Europe. Up to the 1980s, liberalisation in the EU was compatible with big government at domestic level. Pressures for change came from the breakdown of 'organised capital' and the intensification of internationalisation, which has greatly weakened the capacity of national governments for macroeconomic management. The advent of 'disorganised capital' alters the balance of power between different social forces and makes itself felt in party and electoral competition. All European states face the challenge of structural adjustment while maintaining the welfare state, one of the defining characteristics of Europe. Alongside this, they face the challenge of acting within the European integration project – another fundamental part of the European landscape.

Given the circumstances described here, it is clear that the ending of the Cold War, symbolised but not started by the demolition of the Berlin Wall in 1989, intersected in many respects with an existing restructuring of the European state, and with the redefinition of many aspects of European identities. As Chapters 3 and 4 will argue, the ending of the Cold War was a formative event not only in world politics but also in the international political economy. For the purposes of the argument here, two points should be emphasised. First, the reconfiguration of states and nations in Europe after the Cold War has brought together two groups of national societies, in the east and the west, which have been subject to radically different forms of external and internal pressures. Second, the role of the EU in either containing or shaping these restructuring processes has been severely tested by the fact that great expectations of the European integration project have gone alongside high levels of change and challenge. As we have already argued, changes in the EU, arising particularly from the Maastricht process and the TEU, have aroused important forms of resistance, and have heightened a number of underlying uncertainties. It is to be expected that these aspects of 'unsettled Europe' would be further underlined by the impact of radical change in the broader political and economic context.

3 World politics

Introduction

The European Communities and the European Union have, since their establishment, been deeply implanted in the world political arena. In many respects, it is possible to see the foundation of the original Communities during the 1950s as an expression of the emergence and the consolidation of the Cold War; it is thus to be expected that changes both in the 'Cold War system' and in broader world politics would have important implications for the evolution and role of the EC/EU. Not only this, but the linkages between politics at the national or regional levels and the broader world arena are likely to be crucial for the role and status of the EU, both in relation to its own member countries and in relation to outside partners or rivals. Neither wholly 'world politics' nor 'domestic politics', neither wholly political nor exclusively economic in its orientation, the EU stands as a symbol of many of the material uncertainties attending the practice of world politics since 1945, and as a potent focus for such uncertainties in the 1990s. In this way, a focus on world politics opens up many of the issues relating to territory, identity and function explored in earlier chapters, but does so from an 'outside-in' rather than an 'inside-out' perspective (see Introduction, in Chapter 1).

There is clearly a good deal of empirical interest in the extent to which the EU has been and remains implanted in world politics. But there is also a more conceptual and theoretical interest. The nature of world politics has been debated constantly since the Second World War, not only at the level of policy and practice but also at the level of theory and explanation. In this more conceptual sense, it has been clear throughout that there is no agreed grand theory of world politics: rather, there are sets of more or less persuasive competing frameworks, and a wide range of middle-range theories that can provide partial explanations (Keohane 1986; Hollis and Smith 1990; Smith 1994c; Smith *et al.* 1996). The critical study of world politics can thus be seen to show all the symptoms of contention that characterise the social sciences more generally, and many of the conceptual issues dividing scholars of world politics would be very familiar to those engaged in the social and political sciences as a whole.

For the purposes of the discussion here, and in this book more generally, there are a number of central conceptual issues, arising out of the contested nature of world politics, out of the nature of the 'new Europe' and out of the rather ambiguous role played by the EU therein. This chapter first addresses the nature of statehood in the international arena, and the relationship between statehood, world order and processes of change. From this arises a set of issues concerning the transition between 'modern' concepts of world politics and world order and the 'post-modern' consciousness, and a set of more specific questions dealing with the impact of change from the Cold War order to the post-Cold War era, with implications for notions of power, identity and security. These general areas of enquiry are then related to the nature of world politics as reflected in the 'new Europe' of the 1990s, to the ways in which institutions and forces reflect this changing reality, and finally to the challenges facing the EU as a structure of world politics and as a part of the world political process.

The chapter will deal with each of these areas in turn. It should, of course, be recognised that the issues are not contained in a hermetically sealed box labelled 'world politics': they are closely linked to the issues dealt with in Chapters 2 and 4, and many of them will be taken up in the second part of the book, particularly in Chapter 8 on the EU's role in the international arena.

Statehood, order and change in world politics

For generations, the study and much of the practice of world politics has been dominated by what could be described as an ideology of state dominance (Hocking and Smith 1995, Chapters 4–5). There are three central features of this 'ideology'. First, the state (and particularly the nation state) is the central actor on the stage of world politics, represented by its government. It is the central focus of power and legitimacy, and thus of international order. But the phenomenon of state dominance creates a paradox: whilst the state is the source of order and legitimacy, it is also, by virtue of its coercive power, a potent source of disorder and conflict (Northedge 1976; Bull 1977).

Second, states in world politics thus constitute an 'anarchical society' (Bull 1977), in which the search for general order is complicated by the search for national security, and in which competition and cooperation coexist more or less uneasily. This society has important mechanisms of order – diplomacy, law, even war itself – but there is always an uneasy balance between the search for order and potential or actual disorder.

Third, the three key bases of state participation in world politics are: sovereignty, recognition and control. Sovereignty implies the ability to act relatively autonomously, although there can clearly be a disparity in any given case between the claim to sovereignty and the ability to exercise it. Recognition implies the acceptance of a given state and its authorities as participants in the world arena, specifically recognition by other states or groups of states. Control implies the ability to govern: the capacity to establish and maintain borders, and to constrain or to protect the movements and activities of the citizens of a given state.

It is a short step from this sketch of the 'world of states' to the key contested concepts around which this book is organised. Territory, identity and functions are defined sharply as those related to statehood and state power: the notions of sovereignty, recognition and control are effectively inseparable from the assumption that statehood is exercised in a defined area, generating a 'hard' version of national identity and identification and leading to strict control of actions and interactions. These essential characteristics generate a powerful and persuasive version of world politics, in which the world is effectively a world of states. In some ways, it is a quintessentially modernist and positivist view of world politics, since it relies on the satisfaction of certain explicit criteria, and on the capacity of government to exert control over its citizens and resources. That control, it can be argued, is very different in domestic politics as compared to world politics; in domestic politics, state authority is highly developed, whereas in world politics, there are many competing claims and potential threats but no overall structure of governance.

If we accept this view of world politics, we are immediately also faced with important questions about the foundations of European integration and the EU itself. There are strong grounds for seeing the European integration project as an expression of 'politics between states': in particular, the origins of European institutions in the late 1940s and early 1950s can be seen as the expression of an interstate bargain, with France and Germany at its core. Not only this, but the development of European integration during the 1950s and 1960s expressed important trends in interstate politics: the recovery of (West) Germany, attempts by smaller member states to ensure their security and assert their independence, and perhaps above all the resistance of the French under General de Gaulle which led to the 'empty chair' crisis of 1965–66 and the 'Luxembourg Compromise'. What purer expression could there be, in this perspective, of the vigour and power of states within the integration process; and what better expression of the broader interstate system than the central role played by the United States in supporting and shaping the integration project?

During the past twenty years, however (and arguably for a long time before that), strong challenges have arisen both to the assumptions of a state-dominance model of world politics and to the political practices to which these have given rise. Each of the central planks of a state-centric view can be challenged. First, it is clear that states are not the only or even the dominant actors in many areas of world politics. The challenge is most striking in the area of social and economic trans-actions, where major multinational organisations and transnational groupings can be discerned, often with greater resources and mobility than states and governments (Strange 1988; see Chapter 4 below). But even in the most hallowed areas of national security, it can be argued that, on the one hand governments are now incapable of ensuring the security of their citizens – for example against nuclear attack or various forms of terrorism – and on the other hand there are non-state organisations capable of making a dramatic impact on the security of populations (for example, cross-national terrorist groupings or competing national liberation movements) (Hocking and Smith 1995, Chapter 5).

It is clear that the relative tidiness of a state-centred 'anarchical society' does not represent the full complexity of a world in which there are many layers of interaction and many channels of political communication and influence. A widely accepted characterisation of this new reality during the 1970s and 1980s was that of 'complex interdependence' (Keohane and Nye 1987): a world in which there are many layers and overlapping arenas for political action, and in which there are no easy assumptions of hierarchy or precedence. During the 1990s, there has been a powerful trend towards the identification of processes of globalisation, according to which there has been a further erosion of the position of states and (for some) a fundamental transformation of both political and economic processes. In a globalised world, it is argued, immensely powerful forces of production and exchange have 'decentred' the previously relatively predictable patterns of authority and control, to produce new problems of legitimacy, identity and attachment (Dicken 1992; Booth and Smith 1997).

As consequence, it can be argued that the notions of sovereignty, recognition and control are not adequate to the task of describing the new forms of political participation and organisation; David Held has described such arguments in terms of a series of 'gaps' between classical theories of statehood and the realities of global politics (Held 1989, Chapter 8). Whilst the traditional terms are not irrelevant, they need to be supplemented with others that reflect the more complex and fluid reality of the 1990s. Sovereignty is often not as important as autonomy – a property that can be possessed by a wide range of organisations including but not restricted to states and their governments. Recognition may not be as important as representation – the capacity to act on behalf of an interest or a cluster of interests in the world arena, including but not restricted to those of states and governments. Control of the kind implied by sovereign statehood may be less significant in many situations than the ability to exert influence by appropriate forms of mobilisation and communication (Hocking and Smith 1995, Chapter 5; see also Mansbach 1994).

None of this means that the status and roles of states and their governments have been supplanted in the world arena of the 1990s: what it does mean is that they cannot be taken for granted. Power, interest, governance, are not blanket terms describing an unchanging reality: rather, they are situationally specific and dependent on the issues at stake in any given set of circumstances. As Wolfram Hanrieder presciently put it in the late 1970s, 'Access rather than acquisition, presence rather than rule, penetration rather than possession have become the important issues' in the contemporary era (Hanrieder 1978). A number of these processes have become focused very strongly by the European integration project, in ways which challenge the 'state-centric' view of European integration outlined earlier.

In the first place, it is apparent that although the European project may have important roots in interstate bargains, it has generated equally powerful processes involving a multiplicity of actors. The European institutions themselves have elements of 'actorness' at the supranational level, and they also have potent shaping effects on notional governments' strategies; if world politics of the traditional kind exists in the EU, it is powerfully modified by the permanence and complexity of the entanglements between officials and other groupings. However, the EU has also encouraged the growth of a vast range of non-state groupings, whose aims might be to influence national governments, but whose activities are also geared to the existence of resources and power at the European level. These groupings express the qualities of autonomy, representation and influence noted above, but within the particular setting of the EU, which gives them a strong institutional if not formal legal status.

These 'modifications' to conventional world politics in the EU context are carried further into the emergence of a system of multilevel interaction between states and non-state actors. In many ways, this can be seen as a particularly intense version of 'complex interdependence', with multiple channels of interaction, a fluctuating agenda of issues and a focus on non-coercive methods of getting things done. The EU in some ways is an accumulation of several powerful 'regimes', overlapping and constraining and placing a premium on collective solutions to problems of governance and management.

The incomplete but substantial transformation of the international arena has major implications for what might be described as the principles of world politics (Modelski 1972) – the organising ideas, understandings and practices that contribute to order and to the maintenance of stability, and which provide a guide for policy. It has been noted above that the template of sovereignty, recognition and control must be supplemented by the qualities of autonomy, representation and influence. In addition, and equally importantly, there is a tension of historic dimensions between the assumption of self-interest and self-help and the principle of multilateralism. More and more, it appears that the essentially atomised image of world politics represented by a state-centric model needs to be supplemented by acceptance of the limits to self-help. In this situation, the principle of multi-lateralism has an important role to play. It is not new: it is merely that in the last decade of the twentieth century, there is more than ever a perception that many essential values and objectives cannot be achieved or safeguarded on a solely national basis (Ruggie 1993a). The need for concepts and policies that take as central the need to work together rather than the inevitability of competition or even war, is a fundamental part of many theories and approaches in world politics. This does not rule out conflict, although it may mean that conflict is as much about how to collaborate as about anything else. It does not rule out or marginalise states and national governments, but it does see them as part of a broader set of networks and frameworks for the achievement of shared objectives.

Multilateralism is thus not only a principle of world politics for the late twentieth century: it is also part of the day-to-day reality of policy-making, and nowhere has this been more apparent than in western Europe. Many authors have drawn attention to the ways in which world politics is increasingly about rule-making, institution building and the construction of a global 'negotiated order', rather than about hard military security or violent conflict (Young 1982; Krasner 1983; Keohane 1984; Kratochwil 1989). In such a context, it is relatively easy to see the EU as the strongest and most formalised expression of the new 'principles of world politics'. It constitutes a highly institutionalised 'negotiated order', and is based above all on the interlocking interests of its members. A great deal of what goes on in the EU falls precisely into the framework of institutionalised multilateralism: the operations of the European Council and the Council of Minsters in particular can be seen as institutional devices designed to make states adhere to the principles of reciprocity, and the complex legal and institutional mechanisms of the broader European project ultimately rest on this foundation.

The tension between state-centric views of world politics and the image of multilayered and multilateral politics is intimately linked to notions of order and change in the world arena. For a state-centric interpretation, there are a number of possible sources of change or disorder. The number of states can increase or diminish; the hierarchy of states can change; the concerns of leading states, and their willingness to bear the burden of leadership, can change; and, most dramatically, the non-violent mechanisms of international order can be abandoned in favour of violence and war (Northedge 1976; Bull 1977). It can be seen that the central concern here is with the power, hierarchy and interests of states, and with the ways in which these tend towards certain processes and outcomes. This does not, of course, mean that world politics will inevitably degenerate into warfare as the tensions build up in the system, rather as the tensions between tectonic plates in the earth's crust lead to earthquakes. The two saving graces of the system are, on the one hand, the notion of responsible statehood and on the other, the concept and practice of the balance of power.

These two notions are closely linked and are vital to a state-centric under-standing of order and change in world politics. It is assumed that the governments and leaderships of nation states in a competitive world will act responsibly in calculating the costs and the risks of resorting to coercive or violent means and that, as a result, their interactions will overwhelmingly be of such a kind as to generate balance and order (Miller 1981). In this image, interstate politics forms a kind of continuous negotiation in which responsible leaderships are constrained by the objective realities of the international arena, and in which they are anxious to safeguard the interests of their countries by negotiation rather than by the use of force or coercion. Stability, and orderly change, are ensured by this kind of self-denying ordinance, observed even by the most dominant of states, since there is a chance that even the most dominant may be challenged by a coalition of others.

This is a fairly conservative notion of international order and change, built upon the perception that disruption and disorder are costly to all concerned. But it does represent the reality that the maintenance of international security and order rely upon complex calculations by national authorities, operating in conditions of security interdependence. The term 'security complex' has been used to describe this reality (Buzan 1991, Chapter 5), and it adequately expresses what is a sophisticated view of the continuing relevance of states and state authorities in the provision of international order. When we examine this in the context of the EU, it is apparent that the European integration project is in many ways precisely linked to ideas of security and a kind of international 'conservatism'. The initial 'bargain' in the 1950s was about security as much as it was about economic integration – indeed, the two went side by side. Since then, a major feature of the EC's and then the EU's role has been the stabilisation of western Europe and – increasingly – of the 'near abroad' in the wider Europe, the Mediterranean and elsewhere. If we see the EU as an expression of modified interstate politics, it is quite natural to emphasise its contribution to and concern for stability and security.

It is clear, though, that such notions do not always, or consistently, incorporate the pressures created by multilayered and multidimensional politics, as outlined earlier. The emphasis on stability and orderly change can be markedly at odds with the demands of non-state or transnational groupings for various forms of justice, and can be viewed as the basis for more or less repressive forms of containment. The emphasis on the high politics of security can be markedly at odds with the growth of new challenges in the economic, social and environmental fields. In addition, the notion of responsible statehood can be challenged forcefully by notions of group rights and the diffusion of power in a changing world arena (Hocking and Smith 1995, Chapter 14).

It is this set of challenges that has led to some of the most passionate debates in the study of world politics during the past ten years, and which is central to an understanding of what might be called the 'EU order'. The fundamentally modernist and positivist version of the world presented by statist interpretations (and indeed by some interpretations based on the growth of international institutions and cooperation) can be and has been challenged by a view based on the need for awareness of differences and tensions within a rapidly changing world arena. In this light, the EU is more than an expression of modified interstate politics: it is the focus for processes that bring together new varieties of identity and need. One question that arises immediately is the extent to which this variety can be contained within, and expressed by, the existing European institutions (see Chapter 2). Another question follows: to what extent is the EU organised and institutionalised at the appropriate scale for the new variety of world politics?

This question involves a range of rather novel dimensions for the study of world politics, and implicitly for its practice in the EU and elsewhere. First, there is an emphasis on the simultaneous processes of globalisation and localisation or diffusion. The process of globalisation could be taken to underpin a process of global homogenisation, in which structures of governance, production and exchange became more alike everywhere. But equally, it can be and has been taken to express a process of diffusion and difference, in which identities become fragmented, power is diffused, and processes of governance can vary widely at the local, regional and national levels (Dicken 1992; Johnston *et al.*, 1995, Parts II–III; Booth and Smith 1997).

Second, there is a renewed attention to the implications of space and location, and their links to identities. No longer are these defined by the international presence of the (nation) state and its territorial claims; rather, they are defined by reference to group needs, to the pursuit of specific objectives in the economic, social and cultural spheres, and by the ability of individuals and groups to gain 'voice' through channels other than those provided by national authorities (Johnston *et al.* 1995).

Third, these perceptions have fundamental implications for notions of legitimacy and mechanisms of order. It can no longer be taken for granted that the imperatives of state power and the need for security in a competitive 'society of states' are what drive world politics and give them shape: rather, the answers to questions about legitimacy and order are likely to be diffuse and varied in line with the proliferation of identities and 'voices'. As noted in Chapter 2, there is evidence that new territorial forms are being accompanied by new social and cultural demands, with profound implications for the nature of polities in Europe and elsewhere (Ruggie 1993b; Waever *et al.* 1993).

World politics at the level of concepts and working assumptions is thus in a period of profound flux. It has never been an area without contestation, but it can be argued that the contestation is now of a more fundamental kind than ever before. This reflects not only the growth of the academic community studying world politics, but also a number of objective changes in world politics itself.

The global balance

As noted above, the 'Cold War system' has been a defining feature of world politics for most of the period since 1945. It was this system that defined 'western Europe' and by implication the European Communities as they emerged in the 1950s and 1960s; it was this system that shaped the links between western Europe, the European Communities and other parts of the world, to the east, the south and the west (Link 1986; Kegley 1991). It is thus important to investigate the key features and operating assumptions of the system, before going on to suggest some of the ways in which the collapse of the system has affected the place of Europe and the EU in world politics.

The key defining characteristic of the 'Cold War system' was a bipolarity of structure. By this is not meant that the entire world was for political purposes divided into two camps; the reality was never so comprehensive or tidy. Rather, it is clear that the 'Cold War system' relied on the concentration of power – particularly military power – into two main nodes, centred upon the United States and the Soviet Union. The construction of elaborate alliance systems, and of economic regimes, in both east and west supported and magnified this structure. In retrospect, it is possible to question the comprehensiveness and the durability of many of the structures established, but this rather misses the point that perceptions and actions were inexorably shaped by the broad bipolarity of power. This was not merely a bipolarity of power, though; for many involved, it was a bipolarity of ideas and of cultures, expressed in the notions of the 'free world' and the 'communist bloc'.

Such a broad structure gave rise to important operating assumptions. In both east and west, though with different manifestations, it was assumed more or less that the bloc leaders took precedence particularly in defining security postures and policies. It could be argued that this was a rather less tidy process in the west than in the east, but in both cases there was a broad assumption that military muscle and structural power would give precedence if not hegemony to the bloc leader.

This was not, of course, a one-sided bargain: the bloc leader had responsibilities as well as privileges, and there were costs of maintaining formal or informal empires both against the opposing camp and against defections from within. That is to say, the benefits of solidarity and bloc leadership were balanced to a degree by the costs of economic and political leadership (Keal 1983; Calleo 1987). For the EC during the 'high Cold War', this meant that member states were not only engaged in the 'game' within the Communities, but that they were also embedded in the constraints of the Cold War order; both the smaller and the more powerful members of the Community had to take this into account.

The impact of this context was the more powerful because the Cold War system was also in its initial form, Eurocentric; more than that, it was in many respects effectively Germanocentric, with the status and allegiances of the divided Germany a matter of concern to both sides, and the stimulus to crisis on more than one occasion. It has been argued that this element of the structure was effectively stabilised by the mid-1950s, and that from then until the mid-1980s, the European theatre of the Cold War underwent no substantial changes (DePorte 1986). Whether this is wholly valid or not, it is certainly the case that from the early 1960s, the essentially European focus of the Cold War system was diluted. The Vietnam War, the Middle East crises of 1967 and 1973, and the 'new Cold War' of the early 1980s were by no means irrelevant to Europeans, and had their European resonances, but they were redolent of a globalisation of superpower competition (Halliday 1986).

Meanwhile, the attention of Europeans in particular – both EC members and others – became more steadily focused on the future shape of the continent. After the mid-1980s, this was to become an obsession, but to focus entirely on that period is to miss the processes that had been fermenting since the early 1970s. In structural terms, the Conference on Security and Cooperation in Europe (held in Helsinki in 1975) and its follow-up meetings could be seen as consolidating the Cold War system, but in important ways they began to contribute to the recognition of a new Europe (Wallace 1990). Here, it is important to note that, because of the globalisation of Cold War concerns and the increasing attention to the shape of Europe, the structure of strict bipolarity was being questioned from a number of sources from the beginning of the 1970s.

As became apparent after the mid-1980s, the new politics of Europe within the Cold War system were no longer subject to the pereceived structural constraints of bipolarity. General de Gaulle had suggested as much during the 1960s, but it was only in the later 1980s that this became a given rather than a speculation. As has been noted by a range of authors, the objective shift in the system outpaced in many ways the conventional wisdom and categories used by academics and policy-makers to organise their thinking about events; the challenge was as much to concepts and to the capacity to contemplate radical change as it was to institutions and structures (Palmer 1988; Alting von Geusau 1993; Story 1993). This made it, if anything, much less comfortable to deal with. Change was no longer essentially contained within the broader system; rather, the system itself was changing and the foundations shifting in unpredictable ways. The cosiness of the Cold War and nostalgia for the days when one knew who one's enemies were has been much remarked, as has the view that the only way to regain international stability is to refashion something akin to the Cold War system (Mearsheimer 1990).

What precisely were the challenges to world politics posed by the collapse of the Cold War system? Central to the challenges was a new range of problems, some of which bore the familiar marks of radical change within the state system. First, what was to be done with the 'black hole' created by the collapse of the Soviet Union, and with the problems of order created by large numbers of footloose nuclear weapons? Second, what was to be done about the emergence of large numbers of fragile new states, both in central/eastern Europe and in the former Soviet Union? Third, what was to be the position of the United States in the new structure: was it the 'only superpower' capable of dominating the world and willing to do so, the 'lonely superpower' unable to adjust to the demands of international primacy without the focus provided by a powerful rival, or was it the 'uncertain superpower' beset by doubts about its domestic economic performance and its international obligations? (Gaddis 1992; Tucker and Hendrickson 1992; Haftendorn and Tuschhoff 1993; Smith and Woolcock 1993, Chapter 2).

Alongside these ostensibly familiar 'state-system' problems went others of a more novel kind. How should political action adjust to a world in which the balance of economic power had shifted as fundamentally as the balance of military power, but in different directions, with the European Union and Japan taking places alongside the United States? How might governments and other actors deal with the increasingly apparent linkages, suppressed in part by the security concerns of the Cold War system, between economic, cultural and security concerns? How should political actors deal with a change from the politics of bipolarity with a relatively clear-cut set of rules for behaviour, to a politics of interconnectedness and identity, with far less apparent guidance as to appropriate institutional or other solutions for political problems? (Alting von Geusau 1993; Story 1993).

The collapse of the Soviet Union was a profoundly unsettling experience not only for the citizens of this supposedly permanent superpower but also for the leaderships of the United States, the EU and individual European countries. State-centric approaches provide a salient explanation for such uncertainties, with the concept of the 'power vacuum' occurring when a component in the balance of power is eliminated or enfeebled. The outcomes of such a situation are to be sought either in the occupation of the vacuum by other major powers, or in the reconstruction of the failed component. Germany after 1945 displayed elements of both tendencies. But the failure of one component in a wider balance is rather different, however dramatic, from the collapse of one element in a bipolar balance. Not only this, but the collapse of a major nuclear power carried with it the potential for disruption of one of the most apparently stable but also most dangerous of the elements in the Cold War system. There was literally no precedent for such a situation, and not surprisingly the major actors in the balance found themselves unprepared to deal with it (Keohane and Hoffmann 1993, Part I; Story 1993).

During the early 1990s, therefore, a complex set of contradictory tendencies emerged: the United States placed increasing weight on the reconstruction of Russia as a proxy for the former Soviet Union, whilst insisting on observance of nuclear disarmament agreements; and the Europeans, led by the Germans, placed their bets on the economic reconstruction and stabilisation of the Russians and other successor states. The logic of state-centric balance dictated that the reconstruction of Russia should take a central place, but the perhaps equally compelling logic of economic forces meant that this was not simply a matter of security. The stabilisation of the balance was to be achieved by domestic economic and political measures as well as by the application of international agreements and international remedies. An interesting example is provided by the convoluted process of associating Russia with NATO through the Partnership for Peace arrangements; far from being a simple matter of international agreement, these processes became bound up with the internal stability of the Russian state and society, and with the domestic politics both of the United States and west European countries (Keohane and Hoffmann 1993; Peterson 1996, Part II).

No less was this true of the ways in which the new European and Eurasian state system came into being during the early 1990s. The specific impact of change in central and eastern Europe will be dealt with below. Here, it is important to note the ways in which the proliferation of small, often fragile states as a result of the Soviet collapse has borne out another assumption of statist analysis. It will be recalled that 'responsible statehood' was seen as a key feature of world order in a state-dominated system. Whilst the Cold War system validated this assumption in one way, by pointing to the conservative nature of the policies and actions of the United States and the Soviet Union, it is clear that in other ways it undermined it. The states of the Soviet bloc in particular were not allowed to be responsible and sovereign in the true sense, and thus had little on which to draw when the 'security blanket' of Soviet power disappeared in the early 1990s. Not only this, but the creation of many new states from the collapse of the Soviet Empire multiplied the problem. If responsible statehood is taken as a key institution of a state-based world order, then this was undermined in several dimensions in the early 1990s. And it was not clear that the institutional framework provided by Cold War alliances and other bodies was sufficient to sustain the new and unstable equilibrium (Hyde-Price 1996; Webber 1996).

The changing role and position of the United States served only to complicate the picture. By 1991, it appeared that the USA was in a position of dominance comparable only to that which it had occupied in the late 1940s. Militarily, it was supreme not only because of the collapse of Soviet power but also because of its demonstration of crushing power in the Gulf War. Ideologically, it had no rivals given the way in which the ideals of free-market capitalism and liberal democracy were sweeping the world. Politically, it could muster strong leadership not only at home but also through the panoply of international institutions to which it was central. Economically, despite the paranoia induced by the 1987 stock market collapse and the 'double deficits' which were the legacy of Reaganism, the USA was still a major power and capable of generating economic growth of a kind not available to a number of its rivals. However, the consequences of this apparently uniquely favourable position were by no means predictable. Indeed, the mood of national withdrawal and uncertainty in the USA was comparable in the early 1990s not to the crusading years of the early Cold War but rather to the onset of isolationism in the 1920s, after the end of the First World War. This was compounded by US uncertainties in dealing with the shifts of international economic power: the balance between the USA and Japan, and between the USA and the European Union, provided an equally challenging policy dilemma for American leaders, and their responses were an uneasy blend of unilateralism, bilateralism and multilateralism (Steinbruner 1989; Smith and Woolcock 1993, Chapter 2).

The international structure of the early 1990s was thus profoundly unsettled. The collapse of a major component, the emergence of large numbers of new and fragile participants, the uncertainty of the potential leader: all of these contributed to an air of great uncertainty overall, and thus shaped the context of the European Union's development. In both the political and the economic spheres, the increasing interconnectedness of national societies produced a number of compelling 'system frictions' between the leading players, which could not be explained simply in terms of state-centred politics. The linkages between the economic and the security domains, given full voice by a number of groupings in the USA, further demonstrated that it was not possible to see things simply through a state-centric lens. In almost all societies, the end of the Cold War took the lid off two central dilemmas: first, the relationship between politics and markets, and second, the relationship between politics and the military. These could not be accommodated in a simple 'billiard ball' image of national and international security, and the result everywhere was increased questioning of established structures of authority and legitimacy (Waever 1990; Waever *et al.* 1993).

The processes described above not only entailed the collapse of the Cold War system, they also demanded the reformulation of some fundamental aspects of world politics, both on the part of analysts and on the part of policy-makers. Three specific challenges and areas of uncertain response can be identified here. First, there was a need to redefine the key axes of conflict and areas of threat or risk in the world arena – in particular, the need to define new and emerging security complexes, and to attempt to shape institutions that could contribute to their management. Second, there was a need to look very hard at the linkages between security and political authority, and to explore the notions of civilian power, which had been given an artificial air of separation by the application of the Cold War 'security blanket'. Third, there was a need to examine the nature of structures of political authority more generally. The tensions and contrasts between markets, hierarchies and networks have run through this chapter so far, and it is clear that they form a central feature of the developing world politics of the 1990s. It is clear too that the demise of the Cold War system has not led to any easy or complete replacement of one set of assumptions with another; the assumptions of state-centric hierarchical politics are not easy to re-apply in the circumstances of the late 1990s.

The new Europe

As already noted at several points, the logics of change and transformation outlined above were focused in many ways, especially by the emerging politics of a new European order. It would not be going too far to suggest that both in western and in central/eastern Europe the changes and challenges of the late 1980s and the 1990 created a far-reaching crisis of statehood (Smith 1994a, 1996a). There were several components of this crisis: radical structural change in both the relations of European states and their links to the global economic and security systems, the rise of new and often fragile states in Europe and beyond, challenges to the boundaries of the European order itself, linkages between economics, politics and security of a novel and often surprising kind, and questions about the adequacy of existing institutions to contain or to express the new pressures (Smith 1994a; van Ham 1994). These are challenges, as noted, both to policy and to concepts of world politics.

The seemingly stable if not permanent European order of the post-Second World War era was inherently based upon containment and division (Alting von Geusau 1993). Indeed, as has been argued, it was only this containment and division that made the European Communities and the integration process feasible; the Communities were, in many respects, the key building block of a divided Europe, the logical accompaniment to the Marshall Plan and NATO. They represented in statist terms the expression of the interests of key states, with the United States a vital guarantor and catalyst to the process of consolidation and stabilisation. In the east, they were mirrored at least in part by the 'socialist division of labour' in the CMEA and by the Warsaw Treaty organisation. Although there were uncertainties and tensions in the transatlantic relationship, and between the USA and the EC as they developed and prospered, the keystone of the western system was the convergence of interests in a European order built upon the containment not only of the Soviet Union but also of Germany, and centring on the two strands of institutionalisation through the Communities and NATO (Calleo 1970, 1987; Palmer 1988; Story 1993, Chapter 1).

The transformation of the late 1980s and the 1990s threw into question many of the central components of this European order, creating profound issues of stability and policy innovation. Crucially, they went alongside, and some would say were informed by, the process of regeneration and revitalisation in the EC (see Chapter 1). The new architecture of the new Europe would take as one of its givens the movement of the EC towards a single integrated market, and beyond that the new impetus to the building of political and security institutions for the EU. But there was also the possibility not of progress in the building of political order at the European level, but of the regression of European politics to the enmities and conflicts of previous generations, with the removal of the 'security overlay' provided by the Cold War and the superpowers (Mearsheimer 1990; Buzan 1991; Hoffmann 1992).

The challenge to a European order built on containment and division was thus both a practical and a conceptual one. Practically, there was the issue of appropriate responses to the removal of seemingly permanent elements of the order. Conceptually, there was the problem of developing new concepts of 'Europe' and new principles for the generation of order and stability. From a statist point of view, the challenge was especially to state leaderships, and particularly to the leaderships of the most prominent states. If the 'old Europe' of containment and division had been built essentially on the convergence of state preferences and interests, how now could those preferences and interests be reformulated and reconstructed to provide a set of policy principles and institutional mechanisms for a new world? The old congruence of ideas, institutions and state power was no longer to be relied upon, but there was no consensus or settled perception of the new institutional or power framework to act as the guide to policy (Smith 1994a).

To re-emphasise the point made at the start of this section, international order and state policies were thrown into crisis both in the west and in the east. In the west, the crisis might have been more subtle, but it was no less potentially far-reaching than in the east. What were the main symptoms of this crisis? Several can be discerned. One of the most prominent was a nostalgia for the Cold War and for the seemingly clear sense of alignments it expressed, expressed partly by the search for a new 'security blanket' or a new 'pacifier' to replace the overlay provided by the USA and the Soviet Union during the Cold War (Mearsheimer 1990). This was accompanied by a search for new institutional frameworks, leading to what some commentators have referred to as 'organisational interlock', and others as 'organisational gridlock' or 'institutional overcrowding', accompanied by profound uncertainties about the capacity or relevance of existing institutions such as NATO (Smith and Woolcock 1993, Chapter 4). More specific were concerns about the status and role of particular states in the order, focusing especially on Germany (in addition to the broader concern about Russia as a component in the global and European order) (Asmus 1991; Treverton 1992b, Chapters 6–7).

One result of these concerns was a search for new definitions of order and justice, partly expressed through institutions such as the Conference on Security and Cooperation in Europe (CSCE) and the Organisation for Security and Co-operation in Europe (OSCE), but also reflecting the profound tensions between individual, group and national justice which were exploited by those with an interest in conflict and the breakdown of the established order (for example, in the former Yugoslavia or parts of the former Soviet Union). There arose a profound sense of uncertainty about the boundaries of the political and security orders, finding expression not only in unsure responses to regional or ethnic conflicts, but also in tensions around such issues as migration and what has been called 'societal security' in both the west and the east (Waever *et al.* 1993).

These symptoms gave rise to what might be termed a 'post-Cold War syndrome' in the politics of Europe, linking internal insecurities and tensions to the broader European order and expressing both the practical and the conceptual difficulties of adjusting to the new and fluid situation (Waever *et al.* 1993; Waever 1996). In particular, the emergence of a new 'arc of crisis' on the borders of Cold

War Europe, extending from the Balkans to the Caucasus, posed a stern institutional and political challenge, calling into question the boundaries of the transatlantic alliance and the concept of containment that has been implicit in the entire history of post-1945 Europe (Smith and Woolcock 1993; Hyde-Price 1996; Webber 1996).

Statist theory would have at least a partial answer to this sense of crisis: the responsible authorities, particularly of leading states, should appraise the situation and their interests, and apply the required measures of power to create order and stability. Transitions in state systems are inherently messy, and it is to be expected that coercion, defection and the use of apparently random force will characterise the behaviour of important groupings. But a new order will emerge, based on the convergence of state preferences on certain salient territorial and political dispositions, and expressed where appropriate in collective action through intergovernmental bodies, ranging from the UN through the OSCE to the EU itself.

Such an approach can be attacked at its roots: there simply is not the settled hierarchy of states or the acceptance of the principles of responsible sovereign statehood on which such a reformulated order might be based. Balances of power, whether simple or complex, regional or global, depend vitally on the capacity and willingness of the key state authorities to act in accordance with their own and the more general interest (Bull 1977). Often, this trade-off between the particular and the general is difficult, as in 1930s Europe; early 1990s Europe was, if anything, even more broken and mercurial, and not surprisingly state leaderships have subsequently been profoundly unsettled in their thinking about the order more generally.

In this situation, it is quite difficult to see how institutions at the European level (or the global level as applied in the European theatre) can operate effectively. They are inherently linked to the preferences and inclinations of key states, and if those are questionable, then there is little that they can do. Here, statist and broader analyses would agree: whatever frameworks are contemplated for the settlement or resolution of conflict in the new Europe, they cannot achieve effectiveness without recognition of their legitimacy and the provision of adequate material or political resources. Whether these key elements are provided by state authorities or in some way generated from transnational sources 'from the bottom up', it is clear that the Europe of the mid-1990s suffered from a deficiency in all of the significant areas. Whilst this deficiency was most clearly seen in the affairs of the former Yugoslavia, it is a pervasive element in the attempt to construct some form of 'negotiated order' for the new Europe (Smith 1997a; Wallace 1997).

The upshot of this situation appears to be that the new Europe in the late 1990s is a mosaic of order and disorder, institutions and forces, ideas and authorities. Not for nothing have some analysts been attracted to the notion of a 'new medievalism' in which territory, authority and the capacity to act are fragmented and diffused among a wide range of actors (Waever 1996). In a sense, the new Europe, and its Eurasian extension, are akin not to the Europe of the high Middle Ages with the seemingly accepted authority of the church and the Holy Roman

Empire, instead they are more like the 'times of troubles' following upon the challenge to papal authority and the rise of competing religious frameworks. As noted earlier, this is a Europe in which identity is defined by difference and often by fear or antagonism, rather than by the convergence of transnational economic and social forces that might be imagined by a liberal approach.

Is the picture, either politically or analytically, really so negative, though? One apparent beacon of a new conception of order is the European Union. As has been seen, the European integration process for much of its life has been indissolubly linked with the Cold War system, although in the process it has developed many characteristics going beyond conventional world politics. Is there a basis for arguing that, in the new Europe, the EU constitutes the basis for generation of a new and more robust order?

Challenges for the European Union

For many political groupings and for almost as many academic analysts, the presence in the new Europe of the EU constitutes a fundamentally novel element in the generation of a new European order. Briefly put, the argument is this: the EU and before it the EC have transformed relations between the so-far fifteen members of the organisation, on the basis not only of economic integration but also of the building of institutions with essentially political resonances. In the context of the new Europe, it is not only inevitable but also desirable that the EU will form the core of a new European order in which the rule of law, civic statehood and the beneficial effects of economic interaction will be spread. Given this, the EU has not only the position but almost the duty to contribute what it alone can contribute to the evolution of the new Europe, and to the consolidation of principles of multilateralism and reciprocity (Wallace 1992; Allen and Smith 1991–92, 1998).

This sketch of the position contains a number of important components, vital to perceptions and policies in the Europe of the 1990s and to interpretation of change in world politics more broadly. First, it is assumed that whilst the EC and then the EU are based initially on a form of interstate bargain, they have become something else, of greater permanence and embeddedness than a traditional alliance or coalition. Second, it is assumed that this permanence and embeddedness reflect the characteristics of the EU as a 'community of law' based on a novel and pervasive notion of the ways in which responsible authorities deal with each other in a form of continuously negotiated order. Third, it is taken as axiomatic that the novelty and the promise of the EU rests not only upon an interstate bargain but also upon recognition of identities, needs and the potential for action at a variety of levels within and across societies. As such, it is more fully representative of multilayered world politics and of the linkages between politics, economics and security than other forms of state-based organisation. Fourth, and as a consequence of the above, it is argued that the EU is a 'civilising power' (Hill 1990) with the need and the responsibility to generalise and diffuse the benefits of Union membership or of association with the Union.

This, though, encapsulates the ambiguity of the EU as a presence in the new Europe (Allen and Smith 1990, 1991–92, 1998). First, it is indisputable that the EU constitutes an essential structure of the post-Cold War European order. Is it, though, a force for unity and the diffusion of economic and political benefits, or a force for division and containment (Smith 1996a, 1997a)? After all, it is to be expected that existing members of the EU will want to preserve some of their benefits and their 'investment' as well as giving the 'civilising' benefits of membership or association to outsiders. Taken to its extreme, this interpretation could form the basis for a new division of Europe, with several tiers of association or quasi-membership for the states of central and eastern Europe and a complex of 'containing' association and cooperation agreements with states of the former Soviet Union.

Second, the EU – and particularly the EC – can be seen as one of the ultimate 'modernist' projects, looking to the management of technical and economic processes through the erection of rules of law and the allocation of competences. Whilst not a state, the EC/EU takes from notions of statehood the hard (not to say harsh) allocation of powers and authority. In post-Cold War European and world politics, it is not clear whether this 'hard' version of the allocation of powers is appropriate, but it is clear that the series of interstate bargains on which the EC/EU rests creates a pressure to arrive at clearcut and definitive allocations and mechanisms. There are tensions here, between this 'hard' version of EC/EU powers and the 'softer' versions based on subsidiarity or regional governance (see Chapter 1), but the tension is unresolved.

Partly because of the tensions inherent in the systems of authority and allocation on which the EC/EU is based, it is not clear what the relationship is between the EU and change or transformation at the level of action. To be precise, the EC/EU faces the need to muster two forms of capacity to respond: 'carrying capacity' and 'mobilisation capacity' (Allen and Smith 1991–2, 1998). Great expectations and potentially great burdens have been placed on the EU in the post-Maastricht period, and it is unclear whether the EU can sustain them. In terms of 'carrying capacity', it is far from clear that the EU's institutions or its members are willing or able to absorb the implications of multidimensional change. Whilst some argue that 'widening' and 'deepening' of the EU can not only coexist but must go together, there are equally those who argue that a linear sequence of internal reform and widening should be followed. In terms of 'mobilisation capacity', it is not clear what the ability of the EU to extract political support or tangible resources from its members is, in a situation of rapidly changing demands and domestic economic stringency; indeed, further development of the EU is likely to entail complex bargains, for example over Economic and Monetary Union (EMU) or over further enlargement, with existing members extracting the maximum of resources from the EU in return for their acquiescence or support. This leads to major questions about the EU's 'capacity to act' and the 'capacity to interact' in world and European politics, which in turn relate to the 'capability-expectations gap' identified by Christopher Hill (see Chapter 7 below; Hill 1993, 1998).

The EU is thus an ambiguous symbol and presence in the European arena after the Cold War, expressing many of the ties and tensions identified in Chapter 1 of this book at the same time as it expresses many of the contestable features of world politics in the last decade of the twentieth century. It struggles to express new forms of identity and interaction, at the same time as it embeds powerful notions of state interest and preferences. It experiences tensions between the established virtues and benefits of 'civilian power' and the new demands of linkage between social, political, economic and security concerns in a multilevel political arena. It operates to create both a 'magnet effect', attracting new associates and potential new members, and a 'fortress effect' in which the existing investments of members and allocations of competence are safeguarded against both internal and external challenges. It juxtaposes a formal internal negotiated order of considerable complexity against the demands of rapid and sometimes convulsive change in world politics and the European arena.

Not surprisingly, therefore, there has been renewed political and academic attention to the complex and ambiguous relationship between the EU and statehood and the EU and world order (*Journal of Common Market Studies* 1996). What this chapter has attempted to demonstrate are the ways in which the evolution of the EU links with the development of world politics, the global balance and the European arena in the 1990s. To do this, a sense of history and of change is essential, and the chapter has focused on a number of central dimensions in both the history and the changes. By doing so, it has also added a dimension to the understanding of states and nations given in Chapter 2, and it links forward to the treatment of international political economy in Chapter 4.

4 International political economy

Introduction

The European Union (EU) is the product of a long evolution which started in the 1940s with the habits of cooperation fostered by the Marshall Plan, and which continued through the establishment of the European Coal and Steel Community in 1952 and the European Economic Community in 1957. It is currently the world's largest trading power, a principal target and source of foreign direct investment (FDI) and an increasing influence on world currency values and movements (Dent 1997; Piening 1997, Chapter 1; Tsoukalis 1997, Chapter 10). As such, it seems almost redundant to point out that the EU is central to the international political economy, and that the international political economy is central to the EU. The policy agenda for the EU is shaped fundamentally by the development of the global economic arena, and the EU has become an active player in some of the most dynamic parts of that arena.

To state the situation, though, is to raise important questions about the nature both of the EU and of the changing international political economy. In the first place, there are questions about the relationship between the EU's economic weight and its political and economic influence. Given its crucial position in the international political economy, it is inevitable that the EU, intentionally or otherwise, will have significant international effects. It accounts for a large and growing part of the world's production and exchange, and the successive enlargements of the Union have accentuated this trend. Its impact both on member states and on non-members can be felt at the level of the international economic framework and – sometimes acutely – in specific sectors of activity. However, the consequences of the EU's presence and actions are often uncertain and dynamic, contributing to the volatility of international economic developments. There is an interaction between change in the international economic system and change in the Union; not only this, but the differential rhythms of change in the EU and the world political economy can produce both challenges and opportunities. No clearer illustration of this can be found than the intersection in the late 1980s and early 1990s of the Single Market Programme (SMP), international trade negotiations in the Uruguay Round and radical international political change (Treverton 1992b; Harrison 1994; Smith 1994b; Hocking and Smith 1997).

The intersection and interaction of change within the EU and change between the EU and the world political economy are thus major elements in the analysis of international political economy more generally. They are also the source of significant ambiguities. The EU is a major actor in the world political economy, exercising state-like functions, yet it is not a state. It is a highly-structured and rule-governed economic space, yet it is also part of a dynamic global economy. It is a powerful regime and source of order in the international political economy, yet it can also be seen as a barrier and as an obstacle to international exchange. It has many of the makings of a 'foreign economic policy', but it also expresses the complexity of multilevel economic and political activity.

To these ambiguities of EU status and position can be added others relating to the EU's role. It can be seen as a bridge between potentially damaging international rivalry and the broader world economy, yet as already noted it can be seen as a barrier to global economic development. It can be seen as a 'success' in the international political economy, yet also as doomed to failure in the face of external economic and political change. As in other areas evaluated in this book, it is easy to discern the conceptual ambiguities surrounding the notions of territory, identity and function; no less is it possible to identify the ties and tensions surrounding the EU's role in the world political economy.

In this chapter, the aim is to establish a number of approaches to the analysis of the EU's position and role in the international political economy (IPE). First, there is a discussion of some key conceptual debates in the analysis of the IPE, and of the ways in which they might relate to the EU. Second, there is an analysis of key trends within the IPE, both globally and in relation to the 'new Europe' of the 1990s, which form a changing context for the evolution of the EU. Third, there is an evaluation of the relationship between the EU and the IPE, and of the challenges faced by the EU, in three areas: the EU *as* IPE, the EU *in* the IPE, and the IPE *in* the EU. Each of these 'cuts' at the problem is designed to highlight certain characteristics of the EU's status and role. In the final part of the chapter, the elements are brought together to form a general evaluation. It is apparent throughout that the EU's position and role express a number of tensions and contradictions, and that these work themselves out in policy terms. In particular, these tensions and contradictions can be explored in terms of the balance between three types of outcomes: authority, equity and efficiency.

Concepts and controversies in the IPE

The study of the IPE has burgeoned during the past two decades, and it is not the purpose here to give a detailed account of major trends and schools of thought (see for example Gilpin 1987; Stubbs and Underhill 1994; Krasner 1997; Spero and Hart 1997). Rather, it is the purpose, first to identify major conceptual focuses in the analysis of the IPE, and second, to identify important trends and relationships that can then form a background to consideration both of the 'new Europe' and of the EU's position and role.

Perhaps the most time-honoured approach to analysis of the IPE is that which can be labelled 'realism' or, in a more economic vein, 'mercantilism'. For realists, the nature of the IPE is defined principally, if not entirely, by the existence of sovereign states in a kind of proto-anarchy, with no authoritative mechanisms of global governance. Mercantilists make broadly the same assumptions, and define the economic purposes of state activity in the IPE as being the maximisation of national economic security. Traditional mercantilists literally believed that the success of a nation could be measured in terms of the accumulation of 'treasure' at the national level (Gilpin 1987, Chapter 2).

This is essentially a competitive view of the IPE, in which nations engage in a zero-sum contest, using the levers of national authority and power. In such a system, it is possible to define winners and losers and to construct a form of inter-national political/economic hierarchy. It is also logical to see national economic policies in the IPE as closely allied to national security, with the weapons of protectionism and sanctions linked implicitly if not explicitly with those of national military defence. This does not mean that there are no rules of the game in the IPE, since every state is capable of recognising that negotiation, alliances and cooperation of various types are possible sources of national betterment. But it does mean that states reserve the right to control of their own territory, citizens and companies in the cause of national economic interests. Such implications link the approach firmly to the statist analysis of world politics encountered in Chapter 3 (see also Knorr 1973).

A development of this view of unconstrained political/economic competition is that provided by the neo-realists, and more particularly by theorists of hegemonic stability. One description of neo-realism is 'structural realism', and this captures well one of the essential contrasts with realism. States in this view are not free agents: they are constrained by the international power structure. Not only this, but states can rationally recognise that there are advantages to structured cooperation and to the creation of certain types of international rules. In the IPE, such approaches have clear relevance, since they help to explain why inter-national political/economic processes do not degrade into a constant series of trade wars and 'beggar thy neighbour' contests. Force is added to the approach by the concept of hegemonic stability: this argues that the stability of the IPE depends crucially upon the existence of a hegemon, a leading power that is willing and able to lend its weight to the maintenance of international political/economic order. Periods of instability in the IPE can thus be related to the absence of such a hegemon, or to the unwillingness of dominant powers to act in line with their status. It is often argued, for example, that the interwar period in Europe showed the characteristics of such a breakdown, in the context of the decay of British hegemony and the unwillingness of the Americans to take up the burdens (Kindleberger 1973; Keohane 1984; Gilpin 1987).

Both realism and neo-realism are essentially founded on the centrality of states and statehood, and on the ways in which a statist IPE can be managed. This is not the case with the third approach to be examined here, that of liberalism and institutionalism. Vital to such an approach is the assumption that economic processes and economic actors do not coincide with national states, and also that they are at best only imperfectly controlled by such states and their governments. Many economic transactions, in this view, cross national borders, and the key organising feature is not the state but the market and its accompanying institutions. There are two directions in which the argument can go from this starting-point. First, it can take the form of what is sometimes called neo-liberalism, focusing on the logic of the market and denying the right of national governments or international institutions to intervene at more than the basic level. Second, and in contrast, the argument can move in the direction of international rule-making and institution-building, in the attempt to find an alternative to state power and interstate competition. Both of these 'branches' of the liberal approach thus play down (whilst not entirely discounting) the residual power of states; they also play up the impact of non-state actors and organisations both in the market and in the evolution of international governance (Gilpin 1987; Keohane and Nye 1987).

A final approach to the problem of the IPE can be described as the structuralist/dependency school of thought. In contrast to both the realist/neo-realist and the liberal/institutionalist approaches, the structuralist/dependency approach focuses on the underlying power structures created by inequalities of economic status. To put it simply, the world is seen as characterised by permanent inequalities, and by the exploitation of the dependent by the dominant. This is founded on permanent conflicts of interest between the rich and the poor, both within and between nations. The effects can be seen in issues of economic development, but also in terms of the lack of independence and autonomy available to the dependent societies, in government, in culture and in communication (Brett 1985). Not surprisingly, the roots of this approach are to be found in the experience of the Third World, where it has been challenged by the other approaches not only in terms of theory but also in terms of national policy choices.

Each of these approaches thus takes a distinctive position on the IPE. Each has a view on the centrality of various participants and processes, on the ways in which change and contradictions are handled, and on the results in terms of global, group or national welfare. But none of them can be taken in isolation either from the others or from the reality of change in the IPE. During the 1990s, each has had to cope with the fact that the old nostrums about the development and functioning of the IPE seem to be challenged as never before. This has profound implications both for the 'new Europe' and for the EU. They are to be found, as indicated earlier, in three areas: actors and structures; trends and contradictions; and outcomes.

Actors and structures

Attention to actors and structures in the IPE has largely revolved around three areas: the relationship between states and markets, the relationship between the public and the private, and the relationship between production, investment and exchange. The three are not easily separable in practice, but it is important to deal with them here as clearly as possible.

A major preoccupation in the study of the IPE has been the uneasy relationship between states and markets (Strange 1988). A crude model of the nation state has implications not only for the ways in which national political activity is organised, but also for the organisation of economic activity. Realist analysis of the IPE, allied with mercantilist analysis, has perpetuated an image of the state as the gatekeeper between the national and the international political economies, and as the controller of economic activity within its borders. Further, it has generated an image of competition between nationally organised economies in which winners and losers can be identified, and in which national security has an indispensable economic component. But this image has always been in tension with the notion that markets, although influenced by politics and state activities, have their own dynamics: in other words, that the interplay of economic forces is either in tension with the aims of states or is beyond their control. This is a crucial tension, since it feeds directly through into arguments about authority and the distribution of international economic goods and 'bads' (see below).

A second area of debate is that relating to the public/private divide. In a sense, this is a continuation of the states/markets debate, since it implies that there is a dynamic and complex relationship between economic activity in the public domain and that which is generated by private actors and their actions. A 'strong' version of statehood would argue that for all practical purposes, activity in the IPE is governed by the needs and policies of states and governments, but this is clearly far from an accurate portrayal of the situation. States and governments can work alongside private economic actors such as large corporations, as well as other 'governmental' bodies such as international organisations (Stopford and Strange 1991; Strange 1994). Sometimes, there is a form of alliance or convergence between public and private activities, as it has been argued that there was between US governments and large multinational firms in Latin America or elsewhere. Sometimes, there can be decided tensions between public and private aims, as for example in cases where governments impose economic sanctions but corporations see fit to ignore them. At the level of the IPE as a whole, there is a related argument about global economic welfare and the sectional aims of private bodies: how, for example, can ideas of international economic development be matched up with those of corporate profit (Julius 1990)?

A final area of tension in the area of actors and structures is that between the coexisting structures of production, investment and exchange in the IPE. This again cannot be isolated from the discussion of states and markets or that of the public and the private. It is apparent even from the most cursory study of the IPE that there is a fluctuating balance between the processes by which goods and services are produced, the ways in which investment is decided and located, and the ways in which goods, services and knowledge are exchanged. From the Middle Ages, it is evident that whilst much production of necessity has been national or local in character, the growth of investment and exchange has been inherently international. The linkages between the continuing pressures for location of production in national or local contexts, and the contradictory pressures for internationalisation of investment and exchange, are central to the development of the IPE. To take only a few examples, it has been noted that whilst governments place importance on the attraction and retention of manufacturing and service industries, corporations are often more mobile and opportunistic than governments would wish them to be. This links to the tensions that can arise over the process of FDI: attraction and retention of FDI is a prime aim of many governments, but it exposes them to the possibility that FDI may prove 'footloose' and they may find themselves in a competitive bidding process. Given that growth of FDI has outstripped the growth of international trade in recent years, this is clearly important. This is not, though, to argue that trade is unimportant; world trade has consistently grown more strongly than world production in recent decades, assisted by the liberalisation of the global trade regime (Julius 1990; Dicken 1992; Hoekman and Kostecki 1995).

Trade, however, is not what it used to be. In the first place, much 'international' trade is actually carried out between branches of large corporations, subject to conditions set by them. Second, trade in goods and manufactures has increasingly been outstripped by trade in intangibles such as services, financial instruments and information. As Susan Strange has noted, the uneasy relationship between the different structures for production, investment, exchange and knowledge in the IPE is fundamental to judgements about its recent and future development – and it intersects with the activities of public and private actors (Strange 1988).

Trends and contradictions

As a result of the relationships outlined above between actors and structures, the IPE can be seen as expressing a number of important trends and contradictions. Three tensions especially can be identified for our purposes here: between modernisation and underdevelopment; between autonomy, interdependence and integration; and between globalisation and regionalisation.

The growth of the IPE is inextricably linked with processes of modernisation. The emergence of modern political structures, allied to the development of industrial organisation and new technologies, is central to the way in which, from medieval times, there has been a move towards global processes of production, investment and exchange. From the use of gunpowder through the development of maritime transport to the present-day revolution in communications and information technologies, there has been an intimate link between the growth of the modern state and the growth of the modern world economy (Modelski 1972; Strange 1988; Tilly 1992). But at the same time, this has been a generator and perpetuator of inequalities – of development, of distribution and of welfare – which have formed a central part of the history of the IPE. This process of differentiation means that the project of modernisation can be seen as giving rise to often profound inequalities and underdevelopment, not only between regions or countries but also within them.

A second source of tensions and contradictions in the IPE is the shifting relationship between autonomy, interdependence and integration. As already noted, realist approaches to IPE place considerable weight on national independence and the capacity of national governments to preserve the autonomy of their domestic economies. This presumption is at the base not only of extreme variants of economic nationalism but also of many liberal approaches that emphasise the desirability of national economic management and the generation of national welfare. But the development of the IPE has resulted in ever-greater measures of international economic interdependence, not only at the level of national economies but also through the development of transnational structures. To use the term coined by Robert Keohane and Joseph Nye, and already encountered in Chapter 3, the result is 'complex interdependence', in which economic processes in particular are carried out between a multiplicity of actors, through a variety of channels and with no settled structures of authority or hierarchy (Keohane and Nye 1987).

At the same time, these structures challenge the possibility of national economic management and self-sufficiency and limit the autonomy of national authorities in the IPE. They also lead to increasing levels of international economic integration, in which not only are actions and interactions more complex and interconnected, they are also in many cases effectively fused across national and international boundaries. These increasing levels of international economic integration have given new impact to the need for international management, both at the level of processes and at the level of policy. As a number of commentators have noted, the rising levels of both interdependence and integration as 'facts of life' in the IPE have not always been accompanied by appropriate levels of policy interdependence or even the integration of national policies. The result is a continuing set of tensions and contradictions, often sharply felt by policy-makers (Pinder 1983; Henderson 1992; Hocking and Smith 1997, Chapter 1;).

A third area of tension in the IPE is that of globalisation and regionalisation. To a large degree, this reflects the tension between autonomy, interdependence and integration just noted. The study of globalisation has been one of the *leitmotifs* of the study of the IPE in the 1990s. But the increasing attention to globalisation has served to underline the difficulties of defining it and the unevenness of its impact. The global transmission of goods, services and ideas, and the sensitivity of political authorities to the perception that they are losing control of important areas of economic and social life, is clearly central to the problem. But the unevenness of its 'reach' and its impact is equally pervasive. Just as in the 1970s and 1980s it was said that interdependence was a kind of 'American ideology', so it can be argued that, in the 1990s, the concept of globalisation itself is a reflection of the dominant global economic forces, and particularly of those originating in the USA. For some, globalisation has acquired connotations of progress and enrichment; for others, it has carried with it the certainty of exploitation, and the destruction of traditional and reassuring structures of political and social life (Stubbs and Underhill 1994, Part I; Booth and Smith 1997).

At the same time though, there have often been intense processes of region-alisation in the IPE (Fawcett and Hurrell 1995; Bergsten 1997b; Smith 1997b). These are not always new; regional organisations for the handling of conflicts or the resolution of practical problems such as transport or communications have been with us for some time. What is new is the scope and scale of attempts at regional construction, and the ways in which they link with the processes of globalisation outlined above. In some cases, regionalisation can be seen as the defensive response to globalisation, providing national authorities with the means by which collectively they can resist outsiders. At the same time, it can be argued that regionalisation provides a transmission belt for globalisation, a site of expanded scope on which it can have its influence. In this case, the national authorities which come together in regionalisation efforts are the equivalent of King Canute if they attempt to hold back the waves of globalisation. Part of the reason for this paradox is that globalisation raises in an acute form the public/private tension already discussed: national authorities might wish to develop regional bodies to control economic processes, but the proliferation of global networks organised by essentially private interests can profoundly modify if not defeat the regionalist project (Gibb and Michalak 1994; Stubbs and Underhill 1994, Part III).

Outcomes

The product of the relationships outlined above, between actors and structures and between seemingly contradictory tendencies in the IPE, is a series of paradoxes, affecting in particular the balance between three values: authority, equity and efficiency.

In terms of authority, it should be clear from what has been said that the IPE demonstrates high levels of dislocation and differentiation. Dislocation arises from the fact that the national state and national governments are no longer the automatic repositories of authority in the IPE. Although their activities are often more extensive than ever before, they are now only part of a broad spectrum of public and private, local, national and global influences. Governments retain a substantial amount of leverage, but they are not the only source of governance. Both international public authorities and global private governance mechanisms have arisen to challenge and constrain them. The diffusion of authority in the IPE does not mean that authority does not exist, but it does mean that it can arise from various and often unexpected sources (Rosenau and Czempiel 1992).

In such conditions, considerations of equity and efficiency are difficult to balance and even to identify. It has already been noted that unevenness of involvement and benefit is an important characteristic of the IPE, and this means that policies intended to produce either equity or efficiency on even the local scale, for example through the promotion of employment or industrial development, can be self-defeating. Governments have traditionally been concerned with both dimensions, and even corporations have had to balance their efficiency-driven policies with the need for at least some consideration of equity (often encouraged by governments). In the 1990s, it is no longer clear in the absence of incontrovertible national authority that the balance can be struck (Julius 1990).

The outcomes of action and interaction in the contemporary IPE are thus multifaceted and often mutually contradictory. For national and other authorities, both public and private, this produces such apparently paradoxical notions as those of 'global localisation', 'global regionalisation' and 'competitive cooperation' (paraphrased by some authors as 'coopetition'). Each of these labels expresses the essentially multilayered and differentiated nature of the IPE, and of attempts to steer around it (Hocking 1993; Hocking and Smith 1997, Chapter 1). For the purposes of this chapter, the importance of such conclusions lies in the fact that the EU expresses many if not all of the tendencies and contradictions outlined here. It is to this that the argument now turns.

Europe in the changing international political economy

Analysis of the position occupied by Europe in the changing IPE must begin with the recognition that the Second World War, the Cold War and the end of the Cold War were as much economic events as they were events in the political and security domains (Nello 1991; Reinicke 1992). It is impossible in this area to detach the evolution of European political economy from the broader context in which it has been shaped, and in this the key roles are often played by the relations between superpowers and allies not only within Europe but also in the wider world. The analysis can be pursued through use of the three organising frameworks discussed above: actors and structures; trends and contradictions; and outcomes.

In the immediate post-1945 period, it was extremely difficult to conceive of 'Europe' or even major European countries as actors in the IPE. The impact of the Second World War had been such as to destroy the European economy, and also to impose heavy economic burdens on the leading pre-war economic powers. Even the victors had felt the need to liquidate large parts of their economic reserves, and the British, for example, found themselves deeply in debt both to the Americans and to members of the Empire and Commonwealth. The impact was accentuated by the fact that the USA emerged from the War massively strengthened: the combination of wartime boom and the collapse of the Europeans had given the USA a truly hegemonial position. This position was exploited in the construction of the Bretton Woods system of international economic institutions, and in the provision of Marshall Aid to the Europeans in particular (Hogan 1991; Ellwood 1992). As will be seen later, this had important implications for the role played by the first stages of European integration, and for its later development.

The combination of the United States' economic dominance with the development of the superpower confrontation between the USA and the Soviet Union meant that Europe was also fundamentally shaped by the onset of the Cold War (see also Chapter 3). In economic terms, this meant that the continent was divided effectively at an early stage between relatively free-market and command economies; in this process, the Marshall Plan played a major role by demanding commitments to free institutions as a condition of receiving aid. These commitments did not affect simply the countries of the emerging Soviet bloc; in France and Italy, for example, there were fundamental effects on the organisation of the labour movement, whilst in west Germany, there were major impacts on the organisation of production, backed up by constitutional provisions against cartels and in favour of US-style free markets (Berghahn 1986; Ellwood 1992). It is fair to say that the Cold War was fought in many respects at least as fiercely in the economic as in the political sphere, and that European countries recovered beneath an American economic dominance as effective as that provided by nuclear weapons in the security arena.

But this situation of US dominance and patronage began to change from the late 1950s onwards. Paul Kennedy, the historian, has identified this as the period in which the United States began to suffer the effects of 'imperial overstretch', which in the security sphere were to culminate in the Vietnam trauma (Kennedy 1988). In the economic sphere, one of the key developments was in the relative positions of the USA and the countries previously subject to its patronage. In terms of the IPE, from the late 1950s onwards, there were increasing strains in the structures set up during the late 1940s, partly because of a loss of dynamism in the US economy and partly because of the emergence of new competitors to the USA. Initially, the sternest of these competitors were in Europe, and particularly in the emerging European Communities (Diebold 1972; Calleo and Rowland 1973). This in turn, meant that the operation of the main international economic institutions became less trouble-free: the tensions were expressed within the Kennedy Round of General Agreement of Tariffs and Trade (GATT) trade negotiations between 1963 and 1966, and within the system of fixed exchange rates operated under the aegis of the International Monetary Fund.

During the early 1970s, the system began to undergo a fundamental and painful adjustment. The key problem was the asymmetry between the institutional and political dominance of the United States and the increasingly conditional nature of US leadership in the world economy. As the USA ceased to perform the role of 'big spender', suffering increased domestic strains and the rise of forces calling for protectionism, the world economy itself had at one and the same time become more integrated and less manageable (Calleo 1987). In 1971, the Nixon Administration declared a form of 'unilateral independence' through what became known as the 'Nixon Shock': a *de facto* devaluation of the dollar, and the imposition of import restraints that hit particularly at European suppliers. During the next three years, the instability created by unilateral US policies was increased by the end-game of the Vietnam War, which had posed seemingly limitless demands on US resources, and by the oil price crisis which followed the Middle East War of October 1973.

The late 1970s and early 1980s, though, did not lead to the economic collapse widely predicted. This is not to say that there was no trouble: the agenda of trade disputes and of currency fluctuations created a constant pressure on policy-makers both in Europe and in the United States, and the increasing prominence of Japan as an economic competitor was universally noted and feared. But there was a certain amount of rebuilding in the IPE, encouraged by the shared need of all industrial countries to deal with the consequences of the breakdown, and with the policy implications of increasing interdependence. The growth of the western economic summits, the GATT negotiations in the context of the Tokyo Round during the late 1970s, and the efforts to construct a new international economic order dealing with at least some of the problems caused by the disparities between rich and poor countries, did constitute at least a fragmentary new order for the world economy in general (Artis and Ostry 1986; Putnam and Bayne 1987).

It appeared in the early 1980s that this halting progress towards a new order might again be jeopardised, and that the destabilising force would again be the United States. The impact of Reaganism was felt in two interconnected ways. On the one hand, the Reaganite security policy, stressing confrontation with the Soviet Union, meant the rebalancing – for some, the distortion – of government spending towards rearmament. At the same time, the practice of 'Reaganomics' injected a new unilateralism into US international economic policies. The aim was to restore strength to the US economy, on the grounds that this would then diffuse among all industrial and even Third World countries. The policies were frankly inward-looking, with little regard for the wider implications on partners and rivals alike (for differing views, see Bergsten 1981 and Nau 1984–85). As a result, during the early 1980s, there was a series of tensions and recriminations between the USA and its major economic partners, many of them in Europe. Alongside this went the practice of what could be termed 'economic warfare' between the USA and the countries of the Soviet bloc: economic sanctions and controls on strategically-sensitive trade were designed to coerce the Soviets and their dependants into concessions in the more overtly political and security spheres (Kahler 1983; Brown and Rosati 1987; Allen and Smith 1989).

The disruptions in the IPE fostered by Reaganism tended to conceal some more fundamental shifts in both actors and structures. By the late 1980s, it was apparent to some that the international economy had moved far from the situation of US dominance, partly as the result of American relative decline and partly as a result of the emergence of new actors. Nor were these new actors solely the partner or rival countries which had preoccupied American thoughts for nearly two decades. The development of new global markets and processes of production and exchange, facilitated by new technologies, had created a situation in which time and location were less important than before, and had consequently produced a context in which governments were less in control (Strange 1988; Stubbs and Underhill 1994). Governments could and did make efforts to co-ordinate their positions and deal with the impact of interdependence, for example in the Plaza and Louvre agreements on the stabilisation of currencies in 1985 and 1987; they could also attempt to reinvigorate the regulation of world trade, as they did through the Uruguay Round of GATT negotiations from 1986 to 1993. But it was clear that such intergovernmental management efforts were less likely to bear fruit in view of the increasing interconnectedness between local, regional and global actors and structures in the IPE.

It was these contradictory tendencies and trends that contributed to the uncertainties of international economic management in the 1990s. Government policies veered wildly, between efforts to control the activities of private actors, for example over investment or production processes, whilst at the other end of the spectrum there was the admission that little could be done to control the operation of global markets. New phrases began to be heard: in place of the mercantilist nation state, there was reference to the 'regulatory state', the 'competition state' or even the 'post-modern state', in which the emphasis was less on political control and authority than on opportunism and responsiveness in the face of a chaotic IPE (Caporaso 1996).

It was into this set of circumstances that a major political shock was injected by the end of the Cold War. Whilst processes of globalisation and economic restructuring had been going on for many years, the political and security arenas had seemed to be impervious to these forces. With the fall of the Berlin Wall in 1989, the unification of Germany and the emergence of new and often fragile states in the former Soviet bloc, the political foundations were transformed – or at least broken up with little to take their place. This was a major event in the IPE, creating at a stroke new potential markets and new areas of inequality or instability in the world economy. Crucially, this was also a European event (Reinicke 1992; Tsoukalis 1997). For forty years, since the Marshall Plan and the formation of NATO, the world economy and the European economy had evolved broadly on the presumption that there was a 'west' of liberal broadly free-market economies and an 'east' of command economies. This could no longer be upheld; and the coincidence of growing globalisation in the world economy with the sudden release of new 'territory' in the former Soviet bloc was bound to tax the resources and the leadership capacity of the 'winners'.

This discussion tells us something about the ways in which the IPE has reached the rather chaotic and contradictory condition outlined in more general terms earlier in the chapter. It is apparent that the confusion of actors and structures, the tensions and contradictions and the uncertainty of outcomes pointed out in the first part of this chapter have their roots in fundamental problems of political economy; that is to say, in the ways in which political actors, structures and institutions interact with the needs of international processes of production and exchange. It is not clear that any set of political structures in the late 1990s possesses the solutions to the challenges faced. What is clear is that Europe and the European Union have been thrust into the centre of the changing IPE not only through economic but also through political forces.

Challenges for the European Union

In order to identify the challenges posed for the EU by changes in the IPE during the 1990s, it is necessary to make a basic distinction between three perspectives on the EU and the IPE. In the first place, the EU can itself be seen as a form of IPE, manifesting a number of specific and distinctive tendencies. Second, the EU can be placed within the context of the changing IPE, as outlined above. Third, the

EU can be seen as a 'host' for important forces in the IPE, which have penetrated and been diffused in the EU's political–economic space. These are, of course, analytical distinctions which do not hold up in the real world of economic processes. But they do help us to identify the characteristics and the potential of the EU's ambiguous position in the IPE of the late 1990s.

The European Union as international political economy

One way of analysing and evaluating the EU is as the product of international political–economic processes; in other words, to treat the EU as, in itself, an international political economy. Whilst this might be seen as artificial, it gives a sharp focus on processes occurring within the context of European integration, which can then be placed within a broader global context.

It is apparent that one of the driving forces of European integration from the outset has been the perceived economic needs of states, and the ways in which these can be pursued through the achievement of 'political economies of scale' in the context of the EC and the EU. Alan Milward and others have argued that the EC and the EU represent a 'rescue' of the national state, and this is a powerful perspective on the actors and structures encompassed by European institutions (Milward 1992; Milward *et al.* 1993). It is also apparent, though, that the EC and the EU have expressed the needs of actors and structures beyond those associated with states. Alongside the public authorities, represented by national governments, have gone, first, the public authorities constituted by them at the European level, and second, the private networks and organisations that have flourished in the context of European integration (Andersen and Eliassen 1993; Marks *et al.* 1996a, b).

The EU in this context is thus to be seen not simply as the European expression of the economic needs of member states – or an economic mechanism through which member states render themselves capable of meeting political needs – but as the centrepiece of structures that have fundamentally reshaped the European pattern of production, distribution and exchange. These structures have their effects through the exercise not of governmental authority but of the shaping influence of governance and the foundation of a powerful community of law. The EU can thus be seen both as the generator of higher levels of international economic integration and also as the facilitator of the growth of networks and groupings that cluster around the institutions provided by the EU.

It is true, though, that the ways in which the EU has developed have intersected with other trends and tensions in the IPE. One way of conceptualising the EU is as perhaps the ultimate modernist project: a self-conscious attempt to build a community of law and to measure its results in terms of economic welfare and political–social stability (see also Chapter 3). In this, it reflects essentially a nineteenth-century style of political economy, based on the assertion of governmental authority and positive political action in pursuit of welfare gains. It can immediately be seen that this image is in tension with that which has come to characterise the IPE, where, on the one hand, international and transnational institutions and, on the other hand, post-modernist images of chaos and opportunity hold equal sway. One challenge for the EU as an international political economy is thus to adapt what might be seen as an outmoded version of international economic management to the circumstances of the new Europe and the new IPE (Reinicke 1992).

Such an impression is given additional force by reflection upon what is produced by the EU in the area of autonomy, interdependence and integration. It has already been noted that the EU reflects a tension between notions that stress the enhancement of the effective autonomy of member states and those that emphasise the growth of new networks of interdependence and interpenetration. This tension finds its expression in a number of policy problems and dilemmas in the context of the new Europe (Richardson 1996, Chapters 1–2; Wallace and Wallace 1996, Chapters 1–2;). For example, the EU has succeeded in generating considerable administrative and financial resources at the European level, and in developing common policies that give guidance as to the distribution of resources. But these common policies – for example, in agriculture, or steel – have come up against the dynamism of international markets and against the shifting demands for reallocation of resources as the EU has itself evolved. In the EU as IPE, geo-economic forces are sharpened by the shifting centre of gravity between north and south, and they will be further sharpened by a shift to the east through further enlargement. At the same time, the EU has produced high levels of mobility in major factors of economic life, especially through the Single Market Programme (see Chapter 6); but in so doing, it has increased the levels of sensitivity and, partly in consequence, the levels of perceived vulnerability between member states and regions (Dicken 1992; Tsoukalis 1997).

None the less, it can persuasively be argued that the EU has produced a power-ful and institutionalised political–economic authority. This authority has strong powers of regulation over the IPE as encompassed by the EU, and has acquired quasi-governmental powers through the building of legal and administrative structures. This, though, only sets up tensions with national, regional and often local authorities (see Chapter 2). Given this set of tensions, and the coexisting trend towards the penetration of the EU by global economic forces (see below), it is possible to argue that the political–economic structure of the EU can no longer muster the appropriate scope or scale to operate successfully in the IPE. It is either too large and remote for processes that are regional or local in character, or too small for processes that are truly continental or demand pervasive political authority. Not surprisingly, this has contributed in the 1990s to important tensions over major policy developments such as EMU (see Chapter 7) (Wallace 1993).

This brings us to the discussion of outcomes. Throughout its existence, the EC and then the EU has had to deal with the question 'what is it for?' in terms of political–economic development. At one level, this has translated into argu-ments about whether the European integration process privileges the interests of big business, or those of certain regions or countries. At another level, we can see working out in this context the factors of authority, equity and efficiency referred to throughout this chapter. The EU provides a – sometimes contested –

political–economic authority, but it is unclear how far this can be stretched to meet the demands of the 1990s. It provides redistribution and thus promotes equity to a limited degree at the European level, but this is restricted both by the limited resources of the EU authorities and by the rigidities produced by the persistence of national political–economic authorities. Finally, it provides enhanced efficiency, particularly by removing barriers to the movement of factors of production, and by having common structures for the adjudication of claims or disputes, but it is not clear whether the demands of equity and efficiency are in balance. For example, during the 1990s there has been a debate over the possibility of 'social dumping' in the Single Market: the movement of production or other activities from high-cost regions to relatively low cost or otherwise favoured areas, taking advantage of the increased mobility available in a unified market. Such debates raised in a sharp form the tension between equity as expressed in the embryonic EU social policy and the demands of efficiency as propounded by large corporations based both within and outside the EU (Tsoukalis 1997, Chapters 6 and 9).

In the circumstances of the new Europe, the ambiguities noted here are likely to become sharper still, given the broadening of geo-economic scope, the divergences of economic performance and social provision and the consequent dilemmas surrounding the allocation of resources. The EU as IPE represents in this way a microcosm of the strains set up in the broader IPE by the differential impact of change and development (Reinicke 1992; Baldwin 1994).

The EU in the international political economy

The EC and now the EU are inextricably intertwined with the developing IPE. However, as also noted, the position and role of the EU is ambiguous and creates tensions. One of the key elements in the ambiguity is the extent to which the EU is or is not 'statelike': the extent to which it can produce the kinds of policies and actions that have traditionally been reserved to the national state. There are really two sides to this problem. On the one hand, there is the analysis of the 'foreign economic policy' produced by the EU, whilst on the other hand there is analysis of the residual roles of the EU's member states.

The EU does have a number of statelike functions, provided primarily through the mechanism of the 'first pillar' or European Community (Smith 1994b, 1997c). From the outset, the EEC based on the Treaty of Rome boasted a Common Commercial Policy, and procedures whereby the Commission could enter into international trade negotiations on behalf of its members. This enabled the EEC and then the EC to construct a complex web of international trade agreements, both through its participation in the GATT trade rounds and through more restricted bilateral or multilateral agreements. Although member states through the Council of Ministers have control over the negotiating mandates given to the Commission, there has also been the development of a sophisticated Commission 'diplomatic' structure with which to oversee the operation and amendment of trade agreements (Piening 1997, Chapters 1–2).

Although this may make it appear that the EC and the Commission are major actors in the IPE, there are limits to their autonomy and effectiveness. Partly these arise because of the controls exercised by the member states, which mean that the Commission is often in a position akin to that of trade negotiators representing the USA, answerable to 'domestic' forces and institutions. Partly these limitations also arise because of the ways in which international trade and exchange have developed during the 1980s and 1990s. Two trends are central. First, trade in goods as covered by the Treaty of Rome is now only part – and a diminishing part – of total world trade. The explosion of trade in services, and the introduction of 'new agenda items' such as intellectual property or environmental concerns means that there is uncertainty about just where the competence of the Community ends and that of the member states begins. Alongside this goes a second trend: the dynamic growth of investment and international financial transactions, on which the Community has had far less of a purchase and in which member states have a highly developed set of interests.

It can be seen that here, the changing nature of the world economy and the characteristics of the EU (particularly the EC) intersect. There is evidence that the EC/EU has not been able to expand its competence to match the changes and challenges of the IPE, and that attempts to do so would encounter the resistance not only of member states but also of other actors. Such was the case in 1995 when Transport Commissioner Neil Kinnock tried to assert the Community's competence in negotiating international air transport agreements. Most member states refused to consider the issue, encouraged not only by the United States, which wished to conclude 'open skies' agreements with individual partners, and also by national airlines which wished to preserve close links with their home governments. None the less, there evolved a form of negotiated 'division of labour', in which the Community and the Commission were able to assert their right to involvement (Allen and Smith 1996, 1997).

This discussion brings into the open another aspect of the EU's ambiguous role in the IPE. The Union and especially the Community has developed over the years a set of close relationships between European officials and European companies, a fact that vividly illustrates the potential and limitations of public–private links in the IPE. Especially in areas of high technology, there has been a tendency since the 1970s to talk in terms of 'European champions' and to structure policies so that certain areas are privileged and given strategic attention (Sandholtz 1992). This conforms in many respects to the attention given in the 1980s and 1990s to 'strategic trade policy', where national authorities are seen as creating the conditions for firms to exert advantages. But the Community has to wrestle with two limitations on its capacity. First, the financial resources it can devote to such champions are severely limited, and the Community's capacity thus is restricted to the construction of a favourable regulatory and administrative environment. Second, even in this latter activity, the Community is constricted by the persistence of national competences and the increasing strength of international agreements in the GATT. As a result, it is arguably quite difficult for the EC to act as a consistent and effective 'fertiliser' of European corporate activities. This is not as damaging as it appears, however, since this is precisely the situation in which many national governments find themselves during the 1990s (Sandholtz *et al.* 1992).

The EU therefore finds itself both a beneficiary and a prisoner of the IPE in the 1990s. It is a beneficiary to the extent that it has established itself as a legitimate strategic actor, for example in the GATT, where the EU was universally acknowledged as a prime beneficiary of the Uruguay Round (Paemen and Bensch 1995). It also benefits by having developed in the Single Market Programme a sophisticated regulatory regime, which enhances the leverage available through market access policies (see Chapter 6). In addition, it has constructed a complex network of trade and other international economic agreements which some have seen as a tightly controlled 'pyramid of privilege'. But like other national or regional authorities, the EU is constrained by the dynamic growth of non-traditional international economic transactions and by the proliferation of international regimes in new sectors.

In this fashion, the EU expresses many of the trends and contradictions outlined earlier in this chapter. On the one hand, it can be seen as a potential 'fortress Europe', wielding its strategic powers to create advantage for its firms and for its citizens. It can also be seen as acting in a semi-imperial fashion through trade and aid agreements to cultivate clients, first in the Third World and later in the former Soviet bloc, and as potentially building an exclusive bloc through privileged agreements. On this basis, it is also possible to see the EU as part of a 'triangular' world of blocs, engaged in a process of 'competitive cooperation' with the USA and Japan, and manoeuvring to manage the interdependence growing between the 'big three' in the IPE (Smith 1997d). Others might go further, for example on the basis of the prospects for economic and monetary union, and forecast a world in which the US dollar and the Euro form the centrepiece of an essentially 'bipolar' world political economy (Bergsten 1997b).

At the same time, however, the EU can be seen as the harbinger of radically different trends in the world economy. Much of the activity carried on in the EU in relation to the IPE gives it the character of a 'competition state', using regulatory policy and the growth of Europe-wide networks as the basis for enhancing welfare rather than acting as a strategic monolith. In the same vein, the EU can be seen as a 'regulatory state', or in other versions as a 'trading state' (Rosecrance 1993; Caporaso 1996). All of these images detract at least somewhat from the notion that the EU in the IPE should be moving towards a 'real' form of statehood (see also Chapters 2 and 3); they enhance the perception that the EU represents the leverage of complex regime-building and administration, and that this is moving gradually into broader areas as the result both of the internal development of the EU and the changing nature of the world economy. In such a set of developments, it is difficult to talk in terms of outcomes for the EU as a whole, since the emphasis is on the advantage gained within sectors or regions, or by specific groups of economic actors rather than by the EU as a whole. Even (some might say especially) in the potentially highly significant changes brought about by EMU, such asymmetries will be one of the central characteristics (see Chapter 7). This brings us to our final area for analysis.

The international political economy in the EU

One implication of the discussion so far is that the EU suffers from what Robert Reich has termed the 'who is us?' problem (Reich 1991). The surge of inter-dependence and interpenetration in the IPE has meant that notions of 'territory' and of a fixed national or regional base for economic activity have come under pressure. States and statelike authorities have equally come under pressure from the development of new networks and multilevel economic activity, necessitating multilevel policy-making and implementation. The impact of globalisation may be contested by many commentators (see for example Hirst and Thompson 1996), but it seems clear that the mercantilist vision of fixed national boundaries coinciding with control over economic transactions is very difficult to uphold. This means, to coin a phrase, that the IPE is in the EU as much as the EU is in the IPE.

How can this interpenetration be measured? One common yardstick is the extent and location of foreign direct investment (FDI). In the case of the EEC and then the EC/EU, it is clear that the creation of a larger European economic space has led both to an increase of FDI within the EU and to an increase of investment from such sources as the USA and Japan. But this is only part of the picture: the proliferation of strategic alliances, licensing agreements and other forms of indirect access to the EU has created what appears to be a seamless web of economic transactions. The explosion of economic actors and novel structures has created new challenges for EU economic policy-making, but this is an area in which the actions of the EU are strongly conditioned by residual national powers of macroeconomic management and regulation. It is therefore not sufficient simply to say that the EU is penetrated as never before by the IPE; to this must be added an awareness of the linkages between local, regional, national and EU levels, at all of which bargaining can and does take place (Dicken 1992; Thomsen and Woolcock 1993; Mason and Encarnation 1994; Dent 1997).

What confronts the EU in this area are three interconnected problems: issue complexity, agenda complexity and the diffusion of agency in the European economic space. The first implies that the changing nature of issues, of the technical problems they pose and the range of actors they attract is a key factor in the EU's policy environment. The second denotes the increasing linkages between issues and the different levels at which they may be confronted, whilst the third raises, in a sharp and concentrated form, the problem of 'capacity to act' both on the part of the EU and on the part of other institutions, for example in the implementation of EU policy initiatives. It is thus not surprising that European institutions are not always adequate to the challenge; nor are those of other major international actors (Richardson 1996; Wallace and Wallace 1996).

It could be argued, though, that the 'thinness' of the European layer of authority gives the EU problems that do not exist (say) in the USA or Japan. As a consequence, the EU is a site for globalisation in which there are fewer strategic control mechanisms, and also an arena for the policies of other major actors in the IPE. Only in trade policy, it could be argued, is this situation substantially modified, in the absence of an EU common currency or such policy devices as a common investment regime (see Chapter 6). The EU is less able than other actors to balance the demands of equity or efficiency directly, since it has no autonomous agency in key areas of the macroeconomy; indeed, there is a danger that the European institutions and regimes will become little more than a shell for a 'privatised' European economy in which the mobility of capital, persons and production will be a key characteristic.

The challenge for the EU here is clear, if intractable: the maintenance of policy authority in an increasingly interpenetrated system demanding multilevel policy-making. But is the problem essentially different from that confronting other players in the IPE? An argument could plausibly be constructed pointing to ways in which existing national authorities will have to become more like the EU in order to survive in, or profit from, an increasingly globalised economy. And the essentially regulatory powers of much of the EU system are precisely those that are most relevant to a new world of 'soft power' and global mobility. This means that it is perfectly possible to construct an argument based on the flexibility and adaptability of the EU in the face of conflicting forces, and emphasising its ability to respond on the basis of its longstanding experience in international economic governance (Dent 1997, Chapter 1; Piening 1997, Chapter 9). Indeed, there are those who have gone so far as to argue that this gives the EU potential advantages in the complex world of twenty-first century capitalism (Thurow 1992, Chapter 10), and that the potential emergence of the euro as a global medium of exchange and investment might underline this position (Bergsten 1997a).

Conclusions

This chapter has put forward a number of perspectives on the IPE in the 1990s, and examined the ways in which the EU can be explored as a phenomenon within the contemporary IPE. By doing so, it casts further light on the central relationships between territory, identity and function. It is clear that the perceived ambiguity of the EU's status and role is more than simply a reflection of the EU's 'incompleteness' as an economic actor. It intersects with fundamental trends and contradictions in the IPE, which remain unsettled, and cannot be explained simply by reference to a traditional realist/mercantilist model of activity. Increasingly, the EU reflects the impact of globalisation and regionalisation, and the interaction between many levels of political–economic activity. A number of the problems are focused in a distinctive and challenging way by the emergence of the 'new Europe' during the 1990s, which provides both challenges and opportunities for the EU. On the one hand, it might appear that the scope and scale of the EU are inappropriate to the demands of globalisation and localisation; on the other, that the EU combines precisely the qualities of 'regulatory statehood' and multilevel policy-making that are needed in the turbulent IPE of the late 1990s.

Part 2

Process and substance

The focus of this volume shifts, in Part 2, from the context of integration to the processes and substance of integration. Part 1 investigated the broad framework within which the European integration project has evolved, and identified a number of conceptual and policy challenges emerging from the changes of the 1990s. The chapter on Europe's states and nations acknowledged that there is considerable change to the form and function of the contemporary European state but that European integration is just one of the forces impinging on statehood and national identity. Whilst accepting that the contemporary state has a reduced capacity to govern and steer the national economy and society, we rejected the full force of the 'hollowing out' thesis. Rather, the contemporary nation state is learning new strategies of governing, including collective action at the EU level.

Chapters 3 and 4 explored the powerful pressures working on the EU from the outside in, in the shape of world politics and the international political economy. These pressures included decisive shifts in geopolitics and in the international political economy, which have been sharpened but not necessarily created by the end of the Cold War. In these chapters, the EU emerged as an ambiguous symbol and presence in global politics but perhaps one with the capacity to adjust in particular to a rapidly changing international political economy. This very adaptability of the Union, however, may simply mask a decisive shift in the international political economy from states to markets, from the public realm to the private.

The issues raised in Part 1 are further analysed in the following chapters on governance, markets, money and the international role of the Union. Such a focus on distinctive aspects of the integration process leads us to explore not only our general recognition of interconnectedness and contingency, but also the third element of our initial framework for analysis (see Chapter 1): the ties and tensions created by an integration process that is taking place in a much-changed, if not transformed, world. Each chapter thus identifies the specific ties and tensions at the heart of the processes and policies it explores: between a union of states and a market, between a polity and a problem-solving arena, between EU policy-making and multilevel policy-making, and between the EU universe and its global environment. Whilst not all of these ties and tensions will be central to each chapter, they provide the organising framework for this part of our investigation.

5   Governance

Introduction

This chapter addresses the issues of governance in the European Union arising from the broad forces identified in Chapter 2: the reconfiguration of territory, identity and the allocation of functional responsibility in contemporary Europe. Any analysis of European governance is fraught with difficulty, because the Union is always in the process of *becoming* – its constitution, institutions and policy remit have not yet reached, and may never reach, a stable equilibrium. Nor are its geographical limits settled, as it faces the prospect of continental enlargement during the first decade of the twenty-first century. Since the early 1950s, the Union's policy reach, its institutional balance and the relationship between the EU and the member states, have changed considerably in a dynamic character-ised by considerable tension between sovereignty and integration and increasingly between integration and democracy.

This chapter analyses, in particular, two of the ties and tensions outlined in Chapter 1. The focus is on the ties and tensions between the Union as a problem-solving arena and a polity, and those between EU policy-making and multilevel policy-making. We begin from the premise that the European Union is a polity, however novel and original, rather than simply a policy-making arena. It represents the extension of political space above the level of the state, rather than simply another form of international organisation. There is no consensus on what kind of polity is emerging in the Union because the goal of political union itself is contested by the member states and by social forces within them, and it is as yet unclear whose model or vision of Europe will prevail. The Union establishes citizenship rights without a formal constitution, aspires to a common foreign and security policy without an army, erects a pillar on justice and home affairs without a police force. It does not conform to the contours of political hierarchy that we regard as 'normal'. There is thus the constant danger, when analysing the EU, of using inappropriate benchmarks and of seeing weakness and incompleteness rather than originality and innovation.

The lifeblood of governance is generated by authority, resources and legitimacy, all areas in which, from the perspective of a national political system, the Union appears weak. Yet from the perspective of traditional international organisations, the Union appears robust if not positively overbearing. The EU generates a formidable corpus of law, develops and implements common programmes, negotiates international agreements and raises revenue. No other system of regional governance in the world is characterised by equivalent ties in terms either of breadth or of depth. This status has been achieved in an incremental and highly pragmatic manner over time by means of 'a studied change of regime' (Duchêne 1994, p. 20). As a result, the Union is a construction which is 'highly voluntarist, yet pragmatically piecemeal – and yet vaultingly long-range' (Anderson 1996, p. 17).

The purpose of this chapter is to characterise the Union's emerging system of collective governance, to assess how this highly voluntarist, incremental and contested system of governance generates authority, resources and legitimacy (Jachtenfuchs 1995; Kohler Koch 1996; Marks *et al.* 1996b). We will see that EU governance displays considerable innovative features of both structure and process, but that considerable ambiguity remains about the capacity and legitimacy of these structures. This chapter first analyses the enmeshing of the national and the European levels of governance. It then examines the impact of integration on European nation states and the extent to which a Europeanisation of the west European state is occurring. Finally, it analyses the stuff of politics in the Union and the challenges to the Union as a polity.

The enmeshing of the national and the European

The Union lacks almost all of the resources – coercive power, sizeable fiscal recourses, and a strong bureaucratic arm – usually associated with governance. The defining characteristic of the Union as a system of collective governance is rather the enmeshing of the national and the European, or the embedding of the national in the European (see Table 5.1). This process of mutual entanglement has enabled the Union to amass authority with relatively weak bureaucratic and financial resources; it also means that the European Union is intimately linked to, and rests on, the governance structures of the member states. This has been described as a system of interlocking or cooperative federalism – a 'multilevel' system of collective governance (Bulmer and Wessels 1987). The national is ever present in the European, it becomes embedded in institutions, processes and procedures in this new political space. In a system of shared governance, the national and the European are no longer *separate*: 'both levels share in the responsibility for problem-solving because neither has adequate legal authority and policy instruments to tackle the challenges they face' (Bulmer and Wessels 1987, p. 10). The EU thus has to co-opt the resources of the member states to exercise its governance capacity, but in so doing, it penetrates the national legal, administrative and political systems (Rometsch and Wessels 1996). In becoming member states, the west European nation states participate in an extra-territorial constitutional system, a process of collective public policy-making and a system which grants their citizens additional rights and avenues of politics.

Table 5.1 The enmeshing of the national and the European

GOVERNMENT

National executives
European Council and Council of Ministers

Central administrations
Council working parties
Commission working parties and advisory groups

Paragovernmental bodies
Commission/Council Committees

Regional and local government
The Committee of the Regions
Commission committees
Regional Representation in Council of Ministers – Germany, Austria, Belgium

Interest organisations and voluntary groups
Direct representation
Membership of EU federations – general and sectoral
Membership of Commission committees, forums, observatories

Broader political system
National parliaments in COSAC
Party membership of EP groupings
European elections

Constitutional and legal system
Dual constitutional framework – national and European
Article 177 Preliminary Rulings
Implementation and enforcement of EU laws

IDENTITY
State identity can be internationalised
Identity for regions, cities and local units
Impact of EU on individual identities

The Union depends on member state institutions to participate in the Union's policy process, to internalise its legal order in national judicial systems and to implement the *acquis communautaire* and common policies. Central to the process is a system of intensive and iterative negotiations between the Union, central governments, sub-national actors and interests in a policy process that stretches from the European to the local. The multilevelled system of policy-making has produced multiple arenas and a diverse set of policy subsystems rather than a traditional political hierarchy. Although scholars disagree about whether there is a distinctive 'Community method' of negotiation, the system is a 'negotiated order' in that 'Relationships are structured, institutions rather well rooted, rules of procedure operate, judicial settlement of dispute is embedded, and many informal understandings support the formal arrangements' (Hayes-Renshaw and Wallace 1997, p. 264). The growing density of the Union's 'negotiated order' may be gleaned from the growth of different formations and meetings at the level of the Council of Ministers, from the number of working parties under the auspices of the Council, from the innumerable advisory groups attached to the Commission, the growing number of comitology committees and the creation of agencies (see Table 5.2). The iterative nature of the process, a consensual style of bargaining, ample room for package deals, side payments, exceptions, derogations and transition phases all contribute to the capacity to produce collective agreement. This 'negotiated order' has gradually encompassed or shaped most facets of public policy and a wider and a growing array of national actors, operating through the exercise of 'soft power' such as procedural innovation, the establishment of committees and observatories, the holding of conferences, and the use of background research papers. Alongside the process of continuous negotiation outlined above, laws and institutions are central to the enmeshing of the national and the European. This may be seen in the constitutional character of the treaties, the organic development of a novel legal order and the significance of institutions and institutional innovation to the process. The continental model of integration, launched in 1950, was characterised by a pronounced emphasis on common institutions and on the institutionalisation of agreements in common procedures and norms of policy-making. Collective institutions thus bind the system of European governance and give it much of its capacity that is essential to authority.

Why has European regionalism become so institutionalised? First, the European integration project was not based on a hegemon who could control its decision-making processes. No one state had a predominance of power, which meant that no one state could impose its preferences. In fact, the Union's most powerful member states deliberately eschewed traditional notions of 'hard power' and were willing to embed themselves in an internationalised multi-levelled process. European integration from the outset represented a balance between France and Germany and between larger and smaller powers. Collective institutions, procedural correctness and judicial dispute settlement are particularly

Table 5.2 The growing density of the Union as a system of governance

	1960	1975	1990	1994
Council Decisions	10	575	618	468
Commission Decisions	6	838	1,367	2,461
Council Compositions	7 (1967)	12	22	21
Council working groups	10	91	224	263
Council sessions	44	67	138	98
Coreper + WG sessions	602	2,215	2,128	2,789
Comitology number		93	297	409
A-grade civil servants in the Commission	521	2,087	3,642	4,682

Source: Forward Studies Unit, Tables for Integration Indicators, August 1996.

important to small states who cannot rely on hard power. Second, institution-alisation rested easily with the continental state tradition. The west European states traditionally placed a high premium on public law, codification and formal institutions. We should remember that the codification of European law goes back to Roman times. Third, west European states were highly regulated economic spaces. Market creation at the EU level was built on the foundations of national regulation. The generation of EU regulation thus required a sophisticated policy process underpinned by collective institutions, in order to establish its credentials with both the original member states and other potential members.

The Union's institutional design, based on Commission, Council of Ministers, European Parliament, the European Court of Justice and the Court of Auditors, does not reflect the usual separation of executive and legislative power found at national level. Rather, an intermingling and overlapping of functions characterises a policy process that lacks a centre of political authority and contains a number of significant original features. The Commission, the European Parliament and the Court of Justice have most autonomy from national govern-ments and hence represent the *supranational* institutions of the policy process. The independent Commission has responsibility for proposing laws, overseeing their implementation, promoting the collective European interest and acting as guardian of the treaties. The European Parliament has reinforced its demo-cratic credentials following the initiation of direct elections in 1979. The Court of Justice, although it might have remained a weak international tribunal, has in many respects constitutionalised the treaties and ensured that the system would be based on a common legal framework.

The Council of Ministers and the European Council represent state interests, and are regarded in much of the literature as intergovernmental organisations. However, the scale and frequency of meetings in Council serve to distinguish it from similar bodies in international organisations. Wessels argues, with considerable weight, that the Council 'is not an "interstate" body but a body at the supranational level' (Wessels 1991, p. 137). This is underlined by Hayes-Renshaw and Wallace when they argue that:

> There is a shared culture in the Council, in spite of the public and publicised pictures of tensions and antagonistic positioning. Embedded in informal practices, as well as rooted in formal procedures, this is reinforced by forms of socialisation and *engrenage* . . . Our study revels that decision-makers in the Council, in spite of their national roots, became locked into the collective process, especially in areas of well-established and recurrent negotiation. This does not mean that the participants have transferred loyalties to the EU system, but it does mean that they acknowledge themselves in certain crucial ways as being part of a collective system of decision making.
>
> (Hayes-Renshaw and Wallace 1997)

The role of each institution in this Union's policy process is based on treaty provisions, codes of practice, and informal politics. Policy output emerges from a process of inter-institutional bargaining at the EU level, policy processes within the member states and lateral links among the member states. It is thus not surprising that formal treaty change and the expanding scope of EU governance have interacted to exert a major influence on the operation of the Union's institutions, the institutional balance, and inter-institutional relations. None the less, the Union's governance structures are highly fragmented and subject to procedural complexity. The Treaty on European Union introduced the so-called *Pillar* system whereby the Union consisted of the European Community pillar, a second pillar on the Common Foreign and Security Policy (CFSP) and a third pillar on Justice and Home Affairs (JHA). Decision-making rules and the degree of member state control differ from pillar to pillar, as do the role and legal prerogatives of the Union's institutions: thus, institutional roles and decision rules in pillars two and three are designed to limit the role of the Union's supranational institutions and to retain as much national control as possible (see Table 5.3). It should be clear from this discussion that here we encounter one of the ties and tensions central to the discussion: is the EU to be seen as a mechanism whereby the member states pursue intergovernmental solutions to their problems, or as a partial but none the less powerful form of polity? Further exploration of the roles of the major EU institutions during the 1980s and 1990s will help us to develop this point further.

The Commission as 'policy entrepreneur' and 'policy manager'

In the 1980s, the Commission reasserted itself as a source of policy innovation in the EU. Taking advantage of a convergence of interests among the member states, Jacques Delors as President from 1984 enhanced the standing of the Commission as the main proposer of the internal market programme. Not content with market integration, he also succeeded in persuading the member states of the necessity of increasing the structural funds in the form of the Delors 1 package, and championed a vision of Europe that went beyond market integration. Delors' approach has been compared to a 'Russian doll' strategy, which implied 'iterated episodes of strategic action to seize upon openings in the political opportunity structure, resource accumulation through success, and reinvestment of these resources in new actions to capitalise on new opportunities' (Ross 1995, p. 39).

Notwithstanding Delors, the Commission also emerged as an important 'policy entrepreneur' in the 1980s when the member states were faced with policy failure or new policy dilemmas in many areas. Intergovernmental accounts of decision-making in the Union seriously underplay the autonomy of the Commission and its ability to act as a 'policy entrepreneur' or to engage in 'purposeful opportunism' in the policy process (Cram 1994, p. 198). The Commission is in the market for ideas as it strives to promote collective solutions at the European level. Its Directorates-General CDGs carry the institutional memory of past policy proposals, choices and responses of the member states, and if the political circumstances are right, the Commission is in a position to propose packages that

Table 5.3 Institution-building and procedural change in the EU since 1970

Council system
European Council (1975)
Monetary Committee (1973)
Antici Group (1975)
Expansion in the number of Council Formations from 12 in 1975 to 23 in 1995
Greater use of qualified majority voting
Additional decision rules/instruments (constructive abstention, joint actions, etc.)

Commission
Expansion in the members of the College of Commissioners from 9 to 20
Growth in the number of Directorates-General to 23 in 1997
Expansion of working parties, advisory groups and comitology committees
Creation of observatories and forums

European Parliament
Enhanced powers of the Parliament

- Budget treaties 1970 and 1975
- Direct elections 1979
- Cooperation procedure/assent procedure/Ombudsman 1987 SEA
- Co-decision procedure TEU and Treaty of Amsterdam

Court of Justice
Creation of the Court of First Instance 1987
Growth in the number of cases

Other organs
Court of Auditors 1978
Committee of the Regions 1993
Community agencies

Major scope expansion
European Political Cooperation (1970), codifed in Single European Act, transformed into
  the Common Foreign and Security Policy (Pillar 2) Treaty on European Union
Trevi system of cooperation on Justice and Home Affairs, which began in 1975, codified
  and expanded as Pillar 3 of the TEU
European Monetary System (1979)
Expansion of policy scope: regional, environment, R&D, tourism, culture, education

find favour with a sufficient number of member states. There is now a large number of detailed case studies of particular policy sectors in the Union that highlight the central role of the Commission.

The Commission is thus not just another actor among nation states and transnational groups, nor an 'impartial' moderator or agent aggregating member interests: the Commission and also the other EC institutions have autonomous capacities, and are 'biased' towards policy solutions that strengthen the EC as a whole (Schneider *et al.* 1994, p. 494). The right of initiative is, according to Ludlow, a *mandate for leadership*: this allows the Commission to set the boundaries of debate, and their text consequently forms the basis of negotiations in the Council

(Ludlow 1991, p. 64); the ability to frame the arguments and proposals that are subsequently negotiated on in the Council and the Parliament gives the Commission a critical role in agenda setting. Without Commission proposals the Council could not function; in 1995 the Commission sent the Council 600 proposals, and a further 275 communications and reports that review policy and prepare the ground for further policy proposals (European Union 1996, p. 440). Given the multiplicity of states and interests in the Union, the Commission is powerfully placed to devise strategies for dealing with common problems arising from changing international or European circumstances. In one policy area after another it is possible to trace the Commission's search for greater control over the implementation of policy and its desire to steer the Council in the direction of its preferred policy preferences.

The Commission also displays an ability to move into a vacant policy space, in some instances, or incrementally to redirect established policies in a patient manner over time. According to Cram,

> the Commission has learnt to respond to opportunities for action as they present themselves, and even to facilitate the emergence of these opportunities. Much of the activity of the European Commission might be interpreted as an attempt to expand gradually the scope of Union competence without alienating national governments or powerful sectoral interests.
>
> (Cram 1994, p. 199)

Majone argues that, because of the way they are recruited, the structure of their career incentives and the crucial role of the Commission in policy initiation, 'Commission officials usually display the qualities of a successful policy entrepreneur to a degree unmatched by national civil servants' (Majone 1993b, p. 26).

In pursuit of leverage within the policy process, the Commission uses all sorts of devices to enhance the collective nature of the European project and to enmesh national actors by holding conferences, financing research, setting up observatories, financing pilot projects, encouraging transnationalism and stronger administrative partnerships between the Union and the national level and laterally across the member states. The Commission is, in many ways, a classical 'network' organisation that is heavily dependent on working with and through other public and private organisations, and cannot rely on hierarchical dicta either to develop or implement policy. It has limited staffing resources of its own, with fewer staff than the city governments of Amsterdam or Madrid; in 1995 the Commission had just 15,001 permanent staff, some 1,763 of whom were language staff (European Union 1996, p. 440).

To compensate for its weakness and to ensure that it has access to those who are affected by EU regulation, a myriad of consultative committees and advisory bodies – the density of which differs from policy area to policy area – has grown up around the Commission directorates (Pedler and Schaefer 1996). The Draft Budget for 1996, which gives details of all committees that may impose a cost on the Community budget, listed 394 committees in such diverse areas as construction products, spirit drinks, technical standards and regulations, urban waste and toy safety; even this is far from the complete picture, since there are many additional *ad hoc* committees. Although not foreseen in the original treaties, the plethora of committees that have developed around the Commission is an important resource for the Union's system of collective governance. The committees animate the policy process during all phases of the policy-making by helping build consensus in preparation for Council negotiations, by providing the Commission with technical and expert advice and by providing the participants with channels of regular contact, which is necessary in a multilevelled environment (Bücker *et al.* 1996). Although the committee system is vital to the Union's policy process, the secrecy and lack of transparency that characterises its operation raises critical issues of accountability and legitimacy.

In the 1990s, particularly after the difficult ratification process of the TEU, the Commission has had to turn its attention to the management of policy and not just 'policy entrepreneurship'. The Commission has extensive administrative responsibilities to oversee the management of common policies, the competition regime, a vast array of internal and external spending programmes, the implementation and enforcement of Community law and the regulatory regimes arising from the single market. However, the Commission's capacity for policy management is much weaker than its capacity for policy entrepreneurship. In fact, all too frequently, the Council is content to give the Commission additional responsibilities without adequate resources. The paucity of human resources impairs the Commission's ability to engage in stringent monitoring of national implementation, to collect data and engage in *ex post* evaluation, accentuating a bias in the culture of the Commission towards policy innovation and new policy ideas rather than the more mundane work of policy management. From this it is apparent that it is precisely those characteristics which make Commission officials so adept at policy entrepreneurship, that militate against its management capacity.

The Commission's capacity for self-regulation is also rather weak. The high degree of autonomy exercised by the various Directorates-General, limited co-ordination and considerable bureaucratic rivalry lead to a variety of 'policy styles' in the Commission. Coordination is notoriously weak across Directorates-General despite the establishment of task forces and a stronger role for the Secretariat-General. Bureaucratic fragmentation and competition between DGs and between Commission officials and the political tier surrounding each Commissioner undermines the management of programmes. As a result, 'horizontal' directorates (Budgets and Financial Control) in the Commission have difficulty in monitoring the activities of the powerful spending directorates. None the less, there has been a growing emphasis on management and effectiveness in the Commission, stemming from a perceived need on the part of its members to transform themselves from an 'adolescent bureaucracy' into a maturing bureaucracy (Mazey and Richardson 1993; Laffan 1997).

The Commission finds itself in a less benign external environment since the strong integrative impulses of the Single Act and the Treaty on European Union.

Given the major extension of Union policy competence between the Single Act and the TEU, and the fact that integration is contested in public opinion, some have argued that it is time to devote attention to the consolidation of the Union's policy reach and policy regimes rather than to their extension. The political climate of the 1990s has been far less receptive to grand designs, and this chimed with the style and preferences of Jacques Delors' successor as Commission President, Jacques Santer. In contrast to Delors, the Santer approach is aptly summed up in his description of his first work programme in 1995: 'Doing less but doing it better' (European Commission 1995, p. 6).

The European Council and the Council of Ministers

The European Council and the Council of Ministers are the juncture at which the national and the European meet in formal terms to negotiate the terms of EU policies and laws. The Treaty on European Union confirmed the increasingly important role exercised by the European Council, which brought the highest level national office holders into the Union's system of governance, as a source of political authority and legitimacy: article D specified that the 'European Council shall provide the Union with the necessary impetus for its development and shall define the general political guidelines thereof.' This role in strategic goal-setting and political leadership is reinforced in the chapter on the Common Foreign and Security Policy which gives the European Council the responsibility for establishing its 'general guidelines' (Article J, TEU). In many ways, this merely confirmed the growing role of the European Council in the 1980s when summit meetings became the main test of any Presidency and the European Council conclusions became the authoritative documents setting out guidelines for the Union. The cycle of Council meetings sets the pace for the development of the Union agenda and the decisions on the main dossiers. Consequently, the Council has, in effect, become a 'super executive', a quasi-government for the Union.

The Council of Ministers, sometimes described as a hydra-headed beast, is a shorthand term for an array of different Council formations that are buttressed by a myriad of working parties responsible for the early phase of Council negotiations. The Council system extends its tentacles to the member states via the national Permanent Representations in Brussels, which in turn coordinate activity with national administrations and governments. By the beginning of the 1990s, the Council was meeting some 120 days each year, in twenty-one different compositions. The General Affairs Council (Foreign Ministers) and the Economic and Finance Council of Ministers (ECOFIN) were meeting with growing frequency and almost all national ministers were drawn into EU negotiations. Council working groups, numbering some 200, composed of national civil servants, do the preparatory work of responding to a Commission proposal and begin to work out the final contours of a piece of law or policy before it winds its way up to the Committee of Permanent Representatives (COREPER) and the Council where agreements are finalised. The considerable extension of the Council machinery has been accompanied by the enhancement of COREPER's role as the filter to the Council and by the growing importance of the Council Secretariat.

The extension of qualified majority voting in the Single Act and the weakening of the political weight of the Veto altered the 'rules of the game' and the norms of behaviour in the Council. Although consensus is still sought after in the Council and most participants would prefer to reach an agreement that satisfies everyone, it is far easier to arrive at the basis of an agreement with the prospect of a vote rather than where the potential for a veto exists. Between December 1993 and March 1995 the Council adopted a total of 283 legislative acts but only voted on forty of these acts (European Community 1995, Annex IV). The prospect of a vote has, however, moved bargaining from lowest common denominator outcomes to the highest level of agreement and has greatly speeded up decision-making.

The European Parliament

The European Parliament (EP) has steadily built up its presence in the Union's governance structures, notwithstanding the deep-rooted hostility of a number of member state governments, on the basis of three factors: increased democratic legitimacy resulting from direct elections, increased formal powers and the strengthening of its political links to the Commission. In the wake of the first direct elections (1979), interest groups, the Commission and national bureaucracies began to pay far more attention to the deliberations of the EP and its committees. Building on its budgetary role, the EP has inserted itself into the legislative process with the cooperation procedure (SEA) and the co-decision procedure (TEU). Both procedures required the Council and the Commission to take the EP seriously as part of the legislative process. The cooperation procedure was a major improvement on the consultation procedure and the co-decision procedure built on it. The Treaty of Amsterdam (June 1997) further enhanced the role of the Parliament by reducing the number of legislative procedures and by simplifying the co-decision procedure. Much of the work done in the European Parliament is carried out in its committees because the EP corresponds to the continental model of a 'working parliament', rather than a 'talking parliament' akin to the Westminster model. Enhanced powers have transformed the EP's legislative role from one of interested bystander to a player in the bargaining process, although its actual influence differs temporally and across sectors (Judge *et al.* 1994).

The image of governance in the European Union presented so far highlights the development of an arena of public policy-making above the level of the state, one which rests on the member states and is heavily dependent on co-opting the political, legal and administrative resources of those states in the pursuit of collective governance. A common legal system and collective institutions provide the ties that bind the EU as an arena of policy-making and a polity. But the relationship between these several frameworks and functions is far from settled; rather, there is a continuing process of negotiation not only within the framework but about the framework itself.

The tentacles of Europeanisation

The term 'Europeanisation' is increasingly used to describe the interlocking of the national and EU levels in a system of collective governance. It has been defined as 'an incremental process reorienting the direction and shape of politics to the degree that EC political and economic dynamics become part of the organisational logic of national politics and policy-making' (Ladrech 1994, p. 69). The focus here is on the penetration of national policy systems and national politics by the political and policy dynamics of the European Union. A related definition regards Europeanisation as the processes that 'make Europe a more significant political community and thereby European boundaries more relevant politically' (Olsen 1995, p. 21). Others adopt a more disaggregated approach to Europeanisation, focusing on the impact of the Union on different national institutions, policy sectors or facets of politics (Tarrow 1995; Rometsch and Wessels 1996). The fragmented structure of the Union, a multiplicity of policy communities and the Union's myriad decision rules partially hide the breadth and depth of creeping 'Europeanisation', but it is apparent in several key dimensions.

The penetration of national politics

The Union has become part and parcel of domestic politics, to such an extent that the claim made in 1971 that the 'Communities have not penetrated dramatically into the national political scene' is no longer tenable (Wallace 1971). Since the mid-1980s, European issues and constitution-building in the Union have affected government formation in a number of member states, and have become intertwined in party politics, electoral competition and in the design of government programmes. A number of examples suffice to underline this point. The deep-rooted conflict within the British Conservative Party on Europe had a major impact on the governmental capacity and electoral fortunes of the former Conservative Government. European projects such as EMU have become entangled in internal conflict in the Bavarian Christian Social Union (CSU) Party, which in turn have affected the Kohl Administration and hence the movement towards EMU. The unanticipated French general election in May 1997 was motivated by considerations of fiscal austerity that were, in turn, related to EMU.

The growing salience of the Union as an arena of policy-making

The EU has become a more salient political arena for its member states, important for agenda setting and for the generation of European norms that establish the reference point for national policies. This formation of an arena of public policy at EU level creates a permanent challenge to national political systems because they are confronted with the need to adapt to a normative and strategic environment that escapes total control. Rather than amassing extensive and autonomous political authority, the Union gradually alters the exercise of national political authority by enmeshing the member states in a web of collaboration and cooperation. According to Muller and Wright, 'the EU is slowly redefining existing political arrangements, altering traditional policy networks, triggering institutional change, reshaping the opportunity structures of member states and their major interests' (Muller and Wright 1994, p. 6).

The expansion in the range of public policy issues treated in the Brussels arena has been one of the key factors leading to the growing salience of the Union. Most areas of public policy have a European dimension, although as noted above there is only partial and unstable agreement on the assignment of public functions in the EU itself. Enhanced policy responsibility has led to an expansion of policy networks and policy communities around the core Union institutions. The intensification of formal cooperation can be seen in the growth of bureaucratic foliage surrounding all institutions and in the intensification of meetings at all levels of the system.

The mobilisation of national actors at the EU level

There is a significant growth in the mobilisation of economic interests in the Brussels arena. In addition to the traditional Euro-groups, private firms and professional lobbies have mushroomed since 1985. A 1992 Commission document identified some 3,000 special interest groups in Brussels, including some 500 European and international federations employing some 10,000 in the lobbying sector (Commission Sec 1992). Interest representation in Brussels is characterised by a predominance of producer groups; a 1985 survey found that of 654 recorded Euro-groups and associations, 583 represented business interests, far outweighing consumer groups, trade unions, and non-economic interests (Schmitter and Streeck 1991, p. 10). The style and not just the intensity of lobbying in the Brussels system has shifted. Individual firms now play a far more pervasive role in EU lobbying and, because EU regulations matter to firms, they 'have generally been the most active and the best resourced of all of those groups operating at the European level' (Mazey and Richardson 1993). According to Coen,

> there is strong empirical evidence to suggest that this movement to the EU represented a new form of political Europeanisation of business interests, with the institutional economic and regulatory levels of the EU, providing the economies of scale for large sections of European industry, and a legal and political alternative for national market access.
>
> (Coen 1997)

In an effort to counteract the dominance of producer interests, the Commission is active in promoting the mobilisation of non-economic cause groups at the EU level. Voluntary organisations or single issue cause groups in turn see the need to organise at the EU level and not just within the member states. The Commission itself has deliberately created and funds some of these networks, notably, the

European Network of Women, the European Women's Lobby, the European Network of One Parent Families, the European Network of the Unemployed and the Anti Poverty Network. It is quite easy to see that, from the point of view of the Commission, it is preferable to deal with one European network rather than fifteen national ones; it is also logical for the Commission to see these networks as a means of enhancing its own legitimacy. In addition, there are hundreds of non-funded networks active in Brussels (Harvey 1992). Influencing the Commission and EP is the primary but not only objective of these groups; they also use their involvement in Brussels to get access to EU funding, to learn alternative lobbying strategies and to influence national policy, thereby finding empowerment in transnational politics.

There is a growing mobilisation of sub-national governments, paragovern-mental agencies, and public/private partnerships in Brussels. The number of regional representative offices in Brussels has grown from two in 1986 to over a hundred in 1996, and there are parallel forms of representation from countries outside the EU, such as the United States. The Community's regional policies have fostered the growth of inter-regional networks both on the basis of cross-border initiatives and between areas concerned with similar problems such as 'Quartiers en crise', a network of cities experiencing urban decay, and 'Regions of the Atlantic Rim'.

Promoting transnationalism

The Union's budget is increasingly used to promote links and networks between different societal actors and regions within the member states. A series of programmes promote mobility; ERASMUS, COMETT, LINGUA and PETRA (see list of abbreviations) are used to finance students, young workers and university teachers on visits to other member states. Since 1987, some 250,000 students and 15,000 academic staff have undertaken study visits to universities in other countries. There are some 2,000 inter-university cooperation programmes (ICPs) directing this movement. Although this is a small proportion of total student numbers, student mobility serves to add a cosmopolitan flavour to many campuses. The Community's R&D programmes, which began in the early 1980s, have spawned extensive inter-industry and transnational research networks. Innovative Community programmes financed by the structural funds are designed to encourage cross-border cooperation and cooperation of different national groups in a number of member states.

The adaptation of national systems

All of the member states have had to adapt their constitutional systems, government processes and administrations to participation in Brussels policy-making. They have to service the EU's extensive committee system, participate in the continuing process of negotiations and implement EU laws and policies. This has necessitated adaptation at the level of central government, administration, the

Courts, sub-national government, national parliaments and paragovernmental agencies. The mode of adaptation differs across different parts of the state structure and from member state to member state. For example, the Danish Folketing is particularly active in EU business in contrast to the Irish Oireachtas (Rometsch and Wessels 1996). Increasingly, horizontal linkages (partnerships) between the member states to manage the internal market, internal security, the fight against fraud and other policy areas have proliferated. Structured dialogue by the Commission to persuade national authorities to change their domestic institutions, procedures, and systems of public management is a distinctive feature of the post-SEA environment.

Towards internationalised governance

There is compelling evidence from this discussion that the post-SEA Union fosters a further intensification of 'internationalised governance' in western Europe. This process includes a widening policy remit, the enhancement of transnationalism and transgovernmentalism in the Union and the increasing significance of the EU as an issue in domestic politics and as an arena for collective governance. New and varied processes of public management are evolving. Many more domestic actors are operating in multiple arenas – a process that contributes to a further weakening of the integrative processes of domestic policy-making and the capacity of national executives to maintain their role as gatekeeper. In this way, the 'nested games' within each state/society nexus are augmented by transnational 'connected games' (Marks *et al.* 1996b). Europeanisation creates new strategic opportunities for firms, interest organisations, cause groups, regions, cities and paragovernmental agencies. It takes them out of their national containers and enables them to play additional political games, adopt new roles and learn new skills in negotiation and mediation. Those groups, organisations and individuals who are adept at operating in a multilevelled and multicultural environment are favoured by this system.

Integration may not transcend the nation state, the project of the original federalists, but it is transforming the exercise of political authority in an incremental fashion. While nation states are not being 'hollowed out', as noted in Chapter 2, the European project has altered their position in several important respects. First, the member states must accept, however reluctantly in some cases, that they can only govern in conjunction with other states. Although they can theoretically leave the Union, their options are very limited. The strategy of reluctant states has been to limit the scope of institution-building, restrict the reach of the Union and, if all else fails, to negotiate derogations and opt-outs. Second, European governance occurs in contexts that go beyond that of an association of states because of the growing evidence of multiple arenas, transnationalism and cross-national linkages. Third, the implications of the previous two propositions are taken inside each national system in various ways. National actors and agencies have internalised a 'European dimension' to a remarkable degree. Fourth, the conventional wisdom that European integration can be largely explained by the economic and material interests of utility maximising actors ignores the potential importance of collectively shared values and consensual knowledge in the process. Fifth, the significance of institutional learning and socialisation given the innovatory nature of much European public policy-making is very considerable. The process of Europeanisation is conditioned by the multicultural and multinational environment of the Union with very diverse state traditions and institutional configurations at national level.

The enmeshing of the national and the European has been neither smooth nor linear. Rather, it has been partial, patchy and contested. The Union's authority and resources differ from policy sector to policy sector. For example, the Union has extensive regulatory powers in relation to the movement of the factors of production but weak instruments of macroeconomic management. In the social policy domain, there is a consensus about collective action in the area of health and safety but deep division about redistributive policies. The authority of Union competence in any one policy area is accumulated in a gradual manner, sometimes without a strong legal mandate. Even when EU competence is well established, the principles and purposes of EU action may be loosely agreed, leaving important 'grey areas' to be contested in future. Partial and conditional agreement on the objectives and instrumentalities of policy is much more common than broadly based policy agreement. Since the Union has few areas of exclusive competence – external trade and other aspects of commercial policy, and certain features of competition policy – most of its powers are held concurrently with the member states. There is considerable conflict about just how much power the Union should exercise in different policy sectors and about the procedural rules that should govern its activities. Thus, for example, the inclusion of the principle of subsidiarity in the Treaty on European Union sharpened the debate about the sharing of policy competence between the national and the EU level of governance, by seeming to suggest tests that might determine whether policies should be handled at the European or at other levels.

The implementation of Community law is patchy across different policy sectors and different member states. The weakness of the Union's coercive capacity and its dependence on the administrative capacity and will of the member states lead its institutions to adopt a 'softly-softly' approach to the member states when it comes to non-implementation of Community law, or fraud against the financial interests of the Union. The Commission strategy is to establish administrative partnerships and to engage in dialogue with national actors about the implementation of Community law and policies. The purpose of this activity is to generate 'advocacy coalitions' in the member states in favour of institutional modernisation.

Differentiated integration

Managing deep diversity is a key challenge to the Union's distinctive form of governance. Diversity in Europe is complex and multifaceted, manifesting itself in forms of economic management and levels of economic development, in the organisation of welfare, in political organisation and state tradition, in language, religious affiliation, mores and customs. In addition, the member states are characterised by very diverse attitudes to the process of integration itself. The constitutional institutional and policy compromises that characterise the Union highlight the absence of an agreed framework or model for the European project. Managing diversity was relatively easy in the Union of six because of the geographical proximity of the original member states, the scale of the system and their collective commitment to the integration project, underpinned by Christian democratic values. Each successive enlargement, though, has exacerbated the degree of diversity in the Union on the dimensions outlined above.

Because of the need to accommodate diversity from the early stages, the European Communities became adept at constructing package deals, side payments, partial derogations, and transition periods to ease adjustment and to manage the range of interests and preferences in the system. Community law, especially the directive, was designed to allow for a high level of national discretion, and the instruments used to construct the internal market – mutual recognition and home country control – were an acknowledgement that the harmonisation drive of an earlier period was doomed to failure.

During the 1990s, the pressure of diversity has become much more explicit. The Treaty on European Union marked a new stage in the evolution of differentiated integration because the EMU framework was designed to accommodate states that were unwilling to join a single currency and to exclude those that did not meet pre-set criteria. The TEU also included the UK social policy 'opt-out'. At the 1996/97 IGC, it became clear during the negotiations that provisions would be made for 'flexibility' in the Treaty of Amsterdam – the term connoting the desire and capacity of some member states to make more rapid progress than others towards generally agreed objectives. Although many states were extremely cautious about flexibility, all accepted that such provisions were the price of eventual agreement. The flexibility clauses are contained in different parts of the treaty. First, a set of general clauses in the common provisions of the TEU establishes the conditions that must apply where the member states wish to apply closer cooperation. Second, specific flexibility provisions apply in the European Community Treaty. Finally, there are flexibility provisions in Justice and Home Affairs (JHA).

What impact might the Amsterdam Treaty provisions for flexibility have on the pattern of integration? It is important to note that the conditions established under the common provisions on the use of closer cooperation are generally restrictive in tone and character. Closer cooperation may not affect the *acquis communautaire* and should only be a measure of last resort. The Court of Justice is given a review role and the Commission is formally responsible for proposing new actions under this heading. Membership of forms of closer cooperation is open to all member states and those outside can become members at any time, provided they accept the level of existing agreement within the framework of closer cooperation. Given the prospect of future enlargements, the threshold of members for closer cooperation is rather low, being set at a majority of member states.

This being the case, it is difficult to predict the likely impact of the flexibility clauses on the constitutional dynamics of the system. The insertion of such clauses reflected the deep diversity that characterises contemporary Europe and the need to accommodate diversity in the European project. These clauses – together with the EMU provisions, constructive abstention in pillar two, the Schengen opt-outs for the UK, Ireland and Denmark – underline the fact that differentiation is central to the current phase of integration. So far, such differentiation has had an inclusive rather than exclusive character. Whether this is maintained will depend on how the system accommodates enlargement, the shape of EMU and the European policies of those states most reticent about European integration. Depending on the political circumstances, closer cooperation may become a significant constitutional feature of the system or it may remain in the background to be dusted down when the political cycle requires it.

The European Union as a polity

When analysing the process of polity-building in the Union, it is necessary to examine the stuff of politics that animates this system and the challenges facing the Union as it endeavours to domesticate interstate relations in Europe.

The stuff of politics in the Union

The politics of integration encompass the politics of the EU system itself, the regulation of the Union as an economic and social space, and the 'flanking policies' that accompany economic and political integration. The politics of system design and development range from arcane debates about the kind of comitology committee that should govern this or that programme, to the framework decisions of treaty-making. Because the Union is an evolving system, both in terms of its geographical boundaries and in terms of policy scope, a considerable amount of political capacity has been invested in the design of the system. Constitutional politics in the EU were muted until 1985/86 when the Single European Act, representing the first substantial revision of the Rome treaties, was negotiated. This was followed by the Treaty on European Union (1993) and the Treaty of Amsterdam (1997). The intensification of constitution-building has imposed a considerable political and judicial burden on all member states; not only this, but the need for ratification has led to the politicisation of integration politics in many member states. National electorates, constitutional courts and parliaments are taking far more interest in the evolution of the Union than they have in the past.

Constitution-building is characterised by intergovernmental bargaining involving bilateral meetings, the European Council, Foreign Ministers and, in the case of EMU, the Finance Ministers. Specialist officials in the Cabinet offices, and the Foreign Ministries prepare the detailed negotiating texts. The process is permeated with friction about the integration model itself, as there is no real agreement among the member states on the goal of their collective project and the eventual shape of the Union. Substantive issues of policy and the institutional balance are negotiated against a backdrop of national preferences about the shape of the Union. Arguments about the constitutional shape of the Union are a distinctive feature of EU governance, not found for example in debates about the UN, NATO or the WEU.

Much of the substance of EU politics, on the other hand, concerns the regulation of public and private agencies in the member states by means of Community law. The growth of the EU as a 'regulatory state' has received considerable attention in the political science literature. According to Wilks,

> Regulations constitute and define the market, nowhere more than in the EC. The European project is one of market creation in which economic actors are jockeying for favourable treatment, governments are struggling to construct advantageous frameworks, and European institutions are seeking enough authority to impose rules.
>
> (Wilks 1996, p. 539)

There are four main reasons for the importance of 'regulatory politics' in the EU. First, regulatory policies are not costly to the regulators, at least in relative terms; the economic burden falls on the agents whose behaviour is being regulated and on the member states who must implement and enforce the regulations. Second, the Rome Treaty was largely a blueprint for integration consisting of undistorted competition in a free market which necessitated the abolition of a host of barriers to economic exchange. At the outset, it was assumed that the common market could be made by legal prohibitions (negative integration) on activities that distorted competition. It proved far more difficult than anticipated to abolish non-tariff barriers to trade in goods and services. Third, multinational export oriented firms have a preference for European rather than national regulation as this allows them to avoid the costs of diverse national regulations. In some cases, firms are trying to avoid more stringent national regulation by calling for European regulation. Fourth, technological development or regulatory developments in non-European markets can heighten the demand for European regulation (see Chapter 6).

Although market integration was the primary goal of the 1992 process for completion of the single market, the regional, social and environmental consequences of integration increasingly impinge on the agenda. Thus, the 1992 project was accompanied by a widening and deepening of social regulation in the Union (Majone 1993a). Since the 1970s, and more particularly since the SEA, the Union has increasingly engaged in areas of 'social regulation' designed to improve quality of life such as health and safety in the workplace, consumer protection, product safety, public health and environmental policy. Whereas in the past, 'social regulation' was promoted as part of the achievement of the common market, quality of life issues form an increasingly important and autonomous part of the Union's policy agenda.

The dominance of regulation has three important consequences for governance in the Union. First, regulation requires a high degree of administrative and technical discretion (Majone 1993b, p. 27). Hence it privileges administrative power over political power and reinforces the importance of bureaucratic politics in the EU. The fragmentation and sectorisation dealt with above give a particular salience to the relevant policy interests and pushes most of the decision-making downwards to committees. As proposals make their way from the Commission and its expert groups to the Council and EP, considerable *copinage technique* takes place among the relevant policy specialists in the Commission and Council. Second, the predominance of regulatory instruments tends to make the effects of policies less transparent and to make winners and losers less visible. According to Peters: 'Regulatory policy may thus minimise national, regional and even class conflicts over Community policy' (Peters 1992, p. 93). Third, regulatory politics allow the Union to intensify market integration without having to expand Community budgetary resources greatly. The member states are not passive recipients of Community regulation. They engage in 'a regulatory contest to shape European policy, to champion their interests and push through their policy concepts. All member states are interested to a greater or lesser degree in putting their stamp on Community policy' (Heritier *et al.* 1996, p. 331). Others have pointed out that 'the secular rise in the extent of European regulation has raised questions of effectiveness, the costs of compliance and the legitimacy of the regulatory regimes' (McGowan and Wallace 1996).

Market creation in the Union and EU regulation had to be buttressed with elements of positive integration either to complete the market or to make side-payments to those affected by market integration. Despite the Union's limited fiscal resources and the weakness of debate on the left–right spectrum, this process meant that questions of distribution and redistribution impinged on the Union's agenda from the outset. The Common Agricultural Policy (CAP) was the main distributive policy with a direct bearing on the well-being of Europe's farmers – in essence, a compensation mechanism for the agricultural sector. Gradually, the Union's limited budgetary resources have been expanded to include provision for research and development programmes, social policy, the structural funds and external policies. There have been impressive increases in the Union's financial resources since 1988. The Delors 1 and 2 packages underline the fact that major constitutional change in the Union must be accompanied by a budgetary settlement. A commitment to solidarity, which will be difficult to dislodge, is evident in the Delors 1 and 2 agreements which greatly enhanced the flow of finance to Europe's poorer regions.

The problems of polity in the Union

The European Union represents a vigorous and robust system of public policy-making, but with shallow political roots. The enmeshing of the national and the European has produced a Europeanisation of public policy but not of politics. Paradoxically it is precisely those attributes of the system that endowed the Union with an authoritative role in public policy-making and which raise difficulties for it as a polity. Its non-hierarchical, fragmented and loosely coupled institutional setting allowed the Union to develop its policy remit, to spread its tentacles, in an incremental and pragmatic manner, which in turn socialised national actors into further collective decision-making. Governance was characterised by a philosophy of problem-solving with a built-in process of review and evaluation. The Union represented public authority exercised through rules, committees, best practice and the power of the expert.

The intensification of treaty change in the Union has brought polity issues to the fore. The Monnet method of integration described by Pascal Lamy – Delors' chef de cabinet – as 'the people weren't ready to agree to integration, so you had to get on without telling them too much about what was happening', has demonstrated its limits (quoted in Ross 1995, p. 194). The sense that the Union suffers from a 'democracy deficit' and is experiencing a crisis of legitimacy is widespread in the discourse of academics and politicians on integration. Bringing Europe closer to its citizens, making it more relevant to the concerns of its citizens are the constant themes of Europe's politicians and institutions since the Danish 'No' vote on the Treaty on European Union in June 1992. Government leaders and EU institutions have rediscovered citizens and placed them at the centre of their rhetoric about the European project.

The question of how much political cement or glue is necessary for the European project is highly contested politically and in the scholarly debate. Political cement rests on three core attributes: collective institutions, instrumental benefits and affective attachment (Laffan 1996b, p. 83). The Union, as argued above, has invested in collective institutions and has provided considerable instrumental benefits to the participating member states. Early neo-functionalist writings on integration tended to privilege the importance of institutions and practical benefits. However, the politicisation of integration and the expansion in the salience of the Union has led to a renewed emphasis on the affective dimension of integration, on community-building, the 'we feeling' and polity-building. It has also led to an increased emphasis in the academic literature on citizenship and questions of identity (Wallace 1990; Garcia 1993; Meehan 1993).

The problems confronting the Union as it struggles to enhance its democratic credentials are not surprising. Historically, the struggle for democracy took place within national political spaces, whereas interstate relations were characterised by diplomacy. Diplomacy or foreign policy was always treated differently from domestic policy; it was a *domaine reservée* controlled by executives and relatively insulated from national parliaments and public opinion. The ideal of European integration was to domesticate interstate relations, to make EU policy and politics more like domestic policy rather than foreign policy. However, the development of the Union suggests that the transformation from diplomacy to politics is tentative and uncertain. The Union continues to hover between the domestic and the international, between diplomacy and politics, between government and governance in an uneasy tension.

An institutional analysis of the problems of legitimacy leads one to focus on the increased use of qualified majority voting, the reduction of national parliamentary control over the activities of executives, the non-elected Commission, the weakness of the European Parliament, and the obscure procedural rules of the policy process. The Council meets largely in secret and is not collectively accountable for its actions. Negotiations, informal deals and bargains between the three main institutions characterise the process. The vast majority of decisions are taken by delegated officials in Council working parties and in Commission Committees, which privileges expert power. Integration, as a result, has eroded the power and presence of national parliaments. The highly fragmented and opaque decision-making system gives rise to insider groups who are able to take advantage of the opportunity structures created by the diffusion of public power and the multiplicity of levels and arenas of policy-making.

The Union and each institution are tackling the institutional dimension of its legitimacy crisis by enforcing the principle of subsidiarity in the policy process and by attempting to make the decision system more open and transparent. The Commission, having been made a scapegoat during the TEU ratification crisis, has beefed up its information campaigns using electronic means of communication. The search for openness and transparency in the Council, on the other hand, comes face to face with very different national traditions of public access to information and decision-making. The Treaty of Amsterdam (June 1997) contained a specific provision on transparency that may have a major long-term impact on the working methods and culture of the EU institutions, particularly the Council, but the robustness of this provision will depend on the action of the Court of Justice, and the struggle between different national traditions of openness and transparency in the Council. Within the member states, national parliaments have attempted to gain additional power *vis-à-vis* their executives in relation to EU policy. All parliaments have used the ratification of EU Treaties to press for greater parliamentary scrutiny and an enhanced obligation on governments to consult with them about EU business.

The growth of intense patterns of cross-national and transnational policy-making raises a critical problem of scale in contemporary governance. Democracy relies on certain principles of participation and the responsiveness of political institutions to the people, which can be more easily achieved in relatively small political spaces. The undoubted benefits of integration 'could come at the cost of submerging a national democratic government into a larger and less democratic transnational system' (Dahl 1994, p. 23). There is a trade-off between the ability of the citizens to exercise democratic control over the decisions of the polity and the capacity of the system to carry out the tasks that matter most to people (Dahl 1994, p. 28). The separating out of territory, identity and function highlighted in Chapter 2 leads to functional pressures for larger scale policy systems that are not accompanied by comparable institutions and identity symbols. National publics face a trade-off between the consequences of integration for national democracy and their need to participate in structures that enable them to adjust to internationalisation. National electorates and political parties in the Union vary considerably in their attitudes to the trade-off between effectiveness and participation.

The problems of political community and political process in the Union are even more intractable than the institutional dimension of the 'democratic deficit'. A European public interest cannot easily be articulated in this governance structure nor can it easily engage its citizens. The Union treats individuals as consumers, workers and travellers but rarely as political actors. Direct elections to the European Parliament, which have the potential to bind the grassroots politics in the member states, have not done this. Turnout remains low (56 per cent in 1994) and is declining. It is difficult to argue with the conclusion that 'European elections do not provide the kind of democratic validation for the conduct of European affairs that general elections provide in a national context' (Franklin *et al.* 1994).

The link between the nation state and the exercise of legitimate government in western Europe contributes to a weakness of politics in the Union. Democratic politics, embedded in national political cultures and institutions, is still largely national, which makes it difficult for a genuine European political space to emerge. The German Constitutional Court, in its judgment on the TEU in October 1993, argued that when a union of democratic states assumes sovereign tasks it is 'above all the nationals of the Member States through their national parliaments who have to legitimise this democratically. Democratic legitimisation comes about through the feed-back of the actions of the European institutions into the parliaments of the Member States' (German Constitutional Court Judgment, 12 October 1993). The difficulty is that the profusion of administrative and governmental ties discussed in the earlier part of this chapter is not matched by comparable linkages between other parts of the national political systems. Europeanisation is far more pronounced at the level of public policy-making rather than politics. The interlocking of the European and the national is accompanied by a sharp disjuncture between policy-making and politics. The transmission belts that animate and structure national politics, notably political parties and the media, are weakly developed at Union level.

National political players competing for national office and embedded in national politics have little incentive to draw the attention of their electorates to the fact that political authority is shared and that functions are ebbing away to new centres of power. It is far easier to obfuscate on European matters than to address the problem of power in contemporary governance. Defending the 'national interest', 'bringing home the bacon', or scapegoating the Union serves short-term political interests. Equally, governments take credit for Brussels decisions that are likely to be beneficial to national actors. In both cases, national governments portray themselves as central to delivering the goods from Brussels and protecting the nation state against incursions from Brussels. Ministers leaving Council provide a national spin on what has happened to their national media, highlighting their role in securing benefits or limiting costs to their national constituencies. National politicians have, by and large, failed to embed their political activities in their European context, and have yet to begin to communicate politically to their publics about the choices they face in Europe.

The faint outlines of a polity?

EU institutions and the member state governments are beginning to confront the need to enhance accountability and tackle the 'legitimacy deficit'. One could argue that 'the incipient institutions of a "democratic" transnational are faintly visible' (Dahl 1994, p. 32). Despite the continuing salience of national politics, there is a flickering glimmer of a transnational polity emerging in the Union. The Union offers, perhaps, the only prospect in the international system that international governance can be rendered accountable and legitimate. The Union, as an arena of politics, is breaking down the boundedness of national polities. Although the EU is crafted on to national polities, it embeds them in a wider arena of politics. The increasing role of the EP, the development of the concept of 'citizenship', the mobilisation of interests at EU level all suggest that political Europe is struggling to join economic Europe. The need to create a People's Europe and to strengthen the publics' identification with the European project has been a recurring theme in official thinking about integration since the end of the 1960s and was always part of federalist thinking on integration. There have been many reports – for example, the Tindemans Report 1975, the Adonino Report 1985 – which advocated top-down policies to give Europe a 'human face'. This stemmed from a belief that political integration was intrinsic to the European project and that an authentic political community required the development of a 'sense of community' and the 'we feeling'. Moreover, it was motivated by the sense that economic integration needed a measure of political integration.

Top down policies that are designed to enhance the affective dimension of integration rest on three strands of policy: the developments of rights and citizenship, the politics of belonging and symbols (Weiner 1994), and the development and support of cross-national networks (Laffan 1996b). Just as state-builders in the past set out to create an 'imagined community', there are policies designed to construct a 'European identity' in an effort to reinvent Europe. It matters to the future of European integration and to the nature of the incipient polity how this exercise is undertaken, whose views and values prevail and whether European identity is constructed in an open inclusive manner or a restrictive manner.

The development of individual rights has been a slow process, which began with the creation of the common market and the free movement of workers. Gradually, the free movement provisions were expanded and consolidated by the Court of Justice in a series of rulings that went beyond a narrow interpretation of the treaties. A number of landmark judgments expanded the notion of 'workers' and established the framework for the emergence of fundamental rights in the treaty and the Union's legal system. Member state governments acquiesced to these changes although they strongly contested them before the ECJ. The TEU contained, for the first time provision for 'Citizenship of the Union', a form of additional or parallel citizenship that is based on citizenship of a member state but which provides additional rights. None of the rights are absolute, because (for example) the right to free movement and residence apply only if people will not make welfare or other claims in the host state. The development of rights and the concept of European citizenship has displayed considerable dynamism since its inception and makes a tangible difference to Europeans as they move from one jurisdiction to another. In this sense, the development of citizenship rights in the Union is building on the legacy of civic nationalism.

Since the 1980s, political actors and Union institutions have also sought to lever traditional nation-building strategies, in the form of a European flag, passport, driving licence, a European anthem and European sporting events, to create deliberately a sense of identification with the European project. The purpose of these symbols is gradually to alter people's consciousness of political realities and the political domain to which they belong. The blue flag with its golden stars is now flown from public buildings, industrial enterprises and even at beaches that conform to EU standards. Driving in Europe, one is constantly assailed by communal notices ensconced in the gold stars. In forging symbols of collective identity, European politicians are always treading a fine line between remoulding national identities and replacing them. The European passport, the driving licence, even the euro embed European symbols in a national context rather than attempting to replace the national. EU documents refer with considerable frequency to 'Europe's cultural heritage', to 'spreading Europe's messages across borders' and to a 'European identity'. Documents refer to the latter as if it were self-evident and unproblematic, the product of a shared history and common values. Problems of inclusion and exclusion are simply not alluded to, but it matters to the Balts, the Russians and the Ukrainians where they find themselves in relation to 'Europe' and 'non-Europe'. There is a tension between an identity for the EU and the Europe as a whole (Smith 1996a). Apart from the boundary problem, the construction of a 'European identity' is faced with the continuing salience of national identities. It is not clear just how the top-down strategies will find a resonance among Europe's publics.

The relationship between top-down polity-building and bottom-up attitudinal change is difficult to unravel. National identities are 'vivid, accessible, well established, long popularised and still widely believed in broad outline at least. In each of these respects, 'Europe' is deficient as idea and process' (Smith 1992, p. 62). Europe cannot therefore replace national identity, it can complement and shelter multiple identities by assuming diversity and by respecting Europe's medley of identities. A 'European identity' is one of a multiplicity of identities held by individuals. However, those who continue to define identity in exclusive closed terms are unlikely to see themselves as part of a wider polity; they will resist the erosion of their national identities, whereas others will be open to identification with a political and cultural space that transcends national borders. This tension is being played out within national political systems and among different social groups. The generation of a European identity varies across states and among different social groups; some state identities fit easily into the identity structures of the Union, whereas for others there is resistance to the internationalisation of their state identity (see Chapter 2).

European governance: authority, resources and legitimacy

The ties and tensions between the Union as a problem-solving arena and a polity and between different levels of policy-making, run right through this discussion of European governance. It might be argued that the Union's system of collective governance has produced a 'prismatic political system' in which rays of activity and authority are scattered or focused more or less effectively through institutions and social forces. The formal authority of the Union and its institutions is derived from the strong legal underpinnings provided by the treaties, and the principles of Community law elaborated by the interdependent Court of Justice. Its authority is further buttressed by common institutions, a number of which possess a measure of autonomy in relation to the member states. Although prescribed by the treaties and established practices in the policy process, the degree of autonomy that the Commission, in particular, can exercise is heavily dependent on the state of domestic politics in the member states and the extent to which the member states are capable of collective solutions to common problems. Crucially, the authority of the Union rests on the normative underpinnings of the European project. From the outset, proponents of the project cast their endeavour in terms of a peace project necessary to tame the dark side of European nationalism. The rhetoric of integration is a rhetoric of remoulding interstate relations, of going beyond traditional approaches to statecraft, of promoting closer relations between the peoples of Europe and not just their governments.

The Union has proved capable of considerable *adaptation* in the light of changing geopolitical circumstances and the growing internationalisation of the world economy. It has managed to widen its geographical boundaries on four occasions, expand its policy remit to include extensive areas of state activity and reform its foundation treaties on three occasions since 1986. It has survived direct challenges to its authority, such as the 1965/66 empty chair crisis and the sustained hostility of some governments and national populations. Its relevance to European order has, if anything, been accentuated by the collapse of communism (see Chapter 4).

From the perspective of 'big government', the Union appears to have meagre resources to underpin its authority. Governance in the Union is governance with a small budget, which limits the range of policy instruments at its disposal and its capacity for interventionist policies. It lacks independent bureaucratic resources and money, one of the traditional bedrocks of public power. Consequently, it relies on the enmeshing of the national in the European by co-opting national institutions and actors into the Union's multilevelled policy system. EU institutions rely on the ability of the member states to service the Brussels machine and on their capacity and willingness to implement EU laws and programmes. The EU system is designed to encourage governing through networks, which encompass multiple levels of policy-making and public and private actors (Kohler Koch 1996, p. 373). Political hierarchy and steering are replaced by segmented policy-making in multiple arenas characterised by negotiated governance. The member states are induced into the system of multilevelled policy-making in which they have a powerful presence but are also exposed to new styles of governance. The dictates of market integration, the prospect of a single currency and the challenge of continental order, have increasingly exposed all of the member states to more *supranational influences* through the creation of 'advocacy coalitions' at national level, through new strategies of governance and through the framing of discussion of the big issues – competitiveness, unemployment, welfare state reform – in a European context.

A robust system of public policy-making, the extension of political space to the Brussels arena and the Europeanisation of the member states underpin the integration project with authority and resources. In the current phase of integration, however, the *desirability* of the governance structures that are emerging in the Union raises key questions about the legitimacy of these structures. The fact that internationalisation is more pronounced in economics than in politics has various undesirable affects. The present system suffers from technocratic impulsion and an excess of non-transparent informal backroom bargaining. Navigating the stormy waters of EU policy-making is the preserve of 'insiders' who have come to understand the mysteries of the Union's policy process. A weakness of politics and the dominance of regulation transforms fundamental issues of politics into diplomacy.

The weakness of transnational parties and a European media renders democracy and legitimacy highly problematic in the EU. National polities remain the dominant site for political participation and engagement for most Europeans. There is a growing disjuncture between the arena of representative democracy (the national polity) and where decisions are taken (the EU and wider international arenas). National office holders continue to use the language of national interest which hides their embeddedness in the wider European polity and economy. They are loath to confront their publics with the fact that they are locked into collective governance with their counterparts in other member states. National politicians have yet to begin to communicate politically to their publics about Europe.

Conclusions

In analysing the Union as a political system it is important to compare it not just to national democracy but to traditional diplomacy. From the perspective of national democracy, the Union appears to lack essential mechanisms of legitimisation. However, from the perspective of traditional diplomacy and Europe's bellicose and imperial past, the Union appears normatively highly desirable. This is emphasised by Christiansen when he argues that any return to traditional 'non-institutionalised' inter-state relations would 'diminish the rule of law, the transparency of traditional decision-making, the participation of non-state actors, the redistribution of financial resources and other key aspects of the integration process which are widely regarded as normatively desirable' (Christiansen 1996a, p. 2). The Union offers, perhaps, the only prospect in the international system that international governance can be rendered accountable and legitimate. The Union cannot be transformed from a problem-solving arena to a polity in one constitutive act. Rather, the polity is being fashioned in an incremental, contested and patchy manner. The process is not unlike the Monnet strategy of pragmatic and incremental market creation. More polity-like features are being grafted on to the system, bit by bit.

6 Market

Introduction

Any review of European economic policy confronts a number of puzzles. Should we examine it as if it were a national economy, and assess the absence, presence and effectiveness of its policies by that standard? Should we view it as an international organisation, or as a case of international policy cooperation, and evaluate its strengths and weaknesses accordingly? Is there some theory or conceptual scheme that outlines which policy instruments are necessary, and which are feasible in the EU? Approaches of these sorts are partly unavoidable, whether we are discussing the internal market, social policy, cohesion, competitiveness or employment.

The chapter begins by locating the EU in the classical definition of the stages of economic integration. This uncovers the central problem that confronts analysis of the EU: how is deep economic integration achieved and governed in the absence of centralised political authority? We then compare the EU with two other types of economic arrangement: multilateral trade liberalisation and the management of a domestic economy, particularly a continental federation. The EU lies between the international and the domestic, sharing certain characteristics of each. It is emphasised that the preservation of an 'international' dimension frequently requires stronger, rather than weaker, EU rules and more, not less, EU competence.

The third section of the chapter examines the internal market. Having outlined Europe's new regulatory strategy, we turn to some difficult issues concerning its emergence and significance. Should the internal market be understood as the eventual implementation of a blueprint agreed in the Treaty of Rome, or as the novel outcome of the Community's particular evolution? Why is the European internal market so prominent, given the constraints on the EU's powers and the emergence of globalisation? The impact of the internal market on firms and sectors is surveyed, before considering the idea of Europe as a 'regulatory state'.

Attention then turns to three other aspects of European economic policy: the social dimension, cohesion and the – recently developed – policy approaches to competitiveness and employment. The final section of the chapter characterises Europe's emerging economic policy, offers an explanation for its unusual nature and discusses alternative views of its effectiveness and potential.

In examining each of these policy areas, two main questions are explored. How state-like is the EU in its economic governance, and is statehood the standard against which the EU should be measured and to which it should aspire? Second, there is the structure and process of EU policy-making in the economic area, particularly in its core, the internal market. Does the complexity of the legislative and regulatory process in the internal market prevent the EU governing markets in ways which produce efficiency, competitiveness and economic progress?

The EU and the stages of economic integration

The starting point for discussion of economic integration has, for several decades, been Tinbergen's distinction between positive and negative integration and Balassa's five stages of integration. Negative integration refers to the removal of obstacles to international economic activity, while positive integration refers to the creation of institutions and policies necessary to facilitate such activity (Tinbergen 1954). Balassa's five stages of integration are set out in Table 6.1 (Balassa 1961).

This provided the template for economic analysis of integration, since it was based on the definitions of goods markets, factor markets and economic policy, which are used in mainstream economic theory. It is widely recognised that the experience of European integration reveals definite problems with Balassa's stages – although they are still used in trade theory. In particular, it is noted that Balassa's definitions of a Free Trade Area and a Customs Union overlooked the significant elements of positive integration which are normally found in these arrangements.[1] A similar problem existed in Balassa's definition of a Common Market and Economic Union. His Common Market overlooked international trade in services, and this allows a gross underestimation of the degree to which national regulation needs to be harmonised or transferred to Union level. The

Table 6.1 Balassa's stages of economic integration

---

1 Free Trade Area
- tariffs and quotas removed on imports from members
- members retain national tariffs against third countries

2 Customs Union
- tariffs and quotas removed on imports from members
- common external tariff

3 Common Market
- a customs union plus free movement of labour and capital

4 Economic Union
- a common market with some harmonisation of national economic policies

5 Total Economic Integration
- unification of monetary, fiscal, social and macroeconomic policy
- a supranational authority whose decisions are binding for member states

---

common thread in these qualifications to Balassa's stages is their underestimation of the degree of positive integration – policy harmonisation, common policies and union institutions – necessary to achieve market integration. The wide range of economic intervention and regulation in the modern economy dictates that extensive positive integration is necessary to achieve a genuine Common Market.

It is less widely recognised, however, that while Balassa *underestimated* the institutional, policy and political requirements of a Free Trade Area, a Customs Union and a Common Market, he may have *overestimated* the centralisation of economic policy and political authority necessary for an Economic Union or Total Economic Integration. This was because the unitary state was taken as the prototype of economic union, which has turned out to be inaccurate in Europe (Pelkmans 1997, p. 8). This is a central feature of most recent attempts to re-conceptualise European integration. The EU is creating deep economic and monetary union without the development of the kind of political and administrative centre which Balassa, many early integrationists and most conventional concepts of politics and economy, envisaged.

Between international integration and continental federalism

In seeking to understand the EU it is natural to compare it with international economic integration and domestic economic arrangements. International integration, as achieved in this century by multilateral liberalisation under the GATT and the World Trade Organisation (WTO) (and in earlier centuries by the creation of imperial markets), is the most widespread form of integration. The form of domestic governance most relevant to the EU is federalism, particularly federal governance of an economy of continental proportions. Our purpose is not to engage in debates about 'federalism' in the EU, but to bring to light the EU's position between the international and the domestic. For the purpose of this comparison, we put aside the changing nature of European economic integration in recent decades. Its evolution is considered in the next section.

In comparing the EU with a domestic economy, we have in mind both actual federations, particularly continental federations, and the 'economic theory of federalism'. All domestic economies and federations contain a common market, an economic union and a monetary union. These economic arrangements are embedded within a constitutional order that governs the decision-making at federal and state level and defines the legal rights and obligations of the union, states, individuals and corporations. The 'theory of economic federalism' suggests the way in which broad classes of economic policy – allocation, stabilisation and re-distribution – should be assigned to the federal and state levels.[2] While the broad assignment of policy functions in domestic economies conforms fairly closely with these principles, there is significant variation between different federations, particularly in allocative and distributive policies. In allocative or regulatory policies, different federations strike a different balance between liberalisation, harmonisation and centralisation. In distributive policies, federations provide different levels of income support and restrict the fiscal autonomy of the states to varying degrees. Consequently, our comparison is undertaken in the same spirit as Sbragia's discussion of the EU in a comparative federal context. Federalism is not seen as synonymous with a federal state – still less with any particular federal state – but in the institutionalisation of particular relationships among the participants in political life (Elazar 1987; Sbragia 1992, p. 261). In particular, federations can be seen as self-conscious attempts to design institutions in response to the dilemma of size and diversity, to address concerns with territorial or ethnic politics.

There are numerous dimensions on which the EU can be compared with international liberalisation and economic federalism.[3] Our interest is in the institutional arrangements, the assignment of policy functions and the substance of policy, which allow us to characterise the EU.

There are certain respects in which the EU conforms to the pattern of international liberalisation. Its first and major substantive project was liberalisation of trade in manufactures between the member states. The requirement of unanimity on all major steps clearly preserves an international or inter-state dimension, something we discuss further below. Enlargement is a notable feature of modern international liberalisation and a striking characteristic of the EU.[4] A further substantive similarity is that, despite the treaty declaration of the four freedoms, the EU was effectively built for a continent of low labour mobility, a fact that is reflected in the relative underdevelopment of the internal market for labour, and the limited scope of the social *acquis*. One effect of this has been the preservation of national regimes of social security and industrial relations, at least until very recently (see below). A related similarity is the absence of significant fiscal transfers, even in the context of the move to EMU.

There are certain respects in which the EU does not conform to international liberalisation, but displays features of large domestic economies and economic federations. It is an advanced common market, soon to become an economic and monetary union. It has established continental-level common policies of great economic significance, such as competition policy, the Common Agricultural Policy, industrial policy (in politically and militarily sensitive sectors) and an external trade policy (see Chapter 8). International economic relations and organisations traditionally respect and reinforce the right of states to represent and control economic interests within their territory. In comparison with these, the EU contains numerous qualifications to the sway of purely territorial interests. Liberalisation of trade was accompanied by extensive, and open-ended, 'approximation' or harmonisation of national policies and the creation of common policies. Consequently, the EU involves limited forms of regime competition, and such competition is not seen as the best way to achieve harmonisation where it is warranted. The institutional and legal framework means that, like a federation, its policy process has become an ongoing balance between diversity and unity, between territorial and functional interests.

Nevertheless, there are important respects in which the EU differs from existing continental economies and the principles of economic federalism. To date, the broad assignment of policy functions in the EU has not accorded with the normal federal pattern. Major policies with continental-level relevance – such as macroeconomic management and strategic trade policy – have, for most of its history, been the subject of very limited purposive action at EU level. Distributive policies have remained almost entirely at national level, as have the forms of interest articulation and mediation normally associated with distributive policies. In the absence of stabilisation and distribution, European economic policy has been overwhelmingly regulatory (a pattern that is discussed further below). Most importantly, the provisions for the building of a continental common market were strongly conditional, not on *whether* this was an appropriate goal, but on *how* it was to be achieved. The treaty made the common market conditional on harmonisation, specified many exceptions and defined institutional arrangements within which these issues would have to worked out collectively. Examples include Article 36 (which allowed limitations on cross-border trade on grounds of health and safety), numerous qualifications in Title III (on free movement of persons, services and capital), and Article 222 (which provides that matters of ownership will remain at national level). These provisions secure member states from the full force of international competition, in the absence of approximation or harmonisation.

Combining these comparisons, we can establish the sense in which the EU economic system lies between international liberalisation and a domestic economy, sharing certain characteristics of each. In comparison with international liberalisation, the EU's supranational institutions, constitutional order and norms greatly qualify the purely diplomatic and territorial element. Yet, in comparison with a domestic economy, these and other provisions offer an element of protection or reassurance to member states' national and territorial interests. This 'protection' of member states is not necessarily achieved by the *absence* of EU rules or the *minimisation* of Community competence.

A striking example is EU limitation on state aids and public procurement. European limitations on state aids and inducements are greater than those in the US, where states are freer to attract enterprises with whatever packages they wish. American observers are particularly struck by the fact that the EU exerts control on this aspect of state policy. Indeed, over time this aspect of reassurance to member states has evolved into the novel European doctrine of the 'level playing field'. This extends beyond limitations on state aids and public procurement, towards a level playing field in health and safety, environmental protection, some aspects of employment rights and infrastructure. The level playing field doctrine might be seen as European compensation for the lack of fiscal federalism. In several significant areas, the maintenance of the 'international' aspect has been reflected in the assignment of a degree of competence, often of a restraining kind, to the EU level. The less-politically-integrated EU has to go further than the more-politically-integrated USA in enmeshing the member states with one another. The measures necessary to guarantee a level playing field are then determined in the EU decision-making system – which itself balances national and supranational elements in deliberation, law-making, implementation, monitoring and adjudication.

Those greater constraints have a dual, almost dialectical, aspect. On the one hand, they are evidence of the 'strength' of the EU and its powers. On the other hand, those central controls and regulations are, in large part, motivated by the need to limit the possibility that any one member state will be severely damaged by the actions of another. They set a limit to naked regulatory competition, where it might take a beggar-my-neighbour form (Sun and Pelkmans 1995). The formation of the Community involves member states in a deliberate mutual vulnerability, in which, as Sbragia says, 'they submit to one another' (Sbragia 1992). This would be an enormous leap in the dark, if it occurred without a 'constitutional order', which establishes institutional arrangements 'that encourage the parties to make themselves mutually vulnerable by limiting the dangers of vulnerability' (Sabel 1995, p. 101). Vulnerabilities, which in the USA seem only to arise at the point of *international* liberalisation – for example, the concern about labour standards prompted by the North American Free Trade Area (NAFTA) agreement – arise *within* the EU. This can be seen as an example of a greater 'internalisation' of international policy concerns (see Chapter 8). Indeed, subsidiarity, as enshrined in the Maastricht Treaty, can be seen to be consistent with, rather than in opposition to, these elements of EU competence. In these ways the core of economic union is one which enmeshes the national in the European and the European in the national.

The combination of bold ambition and complex qualifications, of supranational institutions and complex negotiated procedure, of strength and weakness, can certainly be read in more than one way. It can be read as strongly integrative, given that reassurance was a condition if agreement to integration was to be achieved. It can be read as systematically encumbered, making EU policy dependent on a coincidence of member state interests. Rather than seek some definitive way of choosing between these readings, it seems better to accept that negotiated order has a dialectical or contradictory nature.

This perspective contrasts with earlier federalist and intergovernmental views – both of which saw a zero-sum relationship between the member states and the Community (Sbragia 1992, p. 269; Armstrong and Bulmer 1998, p. 54). The EU is *between* international liberalisation and economic federalism, but this does not mean that it lies on a one-dimensional spectrum that runs from less to more centralisation. This alone suggests that the standard of classical statehood is inappropriate in assessing the economic role of the EU. But the complexity does not arise only from the side of the EU. While the EU was evolving its novel form, international liberalisation and nation states were also unsettled – changes which are discussed further below. As will be emphasised in Chapter 9, it is difficult in the 1990s to draw the sharp distinction between the domestic and the international, which was the foundation of traditional state-centric approaches to both domestic policy and politics and to external policy-making. The combination of EU development, changes in the international political economy and change in the European nation state has redefined and reconfigured the relationships between territory, identity and function.

The internal market

The common market was the central practical project in both the foundation of the Community in 1957 and its 'relaunch' in the late 1980s. In this section we consider six aspects of the internal market. We begin by describing the internal market programme and the new regulatory strategy that has emerged, often referred to as the Single European Market (SEM). Attention then turns to some difficult issues of interpretation concerning the development from the Treaty of Rome to the Treaty of Maastricht, particularly the balance between constitutive initial agreement and subsequent evolutionary transformation. We then consider the contexts in which the European internal market resides – the political economy of the member states and the wider international system – and how dramatic changes in each of these have enhanced the significance of the European market project. The remaining three sub-sections consider substantive aspects of the internal market. The role of increased scale and globalisation in firms' responses to the SEM help us to identify whether Europe is a nascent 'national' market in the classical sense. We then briefly consider the impact of the SEM on various sectors, noting the varying balance between deregulation and re-regulation. Finally, the idea of Europe as a 'regulatory state' is discussed and some innovative aspects of Europe's regulatory approach are highlighted.

A new regulatory strategy

In 1985 the incoming Commission, led by Jacques Delors, presented a White Paper, entitled *Completing the Internal Market*, to the European Council meeting in Milan. It argued that, in the interests of efficiency and competitiveness, the EC must remove the internal barriers by 'completing' the internal market. The White Paper set out in detail the measures necessary to 'complete' the market and a timetable for their legal enactment. It grouped the 300 measures necessary to complete the market under three headings:

- The removal of physical barriers to trade and competition, including the removal of border posts.
- The removal of technical barriers – the most obvious of these being different national standards for health, safety, environment, consumer protection and sector regulation.
- The removal of fiscal barriers – in particular, the approximation of excise duties and indirect taxes across the EC

The White Paper was endorsed by the European Council and underpinned by the treaty changes introduced by the Single European Act (SEA). In assessing the significance of market integration in the overall process of European integration, there is a strong case for adopting a broad definition of the Single European Market (Armstrong and Bulmer 1998). The SEM, which we often refer to as the internal market programme (for reasons discussed below), should be defined to include not only the White Paper, but also the SEA. In addition, certain market integrating measures not included in the White Paper but added subsequently – such as the internal market in energy, changes in external trade policy and support for trans-European networks – should be included in the SEM. Indeed, some changes introduced in the Maastricht Treaty, particularly the principle of subsidiarity, could also be included in the SEM.

An important aspect of the internal market programme was a revised perspective on the range of national laws and policies that need to be harmonised to create a European market, and several changes in the way such harmonisation would be achieved. 'Mutual recognition' of the legality of products and services, deriving from the *Cassis de Dijon* ruling of the European Court of Justice (ECJ) (1979), was adopted as the default principle. This established the principle of free movement, even where member states invoke Article 36 (EEC) on grounds of health and safety, so long as the national regulatory objectives are 'equivalent'. Where 'approximation' or harmonisation is necessary, qualified majority voting (QMV) was introduced on most internal market matters, by means of the revised Article 100a. The Single Act also introduced QMV in specified areas, such as the common customs tariff, qualifications of the self-employed, liberalisation of capital movements and the regulation of air and sea transport. A second change in method of harmonisation was the adoption of a new approach to technical standards and product safety. This avoided the earlier lengthy process of defining detailed EC standards (see below).

Substantively, the internal market programme involved the deepening of the common market in goods, and the extension of market integration and cross-border competition to services and public procurement. This was a major change, given the importance of services – such as banking, insurance, capital markets, telecommunications, road haulage, air transport, the professions and post – and the scale of public contracts in all member states. The SEM also developed EC policy in the area of social regulation, regional development, environmental protection and research and technological development. While some of this development consisted of codification of policies that had grown without a treaty basis in the previous decade, there were significant initiatives, particularly in 'economic and social cohesion' (see below). The completion of the internal market led directly to the addition of a new Merger Regulation to the Community's existing competition policy.

The complex set of changes embodied in the internal market programme, the SEA and the TEU has given the EU a new regulatory strategy for achieving and governing the internal market. This consists of a political, a judicial and a regulatory panel, summarised by Pelkmans in Table 6.2.

The internal market programme, and this new regulatory strategy, became the 'big idea' around which European integration was revitalised. The programme, and the huge amount of work done on it, have to be viewed in both analytical and rhetorical terms. The enormous 'Cecchini studies' were used to sell the idea of the internal market, disseminate a technical language for discussing it and provide analytical insights into its effects (CEC 1988). Thus, there emerged a language or

Table 6.2 EU regulatory strategy

	Political	*Judicial*	*Regulatory*
Core	Qualified majority voting	Judicial mutual recognition (given equivalent objectives or if Article 36 does not apply)	• Free movement • No internal frontiers • Subsidiarity • Minimum approximation/ harmonisation • Regulatory mutual recognition
Subject to	A few exceptions	Proportionality (member states)	Proportionality (EC level)

Source: Pelkmans (1997).

set of ideas that galvanised political support, motivated business action and, to a significant extent, described the emerging system of European governance. The language includes: 'the single market', 'non-tariff barriers', 'liberalisation', 'deregulation', the 'level playing field', 'mutual recognition', 'home-country authorisation', 'host-country regulation', 'new approach harmonisation', 'minimum essential requirements', 'third-country reciprocation', 'economies of scale', 'intra-industry trade', 'competition-driven innovation'. The dissemination and use of this language is itself a significant aspect of the modern European context.

Constitutive agreement and evolutionary transformation

The development from the Treaty of Rome to the SEM poses the major substantive and interpretative issues concerning European integration. Not surprisingly, it has become the source of, and the focus of, major debates on the nature, dynamics and destination of the European project. One particularly puzzling aspect is whether the economic union should be understood as the result of an initial, over-arching, constitutive agreement or the product of an ongoing negotiated process. This duality between plan and evolution in the creation of a European common market is paralleled by that between incremental change and radical transformation. In the final chapter we consider the link between the internal market as one substantive piece of learning and the new Europe as a learning machine.

At the centre of the Treaty of Rome was the idea of a common market as one of the 'Foundations of the Community' and a route to the key goals. The treaty embodied the analytical idea of a common market as both a customs union and a zone with free movement of goods, services, capital and labour, the so-called 'four freedoms'. The treaty can be viewed as having established a template for the subsequent major steps in integration, by combining market liberalisation with institutional development and flanking policies, a pattern that we discuss in more detail later. Indeed, historically, there is good reason to emphasise the encompassing nature of the initial agreement, since 'partial forms of integration are unlikely to be accepted' (Pelkmans 1997, p. 19). This emphasis on the original treaty design would suggest that the SEM be seen as the eventual *implementation* of an original plan. The long delay might be attributed to the 'failure' of the EC, the essentially intergovernmental nature of the EC or, more pragmatically, the sheer volume of technical, legislative and political measures involved.

This view, however, risks exaggerating the importance and nature of the initial over-arching agreement, or at least of reading it in a partial way. In both the treaty and actual development in the early years, there was a closer focus on removing tariff barriers, and ensuring the free movement of goods (Title I), than on non-tariff barriers and the free movement of persons, services and capital (Title III). There was also much greater progress in developing some common policies, such as agriculture (Title II), than in others, such as transport (Title IV). While the treaty declared the aim of creating a common market, it made its implementation in services, capital and persons conditional on subsequent agreement on harmonisation, approximation, common policies and closer coordination. The constitutive agreement can still be accorded a central role, but its significance lies in the *agreement to ongoing negotiation*, more than an elaborated model of a European economy. This emphasis on the procedural significance of the original agreement allows us appreciate the substantive innovations in regulation and market governance achieved by the SEM.

As noted above, the development from the Treaty of Rome to the SEM also poses difficult questions concerning the dynamics of European integration, the balance between continuous advance and progress-and-regress. Two underlying forces – the advance of technology and functional spill-over – are often considered to create a tendency to centralisation of policy in larger political units (Beer 1973; Dahl 1994). Yet, a conventional view is that European integration has experienced alternating periods of progress and regress. This emerges particularly strongly if we focus on the Council and the Commission, and their legislative role, rather than on the ECJ and judicial review. Overtly political integration certainly experienced significant set-backs, as outlined in Chapter 5. But policy integration continued in a few diverse, but ultimately significant areas (such as the EMS) and major progress was made in the judicial sphere (Pelkmans 1997, p. 22). This element of continuity is underlined when we note the degree to which the drivers of market integration were developed before the internal market programme. Not only were tariffs and quotas on goods removed, but the process of building the Community quickly yielded key principles – direct effect (1962) and the supremacy of European law (1964) – that have endured. Active Commission efforts to reduce the negative impact on cross-border trade of non-tariff barriers, such as divergent national regulations, date from the late 1960s. Indeed, the Commission's adoption of a more pragmatic approach to harmonisation dates from the mid-1970s (Wallace and Young 1996).

Yet there remains a strong sense in which the SEM must be seen as a step-advance in European integration. This is true in two senses. While many elements of the internal market project developed earlier, the SEM established a shared set of ideas and assumptions which galvanised diverse political, administrative, business and other actors. The EU approach to market governance accords an unusually central role to particular kinds of ideas and expertise (see Chapter 5). While the EU approach is incremental and fragmented it seems that the successful operation of this problem-solving approach is dependent on a minimal over-arching agreement. What was true of the original over-arching agreement, was true also of the SEM: the comprehensive nature of the agreement made it possible to achieve change in sectors which had, on their own, proved very resistant (Pelkmans 1997, p. 215).

The second sense in which the SEM was a step-advance, was that the quantitative accumulation of market-opening measures produced a qualitative shift in the degree of integration, the pattern of market governance in Europe and, as we argue in our final chapter, in the nature of the integration process. If the SEM depended on the drivers of market integration developed earlier, it also reconfigured them and combined them with some new approaches and new ideas. It redefined the original treaty goal of a common market. This was possible, indeed necessary, because, as argued above, the Treaty of Rome had made the implementation of free movement of services, capital and labour dependent on subsequent agreement on harmonisation. When the EU came to make real these elements of the over-arching agreement, the economic and political context had changed and new ideas about market regulation prevailed. The SEM necessitated changes in EU external trade relations. Most significantly, it altered the nature of the EU itself, greatly qualified the sovereignty and autonomy of the member states, prompted a significant change in national policy and changed the substantive governance of markets, and some areas of public policy, throughout the Union. Consequently, a process with a significant incremental element became transformational.

These tensions in economic integration – between initial agreement and ongoing negotiation, between continuous evolution and radical shift, between incremental change and transformation, between fragmented policy domains and general principles – are linked to the tensions we see in the overall project of European integration. Our interest is in the extent to which these developments are reconfiguring territory, identity and function on the European continent, and in the nature of the emerging system.

As regards the origin of the SEM, we accept those accounts that cite the changing interests of the member states (Moravcsik 1991b, 1993), and the impact of changes in the international economy on supranational actors (Sandholtz and Zysman 1989). But these forces should not be allowed to occlude the role of the ECJ, the Commission (in its collective, functional and sectoral roles), an emerging international business elite and the European Council (Armstrong and Bulmer 1998; Cameron 1992). Nor should the emphasis on interests and agents blind us to the role of ideas – a renewed belief in market competition and a loss of faith in conventional macroeconomic solutions – in the emergence and dissemination of the internal market project (Garrett and Weingast 1993; Wallace and Young 1996).

Our approach is flexible enough to encompass the undoubted *continuity* of internal market integration, the dramatic *deepening* of inter-penetration (of both markets and market-governing policy) and the *qualitative shift* in patterns of governance. The development of the internal market provides a graphic illustration of the observation, quoted in Chapter 4, that the Union is 'highly voluntaristic, yet pragmatically piecemeal and vauntingly long-range' (Anderson 1996, p.17). Substantively, we are in no doubt that the initial agreement produced an institutional context for open-ended progress in market integration, that evolution has produced a radical shift, that quantitative progress has produced a qualitative transformation, and that fragmented action has yielded systemic change.

Evolving European market in an unsettled national and global context

The significance of the evolution/transformation of the internal market, described above, was enhanced by changes in its context – the political economy of the member states and the international environment. Viewed in this context, the EU of the late 1990s seems quite different from the EC of the mid-1960s.

In the mid-1960s, the EC involved a basic form of internal liberalisation and a common agricultural regime, within a group of settled national political economies and a relatively stable international environment. The settled national models were characterised by a range of, somewhat different, accommodations between capital and labour, approaches to macroeconomic management and sector regulation. Each of the dominant post-war national models of the EC-6 contained a coherent ensemble of macroeconomic management, wage bargaining, enterprise organisation, industrial relations, welfare provision, sector regulation, state intervention and legitimation. Smaller member states usually borrowed significant elements from their larger neighbours (Shonfield 1959; Thompson 1991). These models came under both internal and external strain in the turbulent decades since the late 1960s. The intensity and timing of this pressure, and the responses to it, varied across member states. The international environment in the mid-1960s was one of advancing trade liberalisation in manufactured goods, economic growth and a dollar-based international monetary regime, reflecting the hegemony of the American model of industry. As outlined in Chapters 3 and 4, that international pattern was severely unsettled by both economic and political change from the late 1960s onward, only to be radically transformed at the end of the 1980s.

In the late 1990s, the EU oversees extensive liberalisation and market regulation and a range of economic policies, in a context where the – previously dominant – national models are fragmenting, countries with different models of political economy have joined the Union and the international context has changed radically.

European integration has had a complex and shifting place in this unsettling of national political economy and the international system. By making the national economies more open, it exacerbated the problems arising from the oil price increases. It was, of course, a victim of the differential response of member states to those crises, as non-tariff barriers increased in the 1970s and 1980s. In the EMS, it provided a vehicle for the emergence of common macroeconomic priorities on inflation and public finance, although there were autonomous sources for these new priorities – as evidenced in the UK and the US. While this can be seen as an exportation of the German approach, it should be seen as contributing to the break-up of the 'national' policy models in France, Italy, Belgium, Ireland, Spain and Portugal. In the case of the internal market, European integration can be seen as both an effect of the changing national and international contexts and the cause of further fragmentation. The search for the new regulatory model, outlined above, can be seen as a reflection of a Europe unsettled by global macroeconomic turbulence, intensified international competition and the wider changes in world politics and international political economy, described in Chapters 2, 3 and 4. As is often the case, one disturbance begets another. The move to this new pattern of regulation has, itself, unsettled a vast range of long-established economic, political and social arrangements within member states. While this period of rapid and profound change has revealed the shape of a new European market polity, it should not, of course, be seen as a stable new regime. Later in this chapter we consider some developments in European economic priorities and policy which have occurred since the formal 'completion' of the internal market, and in the next chapter we consider EMU.

Although the EU did not acquire great additional financial resources, this changing domestic and global context was one in which it could acquire significant extra authority and legitimacy in economic matters. It could acquire this mainly from the member states, and only to a limited extent from direct appeal to the business élites, populace or social movements of Europe (although that route has been nurtured with great skill by the Commission and the Court). The demise of the national models of political economy is not necessarily the same thing as the decline of the nation state. The weakening of the domestic ensembles – of macroeconomic management, wage bargaining, enterprise organisation, industrial relations, welfare provision, sector regulation, state intervention and legitimation – has, of course, altered the nation state, in ways that are sometimes described as 'hollowing out'. But its effect on other elements of the national models – trade unions, sectoral lobbies, welfare lobbies, political parties, once-dominant enterprises – may have been even more debilitating. As the coherence, effectiveness and legitimacy of the national models fell away, there remained the state – less effective, broke, but not significantly smaller; still the repository of most of legitimacy that was to be had; desperate enough, but free enough, to see the attraction of the internal market programme. Indeed, it seems that one of the most legitimate things European states could do in the past decade was conduct themselves well at EU level. The development of the EU's economic remit did not, of course, turn the dominant national models on their heads – despite the fears voiced by some in Germany, Britain, France and Denmark. Instead, it adopted significant elements from those national models, but did not combine them in accord with any one national pattern.

Scale and globalisation

The Commission study of the SEM, *The Economics of 1992*, included an inventory of the main non-tariff barriers (NTBs), estimation of the losses in welfare resulting from the fragmentation of the European markets – the so-called 'costs of non-Europe' – and analysis of the likely effects of the SEM programme. The analysis identified two main channels through which the SEM programme would impact on business and the economy: 'size' and 'competition'. 'Size' referred to the possibility that reduced costs, increased demand and better market access would allow firms to exploit economies of scale. The race to acquire scale and the subsequent competition to lower costs could initiate a major restructuring. 'Competition' referred to the possibility that increased competition would force previously sheltered firms into competition with each other, inducing them to differentiate their product by means of innovation. The operation of this mechanism led some to expect that the SEM would have a dynamic impact on those sectors in which non-tariff barriers were high, technological development was significant and the outlook for market growth was good (CEC 1988).

While exploitation of economies of scale and increased competition are not necessarily inconsistent – so long as the market can sustain enough firms – there are, in fact, considerable differences in thinking between those who stress the benefits of economies of scale and those who stress competition and innovation (Geroski 1989). This is one of the most important questions concerning European market integration. If a significant part of the increased competition created by the SEM takes the form of cost reduction based on scale expansion, then the fear naturally arises that small firms will find it difficult to compete. Furthermore, if the SEM implies increased firm size, then barriers to entry of various sorts may be increasing – even though market completion also means increased competition between those dominant firms in a given industry (Venables 1985). If the emphasis on competition and innovation is correct, then the increased competition takes other forms, such as technological activity aimed at product and process development, product differentiation, market segmentation and redefinition of firms' specialisation (Ergas 1984; Geroski and Jacquemin 1985). The argument between these two views turns on a number of analytical and empirical issues concerning the effects of the SEM on the size of firms, the relationship between competition and innovation, the historical significance of economies of scale, the effects of technical and organisational change on scale economies, and the role of small firms in economic regeneration (NESC 1989). While these are complex phenomena, which will take time to work themselves out, some impression of the tensions they create can be gained by reviewing firms' responses to the SEM and the actions of the EU in competition, merger and other policy areas.

Before considering these responses, it is important to clarify what should be expected from the SEM and to note an ambiguity in the term 'Single European

Market'. Although the 'single market' became a powerful rhetorical device, it can be highly misleading if used as a guide to corporate strategy or economic development in the new Europe (Kay 1990). There have long been price differentials across Europe for various products and services – such as cars, pharmaceuticals, insurance and domestic appliances – differentials that would be eroded if there was a truly *single* market. It is unlikely that the removal of a wide range of non-tariff barriers, achieved by the internal market programme, has created a single market of 420 million people for many goods and services. Nor is there a single United States market for most of the goods and services produced and sold in the USA. Several factors explain this. Much of the fragmentation reflects diversity of cultures, traditions and consumption patterns. There is a distinction between a European *market* and a European *industry*. Production is integrated internationally for many goods, such as cars, even where there are segmented national markets. Furthermore, far from seeking a single market, incumbent firms frequently wish to preserve the geographic segmentation of the European market, since the resulting price differentials generate high profits (e.g. airlines, cars). Europe-wide or global markets are more common in commodities, such as grain, or intermediate inputs, than in consumer goods.[5]

> What the single market programme does is to reduce obstacles to the creation of European industries, where these are appropriate (and, for that matter, where they are not) and, to a smaller degree, it has the effect of making segmentation of the economic market more difficult.
>
> (Kay 1990, pp. 22–3)

These analytical distinctions help explain corporate responses to the SEM and why many markets and industries remain national, or even local. But they also explain why many of those sectors in which significant European firms and industries are emerging, also display a strong global dimension (see below). The geographical dimensions of industries and firms are determined by the economies of scale and scope, not just in production but also in distribution, organisation and planning (Kay 1990). Even where sales and production are predominantly national, there may be advantages to global organisation and planning. Where distribution or production or research are continental, there will usually be pressures for global organisation or global sales, or both.

A range of strategic responses to the SEM have been identified. These include cost reduction, product differentiation, mergers acquisitions and alliances, new subcontracting patterns, licensing arrangements and technological collaboration (Lynch 1994; CEC 1996; Jacobson and Andreosso 1996; Welford and Prescott 1996). Mergers, acquisitions and alliances (MAAs) have undoubtedly been the most visible response to this environmental change. While most MAAs in Europe have traditionally been within countries, the SEM sparked a wave of cross-border deals in the late 1980s. While the growth of cross-border MAAs slowed in the early 1990s, it resumed, and spread to new sectors in the later part of the decade. Three features of this phenomenon should be noted. First, the wave of MAAs has distinct national, sectoral and structural characteristics (outlined below). Second, in pursuit of European and global strength, both EU and non-EU firms have been involved in European MAAs. Third, there is, in many cases, a significant global dimension to the restructuring that occurs within Europe (Monti 1996).

Mergers and acquisitions have been particularly strong in chemicals (where economies of scale exist), food products (in which there were high NTBs), packaging (reflecting the Europeanisation of major customers in food and drinks), defence equipment (reflecting the opening of public procurement and the end of the Cold War), distribution, banking and insurance (where new start-ups in foreign markets are difficult) and the media. The increase in strategic alliances has been evident in electronics and information (allowing rapid dissemination of technological information), pharmaceuticals (where R&D costs are high), biotechnology (where scientific synergies and shared research costs apply), airlines and telecommunications (reflecting the deregulation achieved by the SEM) and motors (reflecting global strategy).

While the USA and the UK remain the major countries involved in inter-national MAAs, the SEM does seem to have prompted a change in attitudes and behaviour in other member states. There has been a marked increase in the participation of German and French firms, as both buyers and sellers. However, there remains evidence that it is relatively hard to purchase firms in some member states, particularly Germany and Italy. Firms in the rapidly changing peripheral countries – particularly Spain, Portugal and Ireland – have become attractive acquisitions or partners for firms from the centre.

In the late 1980s, the fear of 'fortress Europe' drove many Japanese and American firms to invest in Europe. In the 1990s, Japanese investment switched heavily to Asia and European firms invested heavily in the new member states, Austria, Finland and Sweden. Although non-European involvement has fallen from the remarkable peak of 1990, the involvement of Asian and American firms in cross-border MAAs within Europe is an important feature of the SEM. It qualifies the idea of Europe as a nascent 'national' market in the classical sense. This idea is further qualified by the third feature of the wave of cross-border MAAs in Europe: the global dimension. In those sectors where there is the emergence of European firms, in European industries, serving a European market, there is, almost always, a significant global dimension to firms' strategies. This is evident in the food industry, where the reduced fragmentation of the European market (reflecting removal of NTBs and some convergence of tastes), and the emergence of pan-European strategies, coincides with the consolidation of the 'global' (European and US) industry into fewer hands – Philip Morris (USA), BSN (France), Nestlé (Switzerland), Unilever (Anglo-Dutch) and Pepsico (USA). The business and economic environment emerging from the SEM is the outcome of a complex interaction between the undoubted Europeanisation prompted by the SEM, autonomous technical and organisational change and the tendency to globalisation evident in many lines of business.

The issues of scale and globalisation raise policy issues that reveal character-istics of the EU approach to economic governance. An important part of the wider SEM was the addition of the 'Merger Regulation' to the EU's competition policy. Mergers and acquisitions with a 'Community dimension' must be notified to the Commission, which decides whether the deal constitutes a threat to effective competition in the EU. In conducting competition and merger policy, the Commission must make a range of decisions that embody a particular perspective on the desirable pattern of business and economic activity in Europe (Cox and Watson 1995). It sees its role as determining the trade-off between the efficiency gains produced by mergers and the increase in monopoly power (CEC 1989). Its processing of 508 cases between 1990 and 1996 shows that it sees benefits from mergers in most of the high technologies and financial services (CEC 1997). Some observers believe that the Commission has been too permissive to merger and acquisition activity, reflecting a 'Euro-champion' philosophy that would subvert competition in the internal market in pursuit of external competitiveness (Kay 1991).[6] The extra-territorial dimension of merger policy is highlighted by the Commission's block to the merger of Boeing and McDonnell-Douglas.

The complex issues of scale and globalisation also highlight the fragmented nature of EU policy. The Union influences the scale and globalisation of business not only through its policies on competition and mergers, but also its approach to state-aids, agriculture, transport, energy, external trade, SMEs, regional development, trans-European networks, research and technological development, harmonisation and standard setting. If nation states traditionally faced difficulty in combining these policies in a coherent and strategic way, this is doubly true of the EU. However, the EU's relative incapacity is qualified by several trends. Technical and organisational change, including globalisation and the fragmentation of national ensembles of economic governance, have undermined national efforts to use these diverse instruments for strategic goals, notwithstanding a heightened concern for national competitive advantage.

The impact of the Single European Market

A central innovation in the internal market programme was the introduction of mutual recognition. But it was clear that, in many sectors, mutual recognition is not acceptable or not wise. Examples include manufactured products that can pose a threat to health and safety and services in which an asymmetry of information, or systemic risk, poses a threat to consumers. In these cases, mutual recognition must be accompanied by harmonisation of national regulatory provisions. A second innovation in the internal market programme was the 'new approach' taken to harmonisation. The traditional approach, of seeking agreement on detailed European standards and provisions, was replaced by an approach that defined the minimum requirements necessary to secure agreement on the internal market. An interesting empirical and analytical question is whether these new approaches produce poor quality, lowest common-denominator, decisions and standards, or high quality, innovative, outcomes. The EU system is prone to sectoral fragmentation and capture, but also has the potential to produce a transformational re-orientation of sectors and sectoral rules.

The balance between mutual recognition and harmonisation determines the balance between deregulation and re-regulation in the internal market. That balance varies across sectors, across member states and across professional groups. Without a detailed account, we can illustrate the possible combinations of deregulation and re-regulation, and effects which these have had. In sectors that had highly fragmented markets, such as defence equipment, the overall process has greatly increased the level of competition. In sectors where there are enduring reasons for a significant level of regulation, such as banking and insurance, the internal market has meant increased competition in the context of a complex re-regulation and a virtual sector policy at EU level, although not of the traditional 'declining sector' type (Moran 1994; Molyneaux 1996). The internal market programme encouraged more vigorous implementation of existing EU policies, particularly competition policy, in sectors that had seemed too difficult or sensitive before, such as passenger air transport. In certain sectors, the internal market programme has provided an institutional framework favourable to high quality production through voluntary quality standards. In sectors where mutual recognition could pose a danger to health, safety and consumer protection, the internal market programme has provided a remarkable new mechanism for establishing standards (see below). The EU has sought to define the regulatory environment in new sectors, such as telecommunications, the development of which is dependent on a clear definition of property rights (Grande 1996). In some new technology sectors, where problems of collective action may limit the emergence of market-driven standards, EU technology policy has actively promoted a European standard (HDTV (high definition television) in televisions and GSM in mobile phones, see Dai *et al.* 1995). The EU is seeking to create a European market in certain sectors, such as energy, which have not been internationalised autonomously by business.

Regulation and innovation

It is now widely recognised that the regulatory method of governance is the dominant approach in the EU and is 'absolutely the character of policy exhibited by the single market' (Armstrong and Bulmer 1998, p. 70). Majone has drawn attention to the growth of EU rules governing numerous aspects of the single market – including rights of establishment and rules of operation in several market areas, competition, technical standards, consumer protection and the environment – and the relative underdevelopment of EU labour market policy, social policy, transport policy and energy policy. This aspect of the emerging European system is, correctly, the subject of much analysis. The dominance of the regulatory approach certainly reflects the weaknesses of the major alternative policy types – distribution, macroeconomic stabilisation and public ownership – which, it turn, reflects the tiny budget available at European level. In part, the growth of regulation in the EU can be seen as a reflection of a trend, led from the USA, of liberalisation combined with new rules and regulatory agencies. As Majone emphasises, the growth of regulation at EU level contains a certain paradox and challenges the dominant analytical approaches to European integration. The paradox lies in the fact that the Treaty of Rome provided for few regulatory policies and in the fact that, for all their complaints about EU regulation, the member states are implicated in its emergence (Majone 1996a, b).

The dominance of regulation at EU level challenges traditional state-centred views of integration, because of its sheer quantitative growth, the extent of policy innovation involved, the fact that it is frequently not the lowest-common-denominator agreement, and the role of the Commission at the centre of vast issue networks that spread well beyond national administrators. It challenges the neo-functional view because there has been a selective, rather than a general, transfer of policy from national to EU level; even the word 'transfer' exaggerates, given the role of the member states in policy formation and implementation. Its quantitative growth is explained, in Majone's view, by the prevalence of 'regulatory failure' at international level. The low credibility of inter-governmental agreements explains the willingness of member states to delegate regulatory powers to the EU. The transfer of regulatory powers to the European Commission, by making stringent regulation more credible, improves both the behaviour of regulated firms and the strictness of enforcement. Its 'qualitative growth' – i.e. its innovative nature – is explained by the role of the Commission as a 'policy entrepreneur', identified in Chapter 5 (Majone 1996b, p. 271).

The concept of the EU as 'regulatory state' may overstate the coherence and familiarity of the EU. While regulatory governance generally tends to segment policy and sectoral areas – indeed, that is part of its logic – this is more pronounced in the EU than elsewhere. Because it lacks an 'overall political architecture specifying relations between citizens and representative institutions', the EU is particularly characterised by 'islands of political authority centring on regulation of economic activity' such as civil aviation or pharmaceuticals (Caporaso 1996, p. 49). Furthermore, the emerging European regulatory agencies – the European Environmental Agency, the Agency for Safety and Health at Work, the Agency for the Evaluation of Medicinal Products, the office for Veterinary and Plant-Health Inspection and Control and the Monitoring Centre for Control of Drugs Addiction – have not acquired the power of rule-making, rule enforcement and adjudication granted to many of the American regulatory bodies. The history of falsified expectations concerning European integration, suggests that we would probably be mistaken to attribute the weak regulatory powers of Europe's emerging regulatory agencies to the immaturity of the EU as a regulatory state, and to expect them to develop in the manner of the post-New Deal USA. On these regulatory institutions, Majone observes something which we apply more widely: that the EU's constraints can also be opportunities.

> With knowledge and persuasion as the principal means of influence at their disposal, the agencies could develop indirect, information-based modes of regulation more in tune with current economic, technological and political

conditions than the coercive instruments of command that have been denied to them.

(Majone 1997, p. 11)

This is particularly interesting, now that some American observers see the regulatory agencies of the New Deal struggling to define, enforce and monitor rules in the face of economic change and social complexity (Dorf and Sabel 1998). While the concept of the 'regulatory state' captures an important aspect of the EU, it clearly has some of the characteristics of a 'post-modern state' (Caporaso 1996).

A particular example of EU innovation is the approach taken to what Pelkmans calls the 'standards/certification/quality nexus' (Pelkmans 1997). Where mutual recognition is not feasible, or not wise – because machinery, medicines and foodstuffs can pose a threat to health and safety – the creation of an internal market requires harmonisation. The Community's traditional approach, seeking detailed European technical standards, was extremely slow and inhibited the development of the internal market and, possibly, the competitiveness of European companies. The new approach involves an interesting division of labour. Member states set only the 'essential requirements' that products will need to meet before being placed on the market. There follows a procedure in which European standards organisations – such as CEN, CENELEC or EMEA (see list of abbreviations) – define a harmonised standard. Firms that comply with it can 'self-certify', subject to the operation of a quality assurance scheme, such as ISO 9000. But the harmonised standard is not compulsory on companies. They can choose to adopt an alternative specification, as long as compliance with the 'essential requirements' is demonstrated, through a third-party certification body. The 'CE' (Communauté Européenne) mark can then be affixed to the product, indicating that it complies with the essential requirements of all relevant directives. At that point the principle of mutual recognition should apply.

In overcoming a particular problem that dogged European integration, this might be seen as a European solution to a problem that only Europe had. But over seventy countries worldwide, including the USA and Japan, have adopted at least some of the EU directives, such that they are becoming global standards, giving a single compliance process for access to many markets. Many EU companies are demanding that their non-EU suppliers comply with the EU directives. The EU directives are simpler than the US system. Rather than writing laws that state the specifics of every product, the EU directives are generic in nature. 'They are written so that they do not need to be updated every time there is a technological advance' (Bailey and Bailey 1997).

Consequently, in solving the problem of technical harmonisation in a diverse, quasi-federal, union, the EU may have solved a governance problem that now confronts business and policy worldwide. It seems that the new EU standards system not only makes it easier for firms to meet irksome rules in an era of rapid technical progress, but can actually assist them in their business coordination. Thus, for example, it has been argued that Du Pont benefits from compliance with the EU's 'New Approach directives', not only because it gives access to markets, but also because implementing the EU standards and quality system allowed it to eliminate over 40 per cent of its test methods. 'There were 27 different methods for determining the pH of a solution; just one was substituted' (Bailey and Bailey 1997, p. 45). The new EU standard-setting procedure would seem to conform to the new principles of business coordination, as identified by Sabel. These principles of 'learning by monitoring', involve disciplined ongoing deliberation in which relatively autonomous business units develop the ability to judge their own progress and judge the value of doing business with other units (Sabel 1994). A further possibility, which remains to be explored, is that the EU has been pushed by its decentralised nature, and other constraints, to itself adopt 'learning by monitoring' – an approach that seems to have relevance in many areas of public policy (Sabel 1995; Dorf and Sabel 1998).

The social dimension

The social dimension of the European integration process has proven extremely difficult to analyse and understand. Some reasons can be suggested for this. At a superficial and rhetorical level, there was an intention to liberalise European markets while preserving the 'European social model' by means of Community-level policy. In reality, European social policy had a scope and nature very different from social policy as understood in European nation states. Second, European social policy has gone through distinct phases – both in terms of its substantive agenda (labour mobility, equality issues, health and safety, etc.) and in terms of its degree of activism (deregulation, harmonisation, re-regulation). This waxing and waning has made it difficult to fix on a definite reading of the social dimension, and has focused attention on the factors allowing or preventing progress at any given moment. Third, comparative research on European welfare states uncovered historical diversity, questioned the possibility of convergence and undermined the notion of a 'European social model' (Esping-Anderson 1990).

In this context, it is interesting that it was an attempt to compare European social policy with approaches elsewhere – and, in particular, to explain it to an American audience – that led to a new appreciation of the extent to which it has unsettled existing social policy regimes in Europe. The work of Stephen Leibfried and Paul Pierson (1995, 1996) has taken issue with the standard minimalist interpretation, and shown that European integration has eroded both the sovereignty (by which they mean legal authority) and the autonomy (by which they mean *de facto* regulatory capacity) of member states. While national welfare states remain the primary institutions of European social policy, they do so in the context of an increasingly constraining multi-tiered polity. The key to understanding this is recognition that three processes are at work: 'positive' social policy, 'negative' social policy and 'indirect' pressures of integration (Leibfried and Pierson 1996).

It is generally agreed that 'positive', activist, social policy at EU level has not developed to any great extent. Efforts to develop European social policy have been intermittent and characterised by a high rhetorical content (Streeck and Schmitter 1991). The existing institutional obstacles (the EU decision-making procedure) and structural obstacles (regional differences in income and development), have been reinforced by a conjunctural obstacle (the weakness of social democracy in most member states in recent decades). European regulation has been confined to the small number of areas designated in the Treaty of Rome and the SEM. The provisions of Article 119 of the Treaty of Rome (EEC) have allowed a significant EU role in gender equality, particularly in the workplace – driven by both directives and ECJ decisions. Some European social policy of this sort was a precondition for the deep market integration that Europe has pursued since the 1950s. However, the full significance of this can only be appreciated when viewed in the context of enlargement. It greatly accelerated the advent of gender equality legislation in member states such as Ireland, Spain, Portugal and Greece.

Another area of activism has been health and safety in the workplace, under Article 118a (SEA). While this underlines the market-related nature of EU social policy, it also provides an example of the Union's innovative policy-making approach. Not only was agreement reached on health and safety requirements, but these were not lowest common denominator regulations. 'Best practice' from several member states (and sometimes non-members, such as Sweden) was combined in a process that Eichener calls a 'new type of regulation' (Eichener 1993; Leibfried and Pierson 1996). At the same time, the introduction of QMV in other social policy areas has led to high-profile conflict between the Commission, the Parliament and the European Trade Union Confederation (ETUC), on the one side, and the Union of Industrial and Employers' Confederation of Europe (UNICE) and key member states, on the other. This undoubtedly led to a slowing of EU social regulation in the 1990s. However, an important aspect of the new reading, suggested by Leibfried and Pierson, is that the analytical focus on the high-profile battles over positive, centre-imposed, social policy (through the Social Charter and the Social Protocol) has been misleading. Indeed, looking below that level, there are developments that may qualify the retreat from the social dimension. One is the use of the 'social dialogue', between trade unions and business associations, as an alternative to Council regulation. Another is the fact that employment and unemployment have moved up the EU's *economic* agenda, a development that we discuss below.

The second process is the pressure to make national social policy regimes compatible with the principles of 'free movement of labour' and 'free movement of services'. Over thirty years, a combination of Community regulations and Court decisions has eroded the sovereignty of member states in the area of social security. As a result, a member state may no longer limit most welfare benefits to its own citizens, nor insist that its benefits only apply to its territory and are consumed there. Member states have lost exclusive power to determine how workers living within their borders are protected and their exclusive right to administer and adjudicate claims for benefit. As Leibfried and Pierson note, neither 'supranationalisation' nor 'harmonisation' are appropriate labels for this dynamic, since each implies more policy control at the centre than really exists. The move to create a genuine internal market in services, initiated by the SEM, seems likely to have a profound effect on national social policy regimes, particularly health care and health insurance. Member states have different combinations of 'national health systems', public insurance, private insurance and state-owned monopolies. These are exposed in differing degrees to cross-border competition, created by the rapidly emerging internal market for private insurance. This, in turn, will challenge existing demarcations between the public and the private spheres – something that was previously determined within sovereign welfare states. Consequently, two core EU principles, free movement of services and institutionally autonomous national welfare states, are in conflict, or at least in tension. The response to this dynamic unsettling of national regimes is likely to involve change by member states, some voluntary coordination of different national regimes, and some EU role in fixing the demarcation between public and private (Bieback 1991).

The third process generating change in social policy is the indirect effect of market integration or other EU policies, such as EMU. The possibility of an indirect effect from market integration is most graphically expressed in the fear of 'social dumping' – a process in which firms in countries with low levels of social provision and protection under-cut firms in countries with a higher 'social wage'. Ultimately, firms may move to member states with lower social standards. This could generate downward pressure on social standards, resulting in a 'race to the bottom'. This fear, felt strongly by unions in the richer Northern member states, can be seen as one reason for the adoption of health and safety standards at EU level. It has been suggested that the evidence for a social dumping effect is limited, since the skills and infrastructure of the richer member states are reflected in higher productivity (Leibfried and Pierson 1996). While this probably held through most of the post-war period, the evidence from Asia and North America (including Mexico) is that the new technologies and organisational patterns are less dependent on the ensemble of infrastructure, education, training and industrial relations provided by the advanced European countries in the post-war period. Another indirect pressure on social policy arises from tax competition. For several decades, tax competition was dismissed or ignored, given the treaty preservation of national sovereignty, the delay in achieving harmonisation of indirect tax, the absence of a genuine internal market for goods and services, the limited migration of workers and the limited mobility of capital and enterprise. All but the first of these conditions has changed, and there is acute awareness of tax competition in certain parts of the EU, as evidenced by the work of the Monti Committee and the emergence of an EU Code of Conduct on corporate taxation. Effects on social policy are likely in member states, such as Denmark, which depend on indirect tax to finance the welfare system. The transition to EMU has also generated significant budgetary change in several member states, and some of this change has, undoubtedly, been felt in social policy.

This broadening of perspective reveals that earlier debate was overly based on the national welfare state as the model of social policy. What is emerging in

Europe is 'a unique multi-tiered system of social policy, with three characteristics' (Leibfried and Pierson 1996). The multi-tiered system is one in which the centre is weak, given the scepticism of the Council and the EU's limited fiscal powers, but the member states have also lost much of their sovereignty and autonomy. While such a combination suggests a high risk of 'joint-decision traps', the new methods of governance explored in this area – in setting health and safety provisions and delegating to the social dialogue – may yield escape from those traps. The 'weakness' of the multilevel part of the system may or may not be compensated for by the second characteristic of the emerging system – the prominent role of courts, the most supranational aspect of the social policy regime. Indeed, the policy-making decisions of the courts are shaped by the third characteristic of European social policy – its emphasis on 'market-building' rather than 'market-correcting'.

Cohesion

Fom the start, the Community recognised the existence of regional problems and had, among its objectives, harmonious development by reducing regional disparities. However, that recognition was primarily a recognition of regional problems facing *member states*. It would be incorrect, however, to infer from this that the relationship between the two objectives was simply that the efficiency objective was uniformly given precedence over the regional objective, and that this reflects a general feature of the Community as a *laissez-faire* project. The extensive derogations in Article 92, and elsewhere, show that *even in the treaty*, let alone in practice, the common market was frequently sacrificed to regional and social objectives. The key point is that, in the first decades of the EC, the common market was sacrificed, not for other Community objectives and policies, but for *national aims*, in regional or industrial policy.

Each major advance in European economic and political integration has involved a significant distributive element and a sharing of the costs of adjustment to market forces. This is a fundamental feature of the European model of internationalisation and integration (see Chapter 9). In the case of the cohesion policies, this generally involves three elements: an analysis of the distribution of costs and benefits of the new stage of economic integration being established; a re-design of Community regional policies; and assignment of increased budgetary resources for economic and social cohesion.

Early European regional policy had a number of debilitating weaknesses. The development of the policy under Article 235 meant that unanimity was required. This was reflected in national quotas, national definition of areas eligible for regional aid, limited additionality and continued national regional policy. Reforms in 1979, 1984 and the development of policies to support the new Mediterranean member states, enhanced somewhat the Commission's role and, more importantly, introduced concepts and procedures that were developed later.

The re-launching of the Community in the mid-1980s included a radical reform of cohesion policies. President Delors explicitly linked the concept of 'cohesion', and greater Community effort to reduce regional and social disparities, to the completion of the internal market. The SEA introduced a new chapter, specifying 'economic and social cohesion' as a goal of the Community and a concern in all policy areas, and pointed towards reform of the structural funds. The 1988 reform, often referred to as the 'Delors I package', was a remarkable development in European integration. It reformulated the goals of policy in terms of five objectives, doubled the structural funds for the planning period 1989 to 1993, concentrated the resources on the most disadvantaged regions, sought coherence and coordination between the various structural funds, and introduced a new approach to management and implementation. This involved the design of multi-annual regional development plans, contractual 'Community Support Frameworks', and both *ex ante* and *ex post* monitoring and evaluation. An important principle in the reform was 'partnership' – between the Community, national government, sub-national actors and the social partners. Further development in cohesion policy occurred in the context of the Treaty of Maastricht and the subsequent determination of cohesion measures for the six-year cycle 1994 to 1999. This included a further doubling of the structural funds, some streamlining of planning, administration and monitoring and the introduction of a new Cohesion Fund to assist member states with incomes below 90 per cent of the EU average.

The agreement to double the structural funds in 1988 can certainly be cast as the type of side-payment likely to emerge from intergovernmental bargaining (Moravcsik 1991a; Pollack 1995). But that reading overlooks the origin, depth and effects of the reform. The deepening of the institutions of the EC in the mid-1980s changed conceptions of fairness and raised expectations about the possibility of addressing inequalities (Marks 1992). While the determination of the 'financial envelope' is the type of zero-sum issue on which intergovernmental bargaining is likely, it is only one small part of EU cohesion policy since the 1988 reform. In most other aspects of the policy, the Commission has a very significant role. The reform was carefully crafted within the Commission, which drew on the most advanced ideas in geography and regional development, and was driven by President Delors. It set in motion a process of institution-building that strengthened the Commission, discussed further below. Substantively, the reform can be seen to have 'openly rejected the chequebook approach in favour of a new core around the integrated approach and partnership' (Hooghe 1996, p. 114). It has been argued that the development of European regional and structural policy was the product of two converging logics: a policy logic, focused on rectifying regional and social disparities, and a political logic, the need to redistribute resources among member states (Hooghe and Keating 1994).

In what sense can the development of cohesion policy since the mid-1980s be described as strengthening the Commission? Cohesion policy involves a particular variant of the EU's unusual division of powers. While Council regulations and decisions provide the framework, 'these resemble a large and virtually empty house which is to be furnished by the Commission' (Scott 1995). The high-level bargains produce ambivalent regulations and an open-ended policy process.

Commission decisions on cohesion are less open to judicial scrutiny and challenge than in other areas. After the dramatic development of cohesion policy in the late 1980s, the requirement of unanimity, usually seen as limiting Community policy and Commission power, has served to thwart attempts to re-nationalise regional policy (Marks 1996). The Commission's influence derives from a combination of its monopoly of institutional and policy design, its administrative power and its analytical resources. Although the Council cedes far more than administration and management to the Commission, member states *individually* remain powerful actors, since regional plans and programmes are designed by member states in dialogue with the Commission. While the earlier regional policy required member states to provide the Commission with mainly financial information, the new approach demands convincing technical and strategic analysis of regional problems and how it is proposed to address them. In the member states that have received the bulk of structural funds – Spain, Portugal, Greece and Ireland – this intense engagement with the Commission has had a positive effect on the conceptualisation of regional planning, especially where the correction of fiscal crises has crowded out developmental ways of thinking. Given the central role of the Commission in advancing the cohesion agenda, designing the institutional arrangements and jointly devising and administering regional strategies and programmes, cohesion policy cannot be understood in conventional either/or terms.

An important aspect of the Commission's new philosophy was the partnership approach: the attempt to mobilise sub-national actors, such as regional govern-ments, local authorities and the 'social partners'. This has sometimes been read as an ambition to 'by-pass the nation state' and build a 'Europe of the regions'. While that reading is exaggerated, this should not distract from the real change that has occurred. In a very real sense, the EU has created a multilevel policy system for addressing regional and social disparities. Yet the influence of sub-national actors on EU cohesion policy varies considerably, making generalisation difficult. That influence is greatest in policy implementation and monitoring, and weakest in the negotiation of legally-binding CSFs, a task generally undertaken by member states and the Commission (Marks 1996). The involvement of regional and local authorities is particularly varied across member states. Their influence is greatest in those member states with well-developed and institutionalised systems of regional and local government (Hooghe 1996; Marks 1996; Bullmann 1997; Jeffery 1997). In part, this reflects the fact that the most important channel of influence, but not the only one, is via the national government (Keating and Hooghe 1996).

Competitiveness and employment

The completion of the European internal market was seen as necessary to re-establish Europe's competitiveness *vis-à-vis* the USA and Japan. Yet develop-ments from the early 1990s suggested that the internal market programme was not, in itself, sufficient to achieve this. Consequently, the issue of European competitiveness was a major theme of the Commission's White Paper, *Growth, Competitiveness, Employment*. While that paper attracted less headlines than other Union initiatives – such as the single market project and EMU – it gave rise to significant developments in EU economic policy.

The Commission's analysis identified numerous dimensions of the EU's relatively poor competitive performance and the many factors that are cited by analysts to account for it. These include macroeconomic imbalances, inadequate level of investment in research and development, relatively low productivity rates, slow structural adjustment, an overly rigid regulatory environment and outdated management practices. Opinions differ on the significance of unit labour costs, relatively low profitability, a poor investment performance, and relatively high long-term interest rates. Policy prescriptions that identify close linkages between one area of policy and the achievement of competitiveness are the subject of intense debate, not only among economists and business analysts, but also between business associations and trade unions. Consequently, in considering possible measures to enhance Europe's competitiveness, the Commission confronted not only the limits of EU competence in policy areas usually thought relevant to competitiveness, but also limited consensus on the determinants of European competitiveness. The White Paper set out possible lines of a policy for enhancing Europe's global competitiveness. These included helping European firms to adapt to globalisation, exploiting the competitive advantage associated with the shift to a knowledge-based economy, promoting sustainable development and enhancing innovation. EU pursuit of these objectives is an important element of European economic policy at the end of the twentieth century.

The White Paper and subsequent developments illustrate the emergence of a significant EU voice in an area in which EU competence is limited, not only because of treaty provisions, but also because of the limited potential for a policy that is both designed and implemented at continental level. EU action on competitiveness consists of aspects of competition and merger policy, trans-European networks, promotion of the information society, policies for research and technological development, the internal market policy (particularly regulation of new sectors), SME policy, the social dialogue and the work of the Competitiveness Advisory Group.[7]

An interesting aspect is the Commission's choice of a bottom-up approach, involving case studies, rather than general empirical or theoretical analysis. It has embarked on a comprehensive benchmarking exercise analysing positive labour market flexibility initiatives. It intends to disclose the possibilities for job protection, job enrichment and especially job creation. These cases suggest that Europe's competitiveness depends on adoption of the new forms of work organisation – involving teamwork, decentralisation, personal autonomy, flat organisational structure and more complex jobs requiring a wide range of skills. While these are primarily dependent on action within enterprises, business sectors and member states, this combination of policy coordination and public/private benchmarking is characteristic of the emerging European approach to both competitiveness and employment.

With this approach the EU can be seen as transcending potentially deep theoretical and ideological disagreements on the causes Europe's competitiveness and unemployment problems. While recognising the need for greater *flexibility*, it is trying to redefine the *security* that citizens require. Rather than choosing between flexibility and security, the Union is seeking, pragmatically, to focus on a number of common themes. One is establishment and encouragement of policies to improve the ability of European firms to innovate and apply new technologies. This will involve action in a wide range of fields including the education system, financial system, labour markets, competition policy, tax system and policies to encourage collaboration between firms. In addition, the EU is seeking to ensure that single market legislation is fully implemented as soon as possible. In this area, the further development of trans-European networks and infrastructure to encourage FDI, are seen as of vital importance. The Union is implementing policies to encourage structural change in European industry into fast growth sectors. Among the most important of these are telecommunications, the efficiency of which is itself a key determinant of competitiveness in other sectors. The EU is seeking ways to encourage firms to adopt new management techniques and competitive benchmarking.

In assessing the feasibility and relevance of continental-level policy, it must be recognised that the major factors that influence competitiveness reside at national or regional level. This is so whether one takes a traditional view, that competitiveness is determined by relative costs; or a perspective that focuses on corporate competition and strategy, emphasising innovation and product differentiation; or the emerging view, that competitiveness is determined by institutional and organisational arrangements (Lazonic 1991; Nelson 1993). Undoubtedly, the internationalisation of markets, companies and technology has altered the generation and exploitation of competitive advantage.[8] But this has not yet yielded a clear picture of the possibility of supranational policies for competitive advantage. Indeed, some argue that internationalisation has increased the relevance of national and local factors. In addition, competitiveness is only partly amenable to regulation – the Union's dominant form of economic governance (Majone 1996a).

Employment

The Commission's 1993 White Paper was the origin of a second significant development of EU economic policy in recent years – the so-called 'Essen Process'. The European Council, meeting at Essen in December 1994 initiated a new EU employment strategy. Although many factors which shape employment and unemployment are international, policy measures that might significantly reduce unemployment remain predominantly at the national level. The Council agreed that member states should promote investment in vocational training, make growth more employment intensive, reduce indirect labour costs (such as pay-roll taxes), increase the effectiveness of labour market policy and reinforce measures to help the groups hit hardest by unemployment. Each member state should adopt a multi-annual programme to achieve these aims, with the EU assisting coordination through systematic information transfer and comparison. The Madrid European Council (December 1995) identified areas of action to achieve these priorities, including investment in training, reorganisation of work, local development initiatives, wage moderation, reduced taxation on labour, active labour market policies and reform of unemployment benefits to remove any disincentives to work while maintaining a high level of protection. The need for a human resource policy to meet the skill requirements of the new information and communication technologies was added in the 'Dublin Declaration on Employment' (adopted by the European Council in December 1996).

This much-increased EU focus on employment was reflected in the Treaty of Amsterdam. It added a new Title on employment, immediately after Title IV on economic and monetary policy, and added to the 'Activities' of the Community 'the promotion of coordination between the employment policies of the Member States with a view to enhancing their effectiveness by developing a co-ordinated strategy for employment' (Article 3). The treaty defines a procedure for developing a coordinated employment strategy. The European Council must consider the employment situation each year and adopt conclusions, the Council must draw up guidelines to be taken into account by the member states, which must, in turn, report annually to the Council. The Union can assist this approach with 'incentive measures', including exchange of information and best practice, analysis and advice, promotion of innovative approaches and pilot projects. Finally, the Title provides for a new Employment Committee, with two members from each member state.

As in the case of competitiveness policy, the emerging labour market policy involves the EU in a range of procedures. Some involve the EU encouraging cooperation between member states and, if necessary, supporting and supplementing their action. Since this involves something considerably less than EU legislation, let alone EU conduct of policy, we are challenged to assess its significance. Conventional state-centred and federalist perspectives would suggest a sceptical view of these developments. The conclusions of the European Council and the guidelines of the Council have no binding force and, consequently, the notion of a European policy for unemployment is a fiction. But this may be too narrow a view of the diversity, nature and potential of EU governance. An alternative view is that major changes to reduce unemployment (such as more active labour market policies, a significant reduction in statutory charges on labour and more solidaristic wage setting) are more likely to be adopted in each member state if they are adopted in all. A related argument is that detailed analysis and discussion of unemployment at European-level has, potentially, a significance in establishing a climate of opinion and analysis which sees employment and unemployment as central problems for Europe. Discussing the role of the European Council in the development of the internal market agenda, Armstrong and Bulmer note that 'Repeated rehearsal of policy commitments can lead to the embedding of ideas in institutions; to the creation of new norms' (Armstrong and Bulmer 1998, p. 17). Although the employment initiative is 'thinner' than the internal market, the *Growth, Competitiveness, Employment* White Paper started a dynamic that led to a new treaty chapter, establishing a 'political framework' for national labour market measures.

The wide-ranging, but thin, EU approach reflects not only the limited consensus on labour market policies and limited EU competence in this area, but also the fact that many labour market policies – such as education, training, and active labour market measures – can be undertaken most effectively at national, or even local, level. These policy initiatives should be interpreted as a pragmatic Union response to limited EU competence, and as a set of policy measures reflecting the complex, indeterminate, state of analytical and political debate on competitiveness and the labour market.

Towards a European economic policy?

The evolving content and procedure of European economic union

The degree of evolution in European economic policy since the 1980s has not been adequately recognised or conceptualised. The evolving economic priorities of the EU since its foundation in 1957 can be summarised as follows.

- The creation of the common market in goods, the CAP and the European Social Fund.
- Exchange rate stability and dis-inflation.
- The completion of the internal market and expanded cohesion instruments.
- Designing the transition to EMU and accompanying cohesion measures.
- Measures to promote European competitiveness.
- The Essen process, addressing employment and unemployment.
- Achieving the transition to EMU.

During the 1980s, European economic policy would seem to have had three primary goals. In order of their appearance on the European agenda these were: the limitation of exchange rate variation, dis-inflation and completion of the internal market – goals that were achieved to a considerable degree. Since then, European economic policy has undergone some change of emphasis. Following the limited fall in unemployment in the late 1980s, and the sharp increase in unemployment in the early 1990s, there was, undoubtedly, an increased focus on European unemployment. In addition, while the internal market was intended to improve Europe's position *vis-à-vis* Japan and the USA, European competitiveness has become a more explicit focus of policy in recent years. However, through much of the 1990s, the political and economic demands of transition to EMU have dominated the new-found emphasis on both employment and competitiveness.

The emerging EU policy focus on employment and competitiveness is less visible than other developments. This is partly because the comprehensive and ambitious nature of the Rome Treaty can lead us to see the history of European economic integration as a continuous, if drawn out, process of *implementation* of a plan in existence since 1957 – a view which we qualified above. The emerging policy approaches come at the end of a remarkable period of European integration, in which the SEA and the TEU stand as major milestones. Each was associated with a strikingly visible, and easily communicated, big idea in the economic area – the single market and monetary union. The extent of change in emphasis is evident in the concepts and language used in Commission documents on the economy.[9]

Including these emerging policies, European economic policy in the late 1990s had five main elements: macroeconomic policy, the internal market, cohesion, competitiveness policy and labour market policy.

A striking feature of the EU since its inception has been the limited role of European macroeconomic policy. Viewed functionally, continental-level policy has a definite relevance in macroeconomic matters. This is because of the difficulty that individual member states, even large ones, have in conducting an effective internal or external macroeconomic policy. We can identify at least two reasons for the attenuated role of macroeconomic policy in the EU. While the standard goals of macroeconomic policy are control of inflation and the maintenance of buoyant demand, European macroeconomic policy has had an additional objective: limitation of nominal exchange rate variability between European currencies (see Chapter 7). A second reason relates to the negotiated nature of EU decision-making. Differences of opinion between member states were compounded by inconclusive academic debate on the feasibility of active macroeconomic policy. In this context, the EU settled on an economic doctrine that emphasises stability – in inflation, public finance, exchange rates and output growth. In the 1980s and 1990s Europe had, in effect, forsaken macroeconomics and macroeconomic policy.

The unusual position of macroeconomic policy means that the EU places particular reliance on internal market policy. The characterisation of this policy has been the main concern of this chapter.

The third element of the emerging European economic policy concerns cohesion. There was a remarkable development of the European structural funds in the context of the completion of the internal market. The institutional developments of the Delors I package – in particular, the deep involvement of the Commission in regional and national planning and the mobilisation of sub-national and non-state actors – were of great significance, both for the recipient regions and member states and for European integration. While a state-centric or bureaucratic conception would emphasise the likelihood of lowest-common-denominator decisions and incoherent (if bureaucratically balanced) policy approaches, the development of EU cohesion policy since the mid-1980s looks more like an innovative, strategic, problem-solving outcome. In our final chapter we argue that the past and future evolution of EU cohesion policy must be viewed in the context of enlargement of the Union and the unsettled political economy of both core and periphery.

The fourth component is the emerging European policies for competitiveness. This involves a wide range of methods, instruments and procedures. Some involve 'Community action proper', in areas such as competition policy, merger policy, EU financial contributions to trans-European networks, and research and technological development. Some involve EU coordination of national policy measures, in areas of infrastructure and technological development. Others involve the EU acting as a *networker* or *broker*, in areas such as SME policy. Finally, some of these policy approaches involve the Union acting as a forum for analysis, discussion and development of shared perspectives on the problem of competitiveness. It is notable that industrial policy does not appear in the list of EU approaches to competitiveness. In part, this reflects the fact that, as noted in the Commission White Paper, 'industrial policy continues to be controversial'. Rather than trying to resolve major doctrinal differences on industrial policy, the Union is forced to develop policy experiments in new areas, such as inter-firm collaboration, innovation and networking (Andreasen *et al.* 1995; Coriat 1995). Despite its limited nature, the emerging EU policy for competitiveness is potentially important, both substantively and procedurally. Indeed, we argue in Chapter 9 that the constraints on EU competitiveness policy may also create opportunities.

The final element of the emerging European economic policy concerns employment. The combination of policy coordination and public/private bench-marking is characteristic of the emerging European approach to the interrelated issues of competitiveness and employment. So is the increased use of the social dialogue and support for European networks of non-governmental organisations. While the EU's approach can be cast as a compromise between the deregulatory approach and the preservation of the 'European social model' – reflecting the absence of intellectual or political support for a full-blooded implementation of either doctrine – it shows signs of being more than the lowest common denominator. It is significant that the EU has begun to act as a forum for analysis, discussion and development of shared perspectives on new problems. The new approach can be seen as reflecting the limited ability of hard law and traditional policy – at either national or EU level – to address adequately the complexity of labour market problems. It may, in time, yield a more formal EU-level policy on employment and unemployment, perhaps involving minimum standards for member states on any measures for the long-term unemployed for which Community support is sought (White Paper, p. 150). The new emphasis on employment is also important in the context of EMU and more coordinated macroeconomic policy. The ultimate test is whether the EU uses its limited, but influential, role to develop innovative approaches to employment, and whether its freedom from the mainstream, large-scale and administratively complex, labour market policy responsibilities of member states is seen as an opportunity rather than a constraint.

Interpreting and evaluating European economic policy

This strange combination of economic policies – macroeconomic, internal market, cohesion, competitiveness and employment – is quite different from that of a classical nation state, a continental federation, a post-war European welfare state and, indeed, the economic theory of federalism. Various explanations have been offered for Europe's unusual pattern of policy competence. These include the old argument that the EU is *sui generis*, the intergovernmentalist view that the unusual policy portfolio is explained by the resistance of member states, the argument that the EU is a neo-liberal project and, more recently, the observation that the EU is not, and cannot be, a 'scaled up version of the nation state' (Hirst 1994). In our final chapter, we discuss these and other explanations, and elaborate our own interpretation. Here, we provide an initial outline of our interpretation and evaluation of EU *economic* policy.

In our view, the emerging pattern of European economic policy should be seen as a new model of internationalisation. The European model of internationalisation involves the freeing of trade and an element of deregulation, combined with the setting of new rules, the transfer of competence to union institutions and the development of distributive instruments. It contrasts with both the freeing of trade under a hegemonic power and with multilateral trade liberalisation. It differs also from the economic union in the US, which has less concern with a 'level playing field' but much larger inter-state distributive mechanisms.

In seeking to understand Europe's unusual pattern of economic policy, it pays to focus not only on the *amount* of policy competence at EU level (and the amount remaining at national level), but also on the *pattern* of policy-making and implementation. In each economic policy area, the existence or non-existence of an EU role is often less revealing than the nature of that involvement, its interaction with national approaches and the patterns of national response to Europeanisation. Not only is the pattern of EU economic policy unusual, but each of its elements – macroeconomic, internal market, cohesion, competitiveness and employment – involves a somewhat different method of governance (see Chapter 9).

For all its complexity, the emerging European economic policy has definite strengths. In a global context, the European model of economic internationalisation may have a particular relevance at the end of the twentieth century. The international economic system now extends beyond trade, to include international investment and globalised technology, information and finance. It is increasingly recognised that this requires an international regulatory framework that encompasses more than trade. The EU can be seen as *the* model for the regulation of deep economic internationalisation. It has shown itself capable of supporting a sustainable, stable and desirable internationalisation of economic activity. While it has emerged in the particular circumstances of the EU, the evolving European approach contains features that have a wider relevance. It may, indeed, be a harbinger of the pattern of economic governance that will become general in an increasingly interdependent world. In our final chapter, we explore further the idea that the complex set of constraints in Europe has turned out to create opportunities, and that the particularities of EU decision-making have yielded principles of policy-making that are of general relevance.

At a European level, two elements of recent EU economic policy – the internal market and EMU – are of historic importance. With the internal market programme, Europe stated that it did not intend to be bypassed by the dramatic changes occurring in business. While theoretical arguments can be conducted about the adequacy of Europe's unusual policy mix, we are in little doubt that in the 1980s and 1990s, prioritising European market integration was appropriate and, in our view, more appropriate than anything the member states were capable of implementing on their own. It brought Europe into line with fundamental changes in economic organisation, public policy, technology and society. Liberalisation and internationalisation of markets was a condition of achieving this. The effect of the SEM on firms, markets and governments was reinforced by the EMU project, because it suspended conflict (between and within member states) on macroeconomic policy.

This interpretation should not be understood to imply that EU economic policy at the turn of the century is sufficient to lay the basis for enduring prosperity in Europe. We cannot assume that the systems' tendency to capture and frag-mentation will be dominated by its ability to reorient sectors in a transformative way. More generally, we do not claim that the EU's unusual economic policy mix is optimal in the long run nor, indeed, that it is the essential nature of European economic policy. It has long been recognised that economic union is uncertain and contested. A functioning internal market can be created with different combinations of deregulation and re-regulation, and a different balance of positive and negative integration. While the actual outcome is determined in part by conflicting national and ideological perspectives, we argue that the indeterminacy in economic integration is resolved, to a significant extent, by particular conjunctures. These include enlargement, global pressures and ideas. The contingent nature of integration is discussed further in our final chapter and incorporated in our overall interpretation. It has, however, one very immediate consequence here. The pattern of EU economic policy, the origin and nature of which we have outlined, is itself contingent and evolving.

Because the absence of macroeconomic policy has been a key feature of the system since the foundation of the Community, the launch of the euro constitutes a major change in the EU's economic policy mix. Indeed, given the political nature of macroeconomic policy, and the apparent close relation between currency and statehood, many believe that EMU constitutes, or demands, a profound change in the degree of political integration. Our characterisation of European market integration, and of European integration as predominantly shaped by market integration, needs to be complemented by an analysis of money, and its place in the European project. This is the subject of the next chapter.

Notes

1 Free Trade areas – such as that between Australia and New Zealand and that between the EC and EFTA – involve joint regulation and some policy 'approximation'. In Customs Unions – such as that between the Benelux countries or the EC – there tends to be extensive forms of joint policy and the transfer of functions to common institutions.

2 Policies shaping the allocation of resources should be shared between the federal and state levels, depending on the extent to which policy preferences differ and the degree of cross-border spill-over in the activity. Macroeconomic stabilisation by means of monetary and fiscal policy should be undertaken at federal level, since it is likely to be ineffective at state level. Redistribution should be assigned to the federal level, to the extent that mobility of capital and labour undermines state-level attempts to follow independent tax and social policies

3 One concerns the legal compatibility of the EU with international liberalisation, as developed by the GATT and the WTO. A fundamental principle of the GATT is non-discrimination, while the EU obviously involves preferential arrangements between members (see Chapter 8). Another question, which has been much discussed, is whether European integration has facilitated or inhibited multilateral liberalisation. Although the EU involves a strong element of preference, most agree that it has promoted multilateral integration.

4 Indeed, short of enlargement, the EU has shown a tendency to extend a significant range of internal economic provisions to non-members. This blurs the distinction between the preferential EU and the non-discriminatory multilateral liberalisation. Although it is notable that large-scale extension of EU provisions to non-members – as in the EEA agreement and the Europe agreements – seem to be a precursor to enlargement.

5 Given these important analytical points, our preferred label would be 'completion of the *internal* market', or the '*internal* market programme'. It is with some reluctance that we use the, widely recognised, term Single European Market (SEM).

6 Other economists argue that the EU merger policy is too open to lobbying and is prone to regulatory capture. They suggest that separate agencies might undertake investigation and adjudication (Neven *et al.* 1993).

7 The Competitiveness Advisory Group was established in 1995 to provide a six-monthly report to the President of the Commission and the European Council on the state of the Union's competitiveness and to advise on economic policy priorities and guidelines (see Jacquemin 1998).

8 The Commission does not assume that European firms have a distinct identity, given their involvement in strategic alliances with American and Japanese firms, and the fuzzy boundaries of traditional industrial sectors.

9 One example might indicate this change. The Delors Report on EMU advocated a single currency, defined the stages of transition and suggested an approach to economic management in EMU. On the latter, it said that 'Governments . . . would refrain from direct intervention in the wage and price formation process' (Delors *et al.* 1989). The Commission's 1993 White Paper *Growth, Competitiveness, Employment*, sees unresolved distributional conflict and lack of organisational innovation as key factors explaining Europe's poor competitive and employment performance. In this context, 'factor mobility and the capacity to combine factors effectively and to organise the social consensus on the share out of value-added are becoming much more important than the initial factor endowment' (CEC 1994, p. 71).

7 Money

Introduction

Macroeconomic and monetary integration pose acute challenges to the study of European integration. The EC was slow to develop any appreciable level of macroeconomic policy coordination; yet it has undertaken a transition to monetary union at a pace that some see as excessive. Much of the dynamic of the Union is explained by its focus on the functional and the economic; yet its progress to monetary union is often seen as submitting economic logic to a high profile political project. The progress to monetary union has been mapped in complex technical studies, yet the European monetary union differs in significant ways from past and existing unions and conflicts with much traditional economic theory. The Union is seen to have developed a complex, multilayered, negotiated, technocratic decision-making system; yet there is a widespread sense that EMU brings the EU across a political threshold which has not been adequately addressed.

These issues can be seen as particular manifestations of the ties and tensions within European integration, which form a connecting theme in our argument. Two of these ties and tensions are particularly prevalent in the project of Economic and Monetary Union (EMU). The tie and tension between a polity and problem-solving arena is at the heart of EMU, producing its peculiar and difficult mixture of technical arrangements, high politics and identity politics. The tie and tension between EU policy-making and multilevel policy is present, if only because it is more definitively resolved in EMU than other policy areas, and yet resolved in a quite novel way. In addition, the links and tensions between the Union's continental project of monetary union and its role in the international monetary system have undoubted relevance in EMU.

In exploring the reconciliation of these economic and political aspects of EMU, this chapter focuses on three sets of issues.

- The origin and motivation of EMU: is it true that the economic logic of EMU is weak and the project must be understood as essentially political? How has support for EMU emerged among a diverse set of member states in an unsettled economic and financial environment?

- The structure and process of policy-making in EMU: is monetary union amenable to the Monnet method, or is it different in ways that require a qualitatively different approach? How are we to understand the distinctive decision-making system and institutions of EMU?
- The character of the emerging European monetary and economic authority: is the European monetary union the German model 'writ large'? Can the European design be defended in the face of diverse critiques? Is there an essential relation between currency and statehood? Does the absence of political and cultural integration confirm that EMU has a 'hollow core'?

Origin and motivation

In attempts to understand the interaction of the economic and the political in EMU, one common view is that the economic logic of EMU is weak and the project must be understood as essentially driven by a political motivation (Krugman 1993; Eichengreen and Frieden 1994; Tsoukalis 1996, 1997). From this view it is a short step to the argument that the difficulties of EMU reflect the limited economic logic of the project, whereas the progress reflects the strength of political conviction of key European governments. While this view is partly understandable – given the key role of political leadership at critical moments, such as the establishment of the EMS or the agreement of the Maastricht Treaty – it is not an adequate starting point for analysing the political and economic aspects of EMU. It would seem to be based on a short time horizon and on excessive credence in a certain strand of Anglo-Saxon economic theory, an approach that seems to generate an enduring scepticism about monetary union. It completely reverses the well known argument that member states seek to preserve sovereignty, without exploring the implications of this rejection of an intergovermental perspective. It invokes political factors, while failing either to analyse them or integrate them with economic issues. In our view, an understanding of the EMU process must begin from a more historical and practical assessment of the economic motivation for EMU, and a more pragmatic view of the approach adopted by the EU. In this section we argue that the economic motivation for EMU is strong and, in the next section, that much of the difficulty of EMU can be attributed to the political complexity of creating EMU in the European context.

Europe's long quest for exchange rate stability

A first step in interpreting European macroeconomic and monetary integration is to view Europe in the context of the changing international political economy, as outlined in Chapter 4. European developments must be viewed as part of an interdependent global monetary system that contains a potential conflict between domestic economic autonomy and international economic stability. It has long been recognised that a stable and efficient international monetary system must solve three technical problems: liquidity, adjustment and confidence (Cohen

1977; Eichengreen 1994b). For a variety of reasons, every international monetary regime rests on a particular political order (Gilpin 1987). The nineteenth century monetary system and the classical gold standard from 1870 to 1914, reflected British interests and hegemony. As Ruggie has shown, the gold standard reflected a world in which 'social purposes' were limited (Ruggie 1982, p. 382). The gold standard solved the three technical requirements, but in a way that imposed costs on certain countries and certain classes within countries. The decline of British hegemony, the rise of the welfare state and the emergence of organised labour and capital removed the prerequisites of the nineteenth century international monetary system. The 'interregnum between British and American leadership' was marked by a nationalisation of the world monetary system, floating exchange rates, competitive devaluations and, in Europe, the rise of fascism. That experience had profound effect on European attitudes to exchange rate fluctuations.

The Bretton Woods system, established in 1944, met these European fears of exchange rate instability and also reflected the new 'social purposes' of growth, full employment and a significant element of national control of macroeconomic conditions. It was founded on American economic and political hegemony. To a significant extent, Bretton Woods provided Europeans with the exchange rate stability they sought and prevented the sort of exchange rate volatility to which they attributed economic, monetary and political collapse. Yet even within the Bretton Woods framework, tensions arose between price stability and exchange rate stability, which remain central issues in European monetary integration. Given the N-1 problem, the Bretton Woods system implied that states which pegged to the Dollar had to accept the US inflation rate. From the first DM crisis of 1956/57, the monetary authorities faced the choice between achieving their domestic inflation targets and losing monetary autonomy by remaining committed to fixed exchange rates. As outlined in Chapter 3, inherent conflicts within the Bretton Woods system and declining American economic and political leadership led to the demise of that international monetary regime in the early 1970s.

The development of European monetary union can be seen as a response to this unsettled international environment and the simultaneous deepening of economic and political integration within Europe. The ambitious plan for macroeconomic policy coordination, set out in Articles 103 through 108 of the Treaty of Rome, was not accompanied by concrete steps (apart from the establishment of the Monetary Committee). This can partly be explained by the fact that Bretton Woods constituted the cornerstone of monetary arrangements; and it can be argued that when Bretton Woods faltered Europe acted on its own account.[1] Indeed, the decisions of the Hague Summit of EEC Heads of State in 1969, agreeing on the principle of monetary unification, was, in part, motivated by the desire for a coordinated European revaluation against the Dollar. In the event, the European response to the collapse of Bretton Woods was far from coordinated. While an unsettled global environment pushed Europe towards a regional monetary regime, unsettled national economic and social conditions prevented a concerted approach (see Chapters 2 and 5). The initial existence of Bretton Woods, followed by the failure of macroeconomic coordination, established a tradition of viewing treaty articles on macroeconomic economic policy coordination as almost entirely aspirational, and divorced from the real business of European integration. This tradition sustained scepticism on monetary union and blinded some observers to the very significant, if low key, advance of policy coordination between 1993 and the selection of EMU members in 1998.

Indeed, from the start, the deepening of economic integration heightened European interest in continental exchange rate stability. European economies were relatively open, within a highly regionalised world trade system. The new European institutions – particularly the Common Agricultural Policy and the internal market – were considered by most Europeans to depend for their survival on exchange rate stability (Giavazzi and Giovannini 1989). To these can be added the immense internationalisation of business and economic life that has occurred in the past decade and a half. Consequently, allowing for the particular global monetary arrangements from the foundation of the Community until the early 1970s, it is clear that the quest for exchange rate stability is an integral part of the overall project of European integration.

Economic union as a motivation for monetary union

The link between the internal market and monetary union is another topic on which political, business and popular perceptions differ from those of academic economists in the Anglo-Saxon world, and which casts doubt on the view that the motivation for EMU is essentially political. Technical studies of the effect of exchange rate risk on trade, production and investment, suggest that the effects are few and small (Willet 1986; Eichengreen 1993). This has supported a wide-spread scepticism among economists about the benefits of EMU. Kenen has recently argued that 'most of these studies, however, looked at the wrong sort of risk' (Kenen 1996). They asked whether short-term exchange rate volatility depresses trade or capital formation. There are, of course, ways to hedge against that sort of volatility. Recent studies of the effects of longer-term changes in exchange rates, have found that they have trade depressing effects. In addition, there are important arguments that weigh with policy-makers, business people, citizens and economic historians, but which are given little credence by theoretical economists, perhaps because they cannot be subjected to conventional methods of technical falsification. Among these is the view that the United States could not have developed as it has, or remain the world's leading economy, if its states or regions retained separate currencies (Kenen 1996, p. 183).

Indeed, this general argument is reinforced when we consider the political complexity of economic integration among diverse European democracies. It is widely agreed that completing the single market in commodities and factors of production, will deliver significant efficiency gains. Even if the majority of those gains are technically obtainable despite the maintenance of separate national currencies, 'a single currency may be required to suppress the political resistance that economic integration would otherwise provoke' (Eichengreen 1994b, p. 108).

The more integrated are national markets, the larger are the import surges that accompany exchange-rate-induced shifts in relative prices, and the greater is the pain experienced by affected firms and workers. The complaints over competitive depreciation and exchange dumping that followed the departure of sterling and the lira from the EMS in 1992 can be seen to illustrate this point. 'Monetary union that prevents "capricious" exchange rate swings, thereby ruling out the associated costs, may be necessary to prevent affected sectors from lobbying against economic integration and to ensure the political viability of the Single Market process' (Eichengreen 1994b, pp. 108–9; see also Helleiner 1994). In addition, the intricate set of transfers and side payments that makes the single market acceptable to all the countries concerned is more difficult to administer when exchange rates vary.

The sequence of events since 1987 strongly supports this link between economic and monetary union. Political and business support for EMU was galvanised by two arguments. First, the liberalisation of capital movements, as part of the internal market project, was widely believed to alter the conditions for the conduct of domestic monetary policy, in such a way that it requires either the abandonment of fixed exchange rates or greater coordination of monetary policy (Padoa-Schioppa 1987; Delors *et al.* 1989). Second, the more the internal market programme was implemented, the more the key actors have come to believe that many of its possible benefits will be lost if separate currencies continue to exist (CEC 1990). Indeed, despite the agonised nature of much economic commentary on EMU, observation confirms that increased levels of trade and capital market integration increase support for monetary union, both over time and across countries (Frieden 1996). While the SEM can be seen to have forced the issue of EMU, it might also be considered to have removed some of the protective measures used to avoid the full effects of a fixed rate regime (Pelkmans 1994).

Motivation for monetary union differs across member states and social groups

In summarising the economic motivation for EMU, we can invoke a principle stated at several places in our argument. The motivation, rewards and costs of European integration are different for different member states and peoples, depending on their history and culture. This applies to EMU also. In their overview of the political economy of EMU, Eichengreen and Frieden say that neither economic theory nor economic evidence provides a clear case for or against monetary unification. 'The absence of a clear economic justification for EMU leads us to conclude that events in Europe are being driven mainly by political factors' (Eichengreen and Frieden 1994, p. 5). While there may be no compelling case for or against a single currency *for the whole of the EU*, it is striking that almost every member state sees a strong individual motivation, given its particular economic history and political culture.

In discussing the variety of motivations for EMU, most member states can be allocated to one of four groups: Germany, the other core northern European states, France and the periphery. Germany's long-term interest in limiting exchange rate movements in Europe emerged from the malfunctioning and eventual collapse of Bretton Wood. The northern European states, which have successfully shadowed the DM, have an undoubted interest in EMU, since if offers the prospect of a similar inflation performance at less cost and with somewhat greater policy influence. France shares much of this motivation for monetary union, having made considerable sacrifices to stay within the EMS and achieve the convergence criteria. In addition, France has a long-term economic and political interest in tying Germany into an integrated Europe, without ceding policy dominance to Germany. A particularly important, and revealing, aspect of the motivation for monetary union is the increased commitment of the smaller and peripheral member states. It is worth considering this in a little detail, since it brings to light some economic, political, financial and analytical developments that are of general relevance.

The experience of Europe's peripheral member states and changes in economic analysis have given rise to a new perspective on the regional effects of integration. To understand the analytical basis of this shift in perspective we make use of the distinction between three different stages of integration – customs union, a common market and economic and monetary union – outlined in Table 7.1. Developments in microeconomics, macroeconomics and regional theory, have served to undermine the perspective that dominated discussion through most of the post-war period: that it is the *monetary* stage of integration that presents weaker regions with the greatest problems. As a result, in earlier decades most discussion by economists of the regional implications of integration focused on the monetary stage and, within that, on the loss of exchange rate autonomy (Williamson 1975). While it is commonly noted that this traditional view was based on a body of macroeconomic theory that many now reject, it is important to see that it was also based on a particular perspective on *free trade* (the customs union stage) and *capital mobility* (the common market stage). It was based on analytical approaches that suggested that these stages of integration would be relatively *benign*.

Table 7.1 Views on the regional effects of integration

Integration stage	Traditional view	New view
Free trade (Custom Union)	All regions gain Adjustment costs only	Uneven costs and benefits
Capital and labour mobility (Common Market)	All regions gain Regional differences eroded	Costs as well as benefits
Economic and monetary union	Possible deflationary effects	Limited effects on output and employment

Source: O'Donnell (1994).

In devising their approach to the simultaneous completion of the internal market and the revival of the monetary union project in the late 1980s, Europe's peripheral and less developed member states – Ireland, Spain, Portugal and Greece – had not only to update the macroeconomics of the monetary issue, but also to take note of new approaches to trade and the mobility of labour and capital. When all three were considered, and combined with their experience in the common market and the EMS, a genuine shift in perspective on the regional effects of integration emerged – although this is more evident in the policy choices of the peripheral member states than in the Anglo-Saxon literature on monetary union. This argument is presented schematically in Table 7.1, which summarises the traditional view and the new view on the regional effects of the three stages of integration.

The traditional view – combining Keynesian macroeconomics with the orthodox theory of international trade and factor mobility – led economists and policy-makers to focus their analysis of the regional effects of integration on the monetary stage. In particular, it was believed that, in weaker states and regions, which previously used exchange rate devaluation to support output and employment, adherence to a single monetary standard would be deflationary (Williamson 1975).

The experience of the peripheral member states, when combined with recent developments in microeconomic, macroeconomics and regional theory, suggests an alternative perspective on the pattern and timing of the overall costs and benefits of integration for weaker regions. This involves, first and foremost, a different view of the regional implications of free trade and capital and labour mobility. It suggests that even free trade can generate large and unevenly distributed costs and benefits in both the short and long run. Furthermore, it indicates that international movements of labour and capital may widen rather than narrow differences between regional economies. Although there remain conflicting views on the causes and effects of exchange rate changes, virtually all schools of economic theory now have less faith in the power of devaluation to sustain output and employment and in the ability of governments in smaller, peripheral, economies to use the exchange rate as an active policy instrument (Eichengreen 1993, 1994b; Tavlas 1993; Cohen 1997; De Grauwe 1997). At the very least, this combination of analytical and practical developments encouraged Europe's peripheral member states to take the emphasis off monetary union as the element of integration that will be most difficult (NESC 1989). Certainly in the Irish case, it prompted a renewed focus on the *real economy* and *political* factors that shape the regional pattern of economic activity in an integrated economic area like the EU, and it yielded a consensus – across both the political spectrum and the social partners – on joining EMU (O'Donnell 1993).

The strong support for EMU in the peripheral member states, and the remarkable measures taken to achieve the Maastricht criteria, are important features of European EMU. They underline and illustrate the contingent, path-dependent, institution-based and pragmatic features of European integration emphasised throughout our argument.

Motivation for monetary union strengthened over time

Not only was there strong, if diverse, motivation for exchange rate stability throughout the process of European integration, but this motivation strengthened over time. In assessing the economic and political motivation for EMU, care must be taken to focus on the actual choices that actors have, or perceive themselves to have, rather than the abstract menu of choice suggested by economic theory. In this regard, Europe's long quest for exchange rate stability, and particularly its experience with EMS, is relevant. It reduces the significance of the wider ruminations – concerning optimum currency areas, asymmetric shocks, etc. – and increases the relevance of comparison between fixed-rate systems (such as the hard ERM) and full monetary union. In making *that* comparison, the motivation for EMU has increased over time. One reason, noted by Kenen, is that the crisis of the EMS demonstrated that even the most virtuous leader can make big mistakes, which impose enormous costs on its partners when the leader is not sufficiently solicitous of its partners' interests (Kenen 1996). Since economic and political actors in Europe do not countenance widespread, large, intra-European exchange rate movements, this experience of an asymmetric fixed-rate system strengthened the attractions of monetary union.

Indeed, the European experience is but one illustration of the fact that fixed-rate systems are increasingly subject to speculative pressure. This largely reflects the profound changes in the structure, technology and regulation of financial markets.

> Above all, changes in technology will work to increase international capital mobility, limiting the capacity of governments to contain market pressures at an acceptable political cost. Together these changes will undermine the viability of the monetary rules under which governments commit to preventing exchange rates from breeching certain limits under all but exceptional circumstances, forcing policy-makers to choose between floating and monetary unification.
>
> (Eichengreen 1994b, p. 6; see also Cohen 1994)

While the depth of this change is widely acknowledged in political economy (Gilpin 1987; Andrews and Willet 1997), business and trade unions, it seems less widely appreciated among economists, many of whom invoke analytical approaches to the choice of exchange rate regimes that derive from the 1960s.

Structure and process

The long process of monetary union has been so beset with difficulties, reversals and uncertainties, that it is tempting to consider monetary union as essentially different from the other main integration projects. At the limit, it might be argued that EMU is not amenable to the normal, pragmatic, institutionalised, bargained approach which, we argued in Chapters 1 and 5, characterises the EU. If this were so, then the Union might have fatally overstretched itself, and may have to confront the need for a qualitatively different type of political, social and symbolic union. This is reflected in the feeling that EMU is a high risk endeavour, especially as it came to be seen as a precondition for progress on other major issues, such as enlargement to the east. In this section we outline a number of distinctive features of EMU. The approach taken to EMU has, despite severe difficulties, produced considerable stability in exchange rates and, most significantly, allowed transition to monetary union. Indeed, the distinctive features of EMU must be viewed in the context of the policy diversity that characterises the Union. This discussion will inform our consideration of the other main issues outlined in the introduction to this chapter.

Distinctive features of EMU

Monetary union differs from most other EU policies because it must be unitary, indivisible and centralised. There is wide agreement that monetary policy must be set centrally. This differs from all other EU policies, with the exception of the CAP. Indeed, over time, the Union has shown reluctance to build new centralised policies like the CAP and, in many respects, the system has become a model of decentralised governance (see Chapter 5). At the very moment when the Union was exploring the implications of 'subsidiarity', it formalised the path to a uniquely centralised policy of great importance. One consequence of the indivisibility of monetary policy was that the move to a single currency was undoubtedly risky, especially in German perceptions, and could only be undertaken in a gradual fashion. But there was a definite tension between the principles of *indivisibility* and *gradualism*, a tension that does not beset other union policies, where gradualism, and the associated multilevel problem-solving, have been the norm. Indeed, this tension was heightened by another feature of the TEU, the setting of an automatic date for adoption of a single currency. Later in this section, it is argued that much of the difficulty of the transition to EMU reflects the tension between indivisibility, gradualism and 'automaticity'. These are reflections of the underlying ties and tensions explored throughout our study.

A second distinctive feature is that monetary union involves co-optation, rather than membership in the traditional sense. The existing variable geometry grants to member states the right to progress more slowly to a common Union policy or standard; in contrast, member states must be invited, or co-opted, to join monetary union. Another principle of European monetary union is *parallelism*: that monetary union must move in parallel with economic union. But economic union can be varied, nuanced and phased to a much greater degree than monetary union. At times, this seemed to make monetary union less amenable to the complex negotiation process that characterises and drives the integration process. Monetary union also involves a different relation between the economic and the political. While this is the core theme of this whole chapter (see especially the final section), we have a specific point in mind here: the wide agreement that monetary management should be independent of politics in certain key respects. Notwithstanding different interpretations of this principle, it undoubtedly marks monetary union off from the vast bulk of EU policies.

Monetary union is also distinctive in the degree to which issue-linkage was possible. In particular, Germany would seem to have had what economists call 'lexicographic' preferences. Although Germany was willing at critical moments to link monetary union to political union (and other issues such as enlargement to the east), no amount of political union would compensate for a monetary union that did not yield price stability similar to that provided by the DM. In this sense, it was harder to handle EMU within encompassing bargains. Yet another difference is in the mix of high politics and popular will. Most EU policies involve a degree of high politics, a lot of technocratic politics and a 'permissive consensus' in European societies. In contrast, monetary union involves a very large degree of high politics, a limited amount of technocratic interest mediation and an unpredictable popular will, which occasionally threatens the whole project (Dyson 1994; Tsoukalis 1996, 1997). Monetary union is also subject to the sentiment and interests of market operators in a different way, and to a greater extent, than other EU policies. While firms are extremely active in shaping, interpreting, and sometimes circumventing, internal market provisions or the Common Commercial Policy, this occurs at a microeconomic or sectoral level and is, therefore, fragmentary. By contrast, efforts to limit exchange rate variation, or to build a single currency, can be undone by the commentary and speculative activity of financial market operators, some of whom may have an interest in preventing a successful transition to EMU.

Monetary union also raises issues of identity to a greater extent than any other Pillar 1 policy. Indeed, since progress on EMU is greater than that on Pillars 2 and 3, monetary union is undoubtedly the first major policy on which European integration confronts issues of identity. In several large member states, notably Germany and the UK, national currency has been an important element of national identity in the post-war period. Turning from the national to the European level, the creation of the euro constitutes a huge increase in the symbolic nature of the union. Related to this is the sense that EMU greatly deepens the degree of political union, or at least requires such a deepening (an idea that is discussed further below). Together, these features suggested that monetary union had the potential to divide the Union like no other previous policy.

Finally, EMU could differ from most other economic policies in having a negative dynamic, rather than a positive dynamic deriving from spill-over. The closer the EU got to EMU via the 'hard EMS', the less immediate interest Germany had in taking the final step to a single currency. Recall the famous comment of former Bundesbank Council member Nolling, 'why does Germany want EMU when she has the EMS?'. This short-term negative dynamic might be considered to have been removed by the move to the wider $\pm$ 15 per cent band in 1993. But the reluctance of other member states to use the exchange rate freedom, formally provided by the wider band, meant that an element of negative dynamic was still possible, at least in the short term. While use of the greater exchange rate freedom might have increased Germany's immediate interest in the euro (as a way of avoiding appreciation of the DM), it would simultaneously have undermined German faith in these countries as members of a currency union.[2]

Overall, it is clear that the policy and institutional arrangements for EMU are distinctive. Several inferences might be drawn from this long list of differences. One is that EMU in not amenable to the Monnet method. Unbalanced development is normally the essence of European integration; recall our description of Europe as always *becoming*, never being. But in the case of EMU, the limited resolution of many important policy issues, and the unbalanced nature of the emerging monetary union, are often considered to threaten, rather than strengthen, the integration process. A related interpretation is that of Giovannini, who suggests that EMU is uniquely vulnerable to a range of 'extraneous factors' (Giovannini 1992). Dyson goes so far as to say that EMU has a 'hollow core', that the TEU locks the project in a design which is too narrow and fatally flawed – an argument that we examine in some detail in the final section of this chapter (Dyson 1994).

Fitting EMU within the integration process

It is important not to exaggerate the distinctiveness of EMU and to place it within the diversity of policy and institutional approaches that characterises European integration. As in other areas of integration, Europe's development of a complex cooperative system, such as the EMS, was a response to global developments. As noted in the next section, there has been quite remarkable incremental progress in monetary integration in Europe, reflecting a persistent political or economic motivation. One of the most important features of the EMS is that it functioned in different ways at different times during the period from 1979 to the present (Gros and Thygesen 1992). Consequently, there are few general propositions that are true of EMS *per se*. Several times this incremental progress involved issue linkage between monetary integration and other policies, most notably at the foundation of the EMS and the signing of the Maastricht Treaty. Within exchange rate and monetary integration there have been complex compromises, including the management of realignments, the Basle–Nyberg Agreement, the Maastricht criteria, other elements of the TEU, and the location of the European Central Bank (ECB) (Sandholtz 1993, 1996).

Ideas played an important role in prompting and facilitating integration. The spread of a sound money doctrine in the 1980s increased the attraction of a cooperative mechanism that seemed to promise low inflation.[3] Furthermore, ideas seem to have played an important role in determining how the system functioned at any given time. Among the relevant ideas were those concerning the teleology of the system – full monetary union. As in other areas, institution building has been a significant feature of the process. In recent years scholars have drawn attention to the network of central bankers that emerged through the practice of the EMS. In the EMS, the member states and central bankers 'learned to cooperate', a development that was highlighted by Britain's relative unfamiliarity with the rules of the game during its brief spell in the system (Cameron, D. 1995; McNamara 1997). The emergence of a shared European understanding of economic issues and a genuinely European-level arena, is highlighted in those works

(Cameron, D. 1995; McNamara 1997). Cameron emphasises the significance of transnational, as opposed to international, actors: in particular, the network of central bankers who shaped key aspects of the TEU.

As in other areas, an initial level of cooperation created pressure for deeper integration. There is little doubt that the EMS, combined with the completion of the internal market, created a dynamic towards EMU. Indeed, in its later days, the EMS depended on the expectation of EMU, and unravelled when that expectation was damaged by the Danish and French referendums on the Maastricht Treaty. Finally, consistent with our overall thesis on European integration, monetary cooperation, like other aspects of integration, changed the macroeconomic identity of some member states. All these similarities between monetary and other areas of integration suggest that the Monnet method, or some variant of it, can be effective in the monetary sphere.

Over and above these differences and similarities between EMU and the other projects of integration, our perspective on European integration suggests that there is no fixed essence from which EMU differs, or to which it conforms. As noted throughout our study, policy diversity is a core characteristic of EU. The Union is always becoming, and its method of becoming is both constitutional and experimental. Thus, given its enormous prominence in recent years, EMU is constitutive of European integration as it moves to the twenty-first century. It is shaping the Union and its institutional balance, accentuating some characteristics, moderating others. Indeed, the EMU project itself would seem to have gone through a rapid, and important, evolution in recent years. The revival of the project by President Delors, and the negotiation and ratification of the Maastricht Treaty, involved the EU in its policy-forming – indeed, its constitution-building – mode. Having tied themselves together in that treaty, the member states had little option but to undertake the enormous task of putting flesh on the Maastricht bones. This has involved the Commission, the European Council and the ECOFIN Council working in the problem-solving mode, which characterises the Union. To appreciate this 'normalisation' of the EMU project – while allowing for its transformative potential – we have to form a view on the balance between its political and economic elements.

The political difficulty of EMU in European circumstances

The central purpose of this section is to identify the structure and process of policy-making in the area of EMU. While the procedures and treaty basis of EMU certainly have distinctive features, we see these as yet another part of the complex and diverse set of policy models developed within the EU. It is also a reflection of the innovative nature of European EMU, which is redefining the relation between territory, identity and function.

In advancing this perspective we dispute the standard view that the economic motivation for EMU is weak and the project must be understood as essentially political. In the first part of this chapter, we have established that there is a strong, long-standing, widely-held, diverse and increasing *economic* motivation for EMU.

This must surely explain much of the *progress* achieved in recent years. The material we need to establish the second half of our argument – that the *difficulties* largely reflect the *political* complexity of creating monetary union in European circumstances – has largely been set out in this section. We have identified ways in which EMU differed from other areas of economic integration. Monetary union involves a different relation between the economic and the political and raises issues of identity to a much greater extent. We noted the tension between the central political principles adopted in the European case: indivisibility, gradualism, parallelism and automaticity. These features of EMU are reflected in the demanding entry criteria and operating rules, a new kind of variable geometry and the limits of issue linkage. The enormous symbolic significance of the euro, and all the attendant difficulties, clearly reflects the political dimension of creating monetary union in a democratic way, in a context of great political, cultural and economic diversity. Consequently, in stepping to monetary union Europe is not only extending the integration project, but is also breaking with international monetary and political history in significant ways. First, it is moving from a traditional asymmetric, or hegemonic, monetary system, such as the EMS, to a non-hegemonic arrangement (Williamson 1983). In this respect, in creating the euro, monetary integration rejoins the mainstream of European integration, which is not characterised by a hegemon. Second, it is creating a *democratic* monetary union incorporating many states – a rare event indeed. Third, it is addressing the fundamental requirements of an international monetary system (liquidity, adjustment and credibility) with a new mixture of policy coordination and harmonisation. Fourth, it is creating monetary union where there is only a part-formed political economy at EU level (see below). In our view, it is these, largely political, factors that explain many of the difficulties experienced on the road to monetary union.[4] Having demonstrated this, we do not want to distinguish too strongly between the economic and the political, since our overall approach is to emphasise their complex interaction.

Towards a European economic–political authority?

In this section we begin the process of characterising the emerging economic and monetary union. First, we outline the main characteristics of the system, identify the combination of strong and weak monetary, economic and political authority. We then ask whether EMU is a replication, at European level, of the German model of monetary and economic management. The European model has been severely criticised, by analysts drawing on various models of national political economy, and these require consideration. Finally, we consider the most profound aspect of EMU, the relation between monetary and political union – in particular, the idea that currency is dependent, in some essential way, on statehood.

The emerging monetary, economic and political authority

In the European Central Bank, the EMU has a definite monetary authority, which seems likely to begin with the technical reputation and political legitimacy that its founders intended. As a central bank, it is somewhat unusual in having a federal structure, but too much should not be made of this element of decentralisation. The more difficult questions arise concerning the effectiveness, authority and legitimacy of the emerging economic authority, centred on the ECOFIN Council and the European Council. While the Union is characterised by governance rather than government, networks rather than administration, regulation rather a classical nation state, multilevel policy rather than centralised political authority, it is not clear that this gives it the pervasive political authority to manage the European economy. Having raised that doubt, it must be said that the years since 1993 have seen quite a remarkable evolution of the ECOFIN Council's effectiveness in 'multilateral surveillance'. Much of this effectiveness depends on socialisation of finance ministers, peer pressure and the emergence of new norms. While the Union has limited power to compel and sanction, it is clear that monetary union has created strong pressure for ongoing reform within member states – pressure that seems likely to intensify. The need to manage the external value of the euro poses a further challenge to the emerging system.

Without a system of fiscal federalism, or other identified instruments to address asymmetric shocks, the Union will approach particular difficulties in its traditional, *ad hoc*, manner. However, efforts at crisis-management are also likely to induce evolution of the system as a whole. Given the limited economic–political authority of the Union, and the internationalisation of finance, the response of business (both financial and non-financial) to EMU is an important feature of the evolving system.

While the Union has emerged as a significant economic–political authority, it is clear that this differs from the pervasive political authority and agency traditionally associated with sovereign nation states. However, the emerging EU system should be viewed in the context in which its member states find themselves. As noted in Chapter 6, this is one in which the ability and willingness to use macroeconomic policy has been severely limited. It is a context in which budgetary decisions are frequently dominated by microeconomic rather than macroeconomic concerns. It is a context in which the commitment to capital mobility, combined with a gobalisation of finance, has greatly constrained macroeconomic sovereignty. In this context, it cannot be assumed that the economic–political authority of the EU will be significantly less than that of most member states. It remains to be seen whether it is sufficient to balance, legitimise and complement the monetary authority in managing the internal and external dimensions of the new European economy.

Is EMU the German model writ large?

Should European monetary union be seen as the German model writ large (Snyder 1994)? In a general sense, there is no doubt that the European monetary union, as designed in the TEU, replicates at European level important features of the German system. In his account of the TEU negotiations, Dyson says that German officials had 'every incentive to ensure that the final EMU bargain reflected German economic priorities and institutions writ large; and the capability, resting on the structural power of its economy and currency and its role as the anchor of the ERM, to get its way in negotiations' (Dyson 1994, p. 149). This is reflected in the priority given to price stability and the adoption of an independent central bank as a key instrument for achieving this.

There are several respects in which we need to qualify the proposition that the new Europe is the German model writ large.[5] First, while Dyson says that 'in effect, the Statute of the European System of Central Banks and the European Central Bank is the Bundesbank writ large', he also qualifies this somewhat – noting that it is both stronger and weaker than the German system (see below). Second, as noted by Garret and others, 'the success of the German model is contingent on much more than the institutional structure of the central bank' (Scharpf 1991; Garrett 1994, p. 48). Labour market institutions, norms and arrangements were critical in securing the effectiveness and legitimacy of independent monetary policy (Soskice 1990; Dyson 1994). The TEU does little to create, at European level, a political economy of wages, inflation, and public finance equivalent to that which characterises the German model (Barrell 1990; Marsden 1992; IAB 1995; Peters 1995). Third, the new Europe is unlikely to constitute the German model writ large in a context in which the German model is itself under severe strain and changing significantly. Finally, note should be made of German attitudes to the TEU. The Bundesbank and, to an extent, the German government, argued that the TEU did not create the political and institutional requirements to guarantee price stability within EMU, and pressed for the creation of a 'stability community' via the new 'Stability and Growth Pact'.

Critiques of the TEU based on alternative models

Commentators of different persuasions have subjected the plan for EMU embodied in the Treaty on European Union to critical scrutiny and argued that it cannot provide an adequate economic and monetary policy framework. The possibility of a gradual transition to EMU by means of a progressive convergence of macroeconomic performance, and tightening of the ERM, was questioned. Related to this, it was argued that the minimal institutional developments envisaged in Stage II would not produce a sufficient pooling of instruments and responsibilities to advance beyond the achievements of Stage I. Many economists argued that the convergence criteria and the treaty rules governing national fiscal policy are arbitrary, unnecessary, or likely to lend a deflationary bias to the European economy (Buiter *et al.* 1993; Portes 1994; De Grauwe 1997). Some believe that central bank independence is based on flawed modern theories of credibility and 'time inconsistency' (Pivetti 1996). In contrast, others consider that the design will not be sufficiently anti-inflationary (Garrett 1994). Dyson argues that the TEU has made monetary union victim to a 'narrow conceptualisation of money as essentially an economic and technical phenomenon' (Dyson 1994, p. xi).

The experience of 1992–93 re-awakened fears that the treaty has designed an unbalanced system, in which there are to be more coherent institutions and policy on the *monetary* than on the *economic* side. Will the Union's economic policies be sufficient to pursue goals other than price stability – especially employment, growth, competitiveness and cohesion? Concern has also been expressed about the fiscal requirements for a successful EMU: can the European Union hope to create an economic and monetary union without the system of fiscal federalism that is found in almost all successful monetary unions? Finally, several of these questions are closely related to issues of political union. Some still doubt that the decision-making procedures set out in the TEU will have the authority, legitimacy or effectiveness to create and, more importantly, to *govern* an economic and monetary union.

While some of these critics raise important questions, we must be careful in basing too much on many of these confident commentaries. Many of them are based on textbook or theoretical formulae of limited relevance to actual policy in successful economies. The failure of the TEU to meet the doctrinal precepts of various theoretical schools may not be very relevant or telling. Other critiques – such as those based on the doctrines of neo-corporatism, liberal Keynesianism, or fiscal federalism – certainly involve more realistic conceptualisation of policy processes and outcomes in various countries in the post-war period. But numerous factors may limit the force of their critiques. First, it is not easy to replicate at European level the policy process, principles and mechanisms that operate in any given national model. Precisely because the political consensus – which underlay the German system in the post-war years – does not exist at Union level, it may be necessary to have a monetary union that is more firmly constrained by constitutional provisions and which is less reliant on political processes. Second, the EU seldom reaches a consensus to adopt a national model, usually reaching a complex compromise of various approaches. The EU is achieving integration in a complex political context by inventing quite new forms of policy-making and governance. Third, the very national models – neo-corporatist, liberal Keynesian (and maybe even fiscal federal) – are themselves disappearing, or at least experiencing severe strain. Consequently, it is not clear that the analytical principles derived from a study of successful economies in the post-war period retain their validity and offer a blueprint for European policy. Fourth, the TEU should not be seen as the end point or the definitive blueprint for EMU, as demonstrated by developments since 1993. The definition of the political requirements, or political price, of EMU is an ongoing process. Despite the force of many of the criticisms of the TEU, it has facilitated remarkable progress on EMU since the crisis surrounding its ratification in 1992–93. It is now necessary to acknowledge its remarkable effect in pushing member states to accelerate their policy reforms in order to meet the convergence criteria. This suggests that there was always a certain core of truth in the 'monetarist' perspective on EMU.

EMU is a novel, experimental, process. It remains to be seen how the process of political evolution will shape the political economy of the new Europe and, indeed, there is little agreement on how it should. Will it add rigid and perverse rules, which is how many see the Stability and Growth Pact, in response to the vagaries of German domestic politics? Will it bring into the picture the labour market institutions so clearly neglected in the TEU, and thereby free EMU from the 'narrow conceptualisation' which Dyson detects. Will it allow the system to incorporate what Helmut Schlesinger calls the 'pragmatic monetarism' of the Bundesbank – a pragmatism that recognises the technical limits, but symbolic importance, of money supply targets, the importance of government and the social partners and the dependence of strong independent monetary policy on a persistent culture of economic stability (Dyson 1994, p. 254)? Most importantly, how can such a pragmatic monetary union be sustained in a European context characterised by fragmented, diverse and rapidly changing labour market institutions and a complex, negotiated, decision-making system at EU level? While there are limited signs of a Europe-wide system of industrial relations or wage bargaining, there has been convergent developments in attitudes to inflation and public finance, among both trade unions and political parties, and in the role of trade unions in wage bargaining and economic policy. One implication of our analysis is that the very process of integration limits the possibility of using any national model as a blueprint for the European Union and simultaneously alters the nature of the national models. Indeed, because of integration and other major changes (in technology, organisation and international competition), there may no longer be any settled national models that might be writ large, even if that were possible. In that unsettled national and global context, the experimental European system of governance may well seem more complete, more effective and more interesting, than it has in the past.

The European Central Bank will operate not only in the constitutional context of the TEU, but also in a political culture, much of which is only taking shape since the treaty. The independence of central banks, such as the Federal Reserve and the Bundesbank, derives from the fact that they are political actors within a political and constitutional system, which gives them some power against other actors, especially other parts of government. Consequently, independence is a matter of degree. It is neither unlimited nor irrevocable (Harden 1990). The success of its management depends on the behaviour of other actors, particularly government and wage bargainers (Dyson 1994). 'Ultimately if a central bank is to remain an autonomous political actor its role must be accepted as legitimate' (Harden 1990). This suggests that the legitimacy of the ECB cannot be considered simply in relation to monetary union; it depends on the broader constitutional framework of the Community. 'In particular, it depends on the allocation of power over economic policy, both as between different Community institutions and as between those institutions and member states' (Harden 1990).

Currency, statehood and nationality

Consideration of EMU would not be complete without taking up the themes outlined in Chapter 1, particularly the relation of currency to statehood and nationality. Does monetary union require a deeper level of political and social integration than has been achieved in the EU, and does the absence of this confirm the view that EMU has a 'hollow core'? As Dyson and others have emphasised, the attempt to reduce EMU to a set of technical issues, has served to obscure the political dimension of the project. Once one is persuaded of this point, it is tempting to argue that there is an essential relationship between the issuing and validating of money, on the one hand, and statehood, on the other. Indeed, there would seem, on the face of it, to be good reasons to connect currency and statehood and to argue that the issue of currency requires a state, which in turn requires a society with a national identity. However, the validity of raising the issues of statehood and identity should not be confused with proof of any particular proposition about their link to currency. In seeking to understand the integration process – or, indeed, make EMU work – it seems important to try to establish the extent and nature of the relationship between currency, state and identity. To establish whether currency is dependent on statehood and identity, we need to consider both the analytical and historical basis for such a relationship.

European monetary and macroeconomic integration touches on central and long-standing issues in economic theory. These include the effect of money on economic activity, the causes of inflation, the effect of exchange rate changes on economic activity and, more recently, the causes of exchange rate changes. These have long been the subject of lively debate in economic analysis. In addition, much of the consensus that did exist has dissolved in recent years, in the face of large-scale exchange rate movements, which proved hard to explain and which had surprising effects. As Gilpin says, the post-war analyical consensus has been displaced by 'a cacophony of economic sects':

> Without the continued dominance of the Keynesian model or any orthodoxy to take its place, rival theories contend on such subjects as the determinants of exchange rates, the fundamental issues of reconciling full employment and price stability, and other basic questions of economic theory.
>
> (Gilpin 1987, p. 161; Isard 1995)

The traditional axis of debate about monetary unions in international monetary economics is the theory of 'optimum currency areas'. Unfortunately, that theory does not offer much of a secure guide to policy. It had been stretched to incorporate more and more criteria and, as a consequence, provided an ever more complex body of contested theories (Goodhart 1989). Its account of the likely costs of monetary union has been challenged by major developments in macroeconomics – particularly the expectations-based critique of the Phillips curve and theories of time-inconsistency (Tavlas 1993, 1994; De Grauwe 1997). Its assumptions about state definition of currency 'areas' has been undermined by the integration of financial markets and the emergence of 'currency internationalisation' and 'currency substitution' (Cohen 1997). Nevertheless, the optimum currency approach has been resuscitated and extended in recent years – largely because of the movement towards European monetary union (Isard 1995). In its revised form, it can help explain why so many European countries have chosen EMU and, in the right hands, it can throw some light on the relation of currency to statehood and identity.

While the dominant traditional approach within the theory of an optimum currency area was to view a choice of exchange rate regime as national optimisation subject to given structural characteristics of the national economy, several authors have, in recent years, treated it in a somewhat more dynamic way. Eichengreen shows that, although the factors cited in optimum currency area theory – factor mobility, size, openness, specialisation, wage flexibility, etc. – emerge from a technical economic analysis (of adjustment to a demand shock), they are not, in fact, purely technical phenomena. Several of them – particularly factor flexibility, other asymmetric shocks, susceptibility to inflation and reliance on seigniorage – are endogenous rather than exogenous. They are themselves shaped by the monetary regime in place, the prevailing doctrines of economic management, the degree of consensus on these and the institutional arrangements of wage setting (Eichengreen 1994b). Consequently, the accepted goals of national strategy, the degree of underlying consensus on these and the willingness to reflect them in industrial relations practices and public finance, should not be seen as mere icing on the cake of economic 'fundamentals', which are given, and technical in nature. This is relevant to Europe, where governments and economic actors have, in the 1980s and 1990s, made heroic efforts to alter the political economy of inflation and public finance. It suggests that our emphasis on the political and popular will to achieve monetary union, and on the transformative potential of participation in European integration, is not inconsistent with an economic analysis of EMU.

Goodhart's use of the optimum currency area theory draws our attention to important, yet ill-defined, relationships between monetary union, social unity, fiscal union and national sovereignty. In his view, the various analytical approaches can be reduced to two common factors determining whether the balance of payments adjustments of some geographical area would be more easily solved as a region within a common currency area, or as an independent country, with a separate, and potentially variable, exchange rate. These factors are size, and social unity with surrounding, contiguous regions (Goodhart 1989, pp. 420–21).

The smaller the size of the region/country, the easier it will adjust within a common currency area and the harder it will find it to run an effective independent monetary and exchange rate policy. Goodhart believes that this approach places too much emphasis on the effects of size, and too little on the role of social unity.[6] Historical experience suggests that if there are adjustment costs involved in maintaining single currency areas greater than some 'optimum' size, these costs are too slight to affect seriously the historical process determining their size. Historically, the more important factor is social unity. If this exists, then fiscal mechanisms will be in place to address regional disparities, at least as effectively as exchange rate changes. Moreover, in such conditions labour migration will be easier, and relative wage–price adjustments harder to bring about under any exchange rate regime. Consequently, 'the "optimal" currency area is a function not so much of geography but rather of social psychology' (Goodhart 1989, p. 422). Given the significant advantages to be expected from large currency areas, particularly the integration of markets, there is a case for advocating common currency areas among all those regional groups with sufficient social unity to make them work well.

Having identified the link between currency union and social unity, Goodhart introduces the issue of national sovereignty, with its monetary and fiscal dimensions: 'Many of the arguments here resemble the question of precedence of the chicken or the egg.' The establishment of a successful monetary union may well require support from a strong, centralised, or at least inter-regionally coordinated, fiscal (and regional) policy to ease regional adjustment. 'Yet it is very difficult to establish a centralised fiscal authority unless there is a monetary union, a single currency, throughout the area.' In order to establish conditions conducive to the successful working of the single currency area, the constituent regions need to exhibit social unity, but the existence of separate currencies is one of the factors tending to divide and separate groups of people. Consequently, 'the problems involved in moving, through a process of political agreement, from a system consisting of several independent currencies to a single currency area are extremely difficult and delicate' (Goodhart 1989, p. 423). However, in Goodharts's view, history suggests two general lessons: (i) that EMU needs fiscal union and (ii) that fiscal union needs a single currency. While he does not offer any practical way out of this chicken and egg problem, the close connection which he sees between monetary union, social unity and fiscal union leads him to say emphatically that 'fiscal and monetary harmonisation will march together, or not at all' (Goodhart 1989, p. 424). He notes that there are, no doubt, exceptions to both rules; and considers that the weaker claim, on historical experience, seems to be the former. The success of the gold standard in the period from 1870 to 1914 shows that it has been possible for countries to establish virtually a common currency area and a fixed exchange rate system, without the support of fiscal policy.[7]

The close connection between currency union, social unity and fiscal union clearly draws our attention to political union. A decision to have a fixed exchange rate between two currencies, or to move to monetary union, places definite constraints on national money creation, the settlement of international payments and requires agreement on means of overcoming adjustment strains.

> It seems unlikely then that a fixed exchange rate system can be maintained on any permanent basis until political harmony and social agreement allow the division of burdens within the area and the direction of policy in each part of the system to be decided by an accepted central *political* process.
>
> (Goodhart 1989, p. 428)

Once that stage has been reached, the next step – eliminating the separate currencies – 'should be simple' (Goodhart 1989, p. 428). Consequently, without extending far beyond the optimum currency area criteria, Goodhart has revealed the interdependence between currency union, social unity, fiscal union and political union. While he has identified certain lines of causation between them, his use of the metaphor of the chicken and the egg suggests a consciously eclectic view.

This approach is of both conceptual and practical relevance to the issue of European EMU, for at least four reasons. First, it allows us to discuss critically whether the issue of currency requires a state. Second, the interdependence between the four factors – currency union, social unity, fiscal union and political union – suggests that their actual relationships, in any given instance, are determined by a historical trajectory and are contingent rather than determinate. Third, this extension, or perhaps abandonment, of the optimum currency area approach supports a more realistic account of what states (or peoples) are doing when they 'choose' monetary union. While the optimum currency area approach suggests choice, in the sense of rational choice or choice off a menu, the reality is that participation in the integration process, including deliberation on treaty re-design, means that most member states do not see themselves with a 'choice' about monetary union, in the sense in which this term is ordinarily meant. The depth of interdependence and interpenetration between the member states of the EU, described in Chapter 5, suggests that a chain gang may be a more apt metaphor. Fourth, Goodhart's approach unpacks 'the political', prompting us to consider its various components.

In one sense, the European process has been characterised by an over-emphasis on currency union and an under-emphasis on political union. This is implicit in Dyson's critique of the 'technicisation' of EMU and in numerous commentaries that emphasise the slow progress towards economic policy coordination. At the same time, as Dyson and others make clear, there has been significant recognition of the political dimension and, at critical moments, the EMU project was driven by political commitment at the very highest level (see our earlier discussion of whether EMU is economic or political). Goodhart's addition of two other dimensions – social unity and fiscal union – reminds us that, in many respects, it is these aspects, rather than the 'political,' in some undifferentiated sense, which have been neglected in the European case. While this might be viewed as evasive or risky, it can also be seen as innovative, experimental and pragmatic. For, as we now show, there may be no definitive relationship between currency and statehood.

Is the relationship between money and the nation state a matter of functional and administrative necessity, or does the relationship owe more to historical contingency? There clearly is an important functional relationship between money and the nation state, whereby the modern state, as a legitimate political authority within geopolitical boundaries, acts as the rule-formulating and sanctioning monetary administrator. Trust in money's abstract properties is, by extension, trust in those agencies responsible for monetary administration. Trust in this sense partly depends on the political legitimacy of the state in question (Dodd 1994). A somewhat different reliance of money on the state arises from the state's economic and fiscal role. Despite the validity of these points, Dodd considers that they provide 'virtually no guidance as to whether a definitive link exists between money and the state' (Dodd 1994, p. 30).

Once again, this suggests a historical examination of the role of the state in the establishment of monetary systems. Such a historical account leads to the interesting proposition that the achievement of a monopoly of monetary administration was as important a resource in strengthening the nation state, given its fiscal requirements, as the political authority of the state was for the validation of money. The institutionalisation of money and credit systems centrally administered by state agencies arose from complex historical trends and pressures, comprising territorial centralisation of the nation state, the expansion of capitalist enterprise, the enlargement of a state's military strength, and the intensification of the fiscal administration. 'To this extent, the historical importance of the transition from absolutism to the nation-states system for the development of monetary systems can be readily established' (Dodd 1994, p. 35). However, it remains difficult to characterise this process in political or economic terms alone and, consequently, to assert that money/currency *requires* a state.[8] There was a significant geopolitical dimension in the historical emergence of money, given the state's fiscal need to secure the territory around a centralised administrative authority. In Dodd's judgement, it is rather less clear whether the relationship between money and the modern state is one of functional necessity as well as obvious historical importance. The historical and conceptual arguments examined 'provide no grounds for regarding the fiduciary assurances provided by a politically legitimate state as indispensable for the operation of money' (Dodd 1994, p. 36).

If we turn from domestic political requirements to the history of the international monetary system, we confirm the contingent relation between money and statehood and find that the political nature of money is as much international as domestic. In the pre-modern era, precious metals or specie money provided the basis of the international monetary system. As Gilpin says, 'for millennia, the international monetary system was largely apolitical' (Gilpin 1987, p. 120). This automatic system began to break down in the sixteenth century, and was revolutionised in the modern era due to a number of economic and political developments (Williamson 1983). 'Stated simply, money had been transferred from a gift of nature to a creation of the state' (Gilpin 1987, p. 121). Government issue of paper money ushered in an era of 'political money', which transformed the relation between state and economy and had a profound impact on international economics and world politics. It created the conflict between domestic economic autonomy and international economic stability, which became the 'fundamental dilemma of monetary relations'. The various efforts to resolve this dilemma at the international level produced shifting relations between money and statehood at the national level – with the causation frequently running from the international to the national.

The classical gold standard subordinated national autonomy (except in Britain) to international monetary discipline. The interregnum between British and American hegemony, from 1914 to 1944, saw a nationalisation of money, nation state control over the resources of society, the 'warfare state', and paved the way for the modern welfare state (Gilpin 1987, p. 121). The Bretton Woods system attempted, with initial success, to combine international stability with national monetary autonomy and domestic interventionism – a period which seems to sustain the notion of an essential link between the nation state, domestic politics and currency. The 'non-system' of flexible rates since the demise of Bretton Woods was expected to 're-nationalise' money and 'de-link' national macro-economic policies – an outcome designed to exploit the supposed link between the nation state, national policy preferences and money. However, it proved impossible to keep the pursuit of domestic objectives separate from the stability of the international economy and monetary values, largely because of the increased integration of world financial markets (Gilpin 1987). This has produced a range of policy responses and proposals – including benign neglect, dramatic exchange rate movements, various schemes for policy coordination, currency substitution and internationalisation, the building of regional monetary blocks, and a return to a gold standard and apolitical money (James 1996). Each of these involves a somewhat different relation between the nation state and money, and none assumes that the creation, validity and management of money are linked one-to-one with classical statehood. All, except the purist gold standard proposal, recognise the political dimension of money; but the political element can be national or international, and can rely on a combination of each to produce liquidity, adjustment, credibility and legitimacy.

History confirms that there are, indeed, political requirements for an effective monetary regime. But it provides no definitive model of what those political requirements are. The argument that money requires to be produced and validated by an individual nation state, or that any monetary authority must have classical state-like features, has no compelling foundation. One view is that further exploration of the relationship between money and the modern state requires examination of money's symbolic importance (Dodd 1994). It is argued below that we have, so far, made little progress in analysis of the national element of this symbolism and its implications for EMU. Two more immediate points flow from these considerations. First, achievement of a monopoly of monetary administration in Europe by the EU has the potential to radically 'strengthen' the Union, and that may include its 'state-like' features. Second, given money's undoubted symbolic importance, and pending a better analysis of what this means, it does seem likely that the euro can become a major symbol of European integration.

Is EMU an elusive union with the 'hollow core'?

Much the most complex study of the political economy of EMU is Kenneth Dyson's (1994) *Elusive Union: the Process of Economic and Monetary Union in Europe.*

Indeed, Dyson's methodological and substantive orientations are very similar to those which inform this book. His analytical approach is one that acknowledges the worth of various structural explanations of the process of European monetary integration,[9] but emphasises that each reveals a different facet of the process, and offers too limited and sometimes too static a picture of the evolving bargaining relationships underpinning the EMU policy process: 'Inherent in acceptance of them is the illusive search for a single theory of European integration.' In contrast, Dyson believes that 'the search for an all-embracing theory of European monetary integration is a will-of-the-wisp, and that what is required is a method of analysis that leaves theoretical choices open' (Dyson 1994, p. 315).

He summarises and concludes his account with two propositions that bear directly on the issue of currency, state and identity. The first is that the difficulties of achieving EMU arise because of the EU's neglect of the political, cultural and symbolic nature of money. The second is that the process of monetary integration has a 'hollow core'.[10] Given the status of his overall account, it is significant that these two propositions remain relatively undeveloped and, in our view, confront certain counter-arguments.

Consider first the argument concerning the political, cultural and symbolic nature of money. 'Money is political in being a key expression of statehood. States express their sovereignty in issuing and managing their own currency' (Dyson 1994, p. 5). Hence, central banks have a symbolic, as well as technical importance, often expressed in their imposing façades. 'Money is also cultural; it expresses nationhood and identity.' Currencies like the French franc, the pound sterling and the US dollar possess an emotional and psychological power – with coins often representing elaborate national mythologies.

> Correspondingly, a single European currency is evocative of a claim to 'statehood' and 'common culture': a claim that was always bound to be disputed, but a dispute for which EC policy-makers – blinkered by the technical economics of EMU and the technocratic policy style of the EC Commission – were unprepared.
>
> (ibid., p. 5)

These claims concerning an *essential* link between currency, statehood and identity remain unanalysed in Dyson's work. We argued above that the notion of a *definitive* link between them is problematical. Empirically, the extent to which currency and identity are linked, 'representing elaborate national methodologies', is variable within the European Union. While they seem closely linked in Britain and Germany, no such link exists in Ireland or some other smaller member states. More importantly, even if national money was generally an expression of sovereignty and culture, this would not be sufficient to sustain Dyson's inference that 'correspondingly' the single European currency represents such a claim. We do not dismiss the possibility or significance of such links, where they exist, but emphasise their contingency and the fact that we have relatively little grasp of the origin or nature of the relationships involved.

Significantly, rather than providing an analysis of the relationship between money and identity, Dyson buttresses his observations with *different* arguments, which themselves require scrutiny. He argues that the neglect of the symbolic nature of money was manifested in the rejection of evolutionary approaches to EMU. A 'precondition of union' was an opportunity for the European publics to learn more about the benefits of monetary union. 'In political terms, EMU remained too much an abstraction, lacking the roots in daily life and affective identification that national currencies continue to possess' (Dyson 1994, p. 7). In the absence of a European citizenry 'accustomed to European-wide political and economic transactions and recognising its established practical benefits, there were only high risk strategies – and serious dangers of failure for the integration process' (Dyson 1994, p. 8). Here, in Dyson's view, 'was the Achilles heel of EMU after Treaty ratification' (Dyson 1994, p. 360). While this might describe the experience of some UK citizens, it is scarcely an accurate account of the experience of those in countries that had participated in the EMS for a full thirteen years before the TEU, and twenty years before the locking of currencies in January 1999. In those countries, EMS was seen precisely as 'practical experience of the benefits of a common currency'. Elsewhere in his text, Dyson notes that there is a connection that holds together the Snake, the EMS and the EMU project, 'constituting an enduring learning experience'; but he seems to refer only to policy-makers, excluding economic actors.[11]

The second argument that requires scrutiny concerns the 'hollow core'. Given his account of the complexity of bargaining relations and structural constraints, Dyson considers that, looked at as a whole, the EMU process walks a tightrope: unsettled by the pressures consequent on hierarchical coordination at the national level and on the operation of the financial markets, and yet steadied by a corporatist policy network. As a result, the EMU policy process has a 'hollow core': no single actor is capable, on a continuing basis, of being the policy-brokering centre, promoting compromise or imposing settlements (Dyson 1994, p. 15). As a result, there is a policy process at the heart of European integration that is beset by enduring uncertainty and complex turbulence, disposed to pursue a scale of policy steps which fail to match the challenges – fiscal, monetary and political – that confront it. While this description has a certain appeal, and is consistent with some elements in our argument, it is not clear that it warrants the concept of the 'hollow core'. Dyson, and others, have offered sufficient evidence of the complexity and difficulty of the path to EMU to account for the halting nature of progress.

Among these difficulties are some, substantive, issues that should be considered, before taking recourse to the traditional, but unanalysed, notion of a definitive link between currency, statehood and identity, and the idea of a definite gulf between this and an EMU process with a 'hollow core'. Indeed, these substantive issues are elaborated persuasively by Dyson: if the EC is to reflect the real complexity of economic policy values, and to be responsive to democratic politics, its policy process for EMU must provide a broad framework for policy development. Such a policy process would be 'a complex and subtle mechanism' for reconciling the conflicting requirements of stability (to savers), wealth-creation (to satisfy those in manufacturing and commerce) and equity (to satisfy those who are disadvantaged by change). 'The Treaty on European Union', he says emphatically, 'was not that mechanism' (Dyson 1994, p. 259). But it seems likely that it was, indeed, anxiety about stability, wealth creation and equity that created both divergent economic policy approaches in member states and worries about EMU. This view is consistent with the idea that economic actors in most member states had accepted that monetary union was ultimately desirable. Indeed, it is consistent with Dyson's argument that there is a 'need to root effective monetary policy in a strong political infrastructure, not least to provide the protective constitutional framework of democratic legitimacy that such policy requires' (Dyson 1994, p. xii). However, because we see a weaker link between currency, statehood and identity, we are sceptical of the view that political objection to the costs of a stability-oriented policy might 'simultaneously demystify not only the ideology legitimizing central bank power but also the ideology of European integration itself' (Dyson 1994, p. 259).

It remains necessary to explore how the issues of stability, wealth creation and equity are linked to questions of currency and identity. Indeed, one of the motivations for this book is to develop an account of European integration that does not rigorously separate the material and self-interested dimension from the cultural, conceptual and idealistic aspects.

This section has discussed aspects of money – its relation to statehood and identity – which are frequently taken for granted, rather than critically analysed, but which may be critical to an understanding of the EMU project. Our approach suggests that it cannot be assumed that exploration of these aspects of money will lead entirely back to the national level. Much of the analytical advance of recent years lies precisely in embracing the emergence of a genuine European-level sphere of analysis and activity. The symbolic and political aspects of currency, and the link to statehood, undoubtedly require attention, given their importance in some member states and the needs of the EU. But they should be seen as contingent, rather than necessary, relationships, and should certainly not be invoked as reflections of an underlying reality of nationality, which sets definite limits to the possibilities of European integration.

Conclusions: the analysis and consequences of monetary union

The issues of macroeconomic and monetary union examined in this chapter underline the relevance of our overall approach. The re-launch of the EMU project in the late 1980s was a reflection of the 'unsettled Europe' created by deepening market integration and an unsettled international economic and political context – while the agreement of the Maastricht Treaty was undoubtedly related to the transformation of eastern Europe. The process vividly illustrates the unsettled state of analysis, both of macroeconomic mechanisms and of the European integration process. It brought to the surface the uneasy way in which economic and political factors are distinguished, and combined, in the study of European integration. On this, we take issue with one influential view, that the economic logic of EMU is weak and that the project must be understood as essentially political.

Europe's experience of macroeconomic and monetary integration also confirms and illustrates our four analytical assumptions. Europe's economic and monetary union confirms that the integration process is contingent on the material, political and intellectual circumstances of the 1980s and 1990s. This is a context in which textbook ideas about the requirements of monetary union count for little against the dynamic which pushed the EU forward from the EMS. The emerging international financial situation may change this context and prompt significant change in Europe's approach. The story of European efforts at monetary stability underlines the way in which integration can both progress and regress, and the degree to which integration can be a residual in the play of larger national or international forces – in this case a radically changed, and potentially unstable, international monetary system. Europe's chosen approach to EMU strongly confirms the 'interactive' view outlined in Chapter 1. Contrary to what many suggest, the emerging European model cannot be characterised as the German model writ large, since few of the social, political, economic and financial structures which underpinned the German model exist at European level. The European model emerges from the interaction of various national approaches, but also from the fact that integration, in combination with other forces, is altering national approaches themselves. As in the economic sphere, monetary integration is characterised by both transfer and transformation.

The process of macroeconomic and monetary union also displays the ties and tensions that characterise the current phase of integration. Two of these ties and tensions are particularly evident, and a third plays some role. The arrangements for technocratic management of exchange rates, with ECOFIN and the various monetary institutions increasingly providing a problem-solving arena, stand in definite tension with the feeling that a European economic and monetary union requires more of a polity, in which institutions are accountable and reflect values and identity. The tension between EU and national policy-making has been resolved in a quite novel – and unproven – way. This involves centralisation of monetary policy, decentralisation of fiscal policy and a complex system of EU-level economic policy guidelines and rules. This approach to monetary union is, in many respects, typical of an emerging policy system characterised by innovation and experimentation.

A third of our ties and tensions has some relevance: that between the EU's continental and global roles. At a purely quantitative level, the EU is undoubtedly large enough to affect global monetary relations. While the euro will certainly erode the dominant position of the dollar as a reserve and vehicle currency, many expect that this effect will be gradual (Gros and Thygesen 1992). It might be expected that EMU will increase the influence of the EU in global monetary management and improve the quality of international policy coordination, thereby propelling the EU to centre stage in monetary as well as other international affairs. However, EMU will reinforce the move to a more symmetric, less hegemonic, global monetary system, and this could increase, rather than decrease, the difficulties of policy coordination. Indeed, there is evidence that the success of international coordination depends on the quality of internal coordination between central bank and government (Dobson 1991). However, *internal* coordination in the EU – between monetary and fiscal policy, and between monetary policy and exchange rate policy – is precisely one of the unresolved issues in the EU. Indeed, the EU may have limited interest in exchange rate management at the global level, as the ECB builds its credibility. While EMU undoubtedly increases the international role of the Union, it remains to be seen whether this implies greatly increased levels of international policy coordination (Gros and Thygesen 1992; Kenen 1996). While the Union may prefer to build the euro, international financial instability may force it to adopt a more active global role.

Implicit in the paradoxes of monetary union outlined above, and in much of the literature, is a particular view of a deep connection between currency and statehood. Our approach throws this connection into question, partly by distinguishing between three facets of statehood: function, territory and identity. In the case of monetary integration, there has been a complex fragmentation of functional responsibility and something of a split between the technical functions and the social and political underpinnings of price stability. The internationalisation of finance, and the removal of exchange controls, has radically altered the territorial element of finance. Finally, EMU raises issues of identity, particularly in Germany, the UK and Denmark, although these remain to be adequately analysed or resolved. In monetary matters, this recent European unsettling of territory, identity and function should be viewed in a longer historical context – a context that reveals varying relations between money and statehood, and an international as well as national dimension to the political foundations of money.

While much of the analysis of this book suggests that the complex, multilayered, negotiated pattern of governance emerging in the EU is particularly suited to the late 1990s, the difficulties of monetary union are often invoked to draw attention back to certain irreducible, state-like, functions, and to the need for deep, and routinely accepted, relations between state, society and nation. While we too find our attention drawn back to the connection between currency, statehood, identity and social unity, we believe that these factors are poorly understood, and our analytical approach forces us to question whether these relationships are, in fact, irreducible.

Much of the academic and public debate on EMU displays a peculiar distance from the transition to EMU as experienced by governments, firms, unions and citizens. At times, it is as if the academic economists, journalistic pundits and crank politicians occupy a different world from the actors who are driving and anticipating EMU.

In part, this reflects a failure to grasp the fact that the EU is shaped by both constitutive events (such as treaty revisions and epoch-making bargains) and continuous evolution. The commentary is out of touch precisely because its authors take insufficient account of the evolution of cooperation, institutions and socialisation in monetary matters, and the way these put flesh on the bones of the TEU.

A second problem, reflecting a deeper issue discussed above, derives from the assumption that, in monetary matters, both legitimacy and effectiveness exist first and foremost at national level. Only in rare circumstances will sufficient consent, capacity or authority be *passed upwards* to the European level. This misses the fundamental point that currencies are essentially relational; they begin life with a significant international dimension, they do not acquire that dimension through political, still less popular, choice. Indeed, in the EU the international dimension has, for several decades, gone much further. In many member states, the effectiveness, legitimacy and credibility of monetary policy is determined more by its conformity with the EMS or a DM-peg, than by anything at the national level.

Journalistic commentary and academic economics in the Anglo-Saxon world have consistently and grossly underestimated the capacity of the EU to create monetary union. What was taken by Europe's leaders, businesses and citizens as a definite plan, was seen by these commentators as a faint probability. It is interesting to reflect on the dimensions and origin of this error and the tenacity with which it was repeated. It is hard to think of parallels. While the years of Euro-sclerosis fuelled intergovernmental scepticism, the re-launch of the Community quickly led to an explosion of research on the dynamics of integration. Only among a minority of Anglo-Saxon economists was there an equivalent response in the analysis and discussion of monetary union. There was, of course, accuracy in the some of the critical and sceptical points that were made – the divergence of national economic policies and the reluctance to coordinate, the incomplete and contentious nature of the TEU, its non-conformity with various economic doctrines. But these were only ever half of the story. It required a better understanding of the Union to sense that there was more, and a wider framework than mainstream macroeconomics to find out what it was.

The idea of the EU as a new model of internationalisation expresses both its systemic and novel nature. While open economy macroeconomics tells us a certain amount, in retains the traditional macroeconomic notion of the national economy. The path to EMU is more akin to the political economy of the international monetary *system*. In contrast to national macroeconomists, observers who came at EMU from the global end seem to have appreciated its dynamics much better (e.g. Eichengreen 1994b, 1996; Cohen 1997). But even when viewed as an international monetary system, European EMU has strikingly novel characteristics: it is democratic, it lacks a state, it is moving from (rather than towards) hegemony. When this novelty was noticed, it was seen as further evidence of how out of step the leaders of EMU were with various theories. In contrast, our pragmatic instinct, and our view of Europe as an experimental union, suggest that when theory and practice are in conflict, it is theory rather than practice that requires scrutiny and revision.

Notes

1 Action was taken to prevent exchange rate volatility disrupting the CAP. In 1964, the role of the Monetary Committee was extended and the Committee of Governors of the Central Banks of the member states was established. The 1967 devaluation of sterling, was used by General de Gaulle as an argument to justify his veto of UK membership. By the end of the 1960s, the rising concern that exchange rate fluctuations would jeopardise the working of the common market and the Common Agricultural Policy led to active discussion of economic and monetary union. After revaluations of the mark and devaluation of the French franc in the 1960s, the 1969 Hague summit of Community leaders decided that the Community should seek to move towards EMU. Finally, soon after the collapse of Bretton Woods, the Community devised its own arrangements to limit exchange rate volatility, the snake and the EMS.

2 A second possible negative dynamic was identified by Allesina and Grilli (1994). States that did not qualify at the outset, might find it more difficult to meet the convergence criteria over time.

3 The literature on EMS is now enormous and, as Frieden says, 'almost all of it is purely economic in content' (Frieden 1991, p. 447). Economic analysis of the EMS, has focused on six questions (see Gros and Thygesen 1992). Did it succeed in creating a zone of monetary stability? How important were capital controls in creating the stability of the system? Did the EMS help reduce the cost of disinflation (i.e. getting inflation down)? Did the EMS operate as a mechanism jointly to absorb shocks coming from outside? To what extent, and in what ways, was EMS an asymmetric system? Did the EMS contain a deflationary bias? Studies that analyse it as a political development, or apply a political economy perspective, include Ludlow 1982; Frieden 1991, 1992, 1994; Giovannini 1992; Williamson 1992; Jacquet 1992; Eichengreen and Frieden 1994; McNamara 1997; Sandholtz 1993, 1996; and Cameron, D. 1993, 1995.

4 This view is implicit in Eichengreen's argument that the binding constraints on European monetary union are political, rather than economic. (Eichengreen 1994b, pp. 106–8).

5 Even the EMS, which Germany undoubtedly dominated, should not be seen as a large-scale version of the German model. An international system hegemonised by a particular state involves different governing mechanisms than are used *within* that hegemonic state. This is an illustration of our general argument that interdependence somewhat alters the nature of each of the interdependent states or societies.

6 If size were so very important, one might expect a convergence towards some common size for each single national currency area.

7 While views differ on the adjustment mechanism that operated under the gold standard, Goodhart believes a partial explanation lies in the enormous, cyclical, migration flows of that time.

8 The state's role in monetary administration can be interpreted in terms of two 'opposite causal patterns' entailing, first, a flow of power upwards from civil society towards the state, and second, a reversed tendency extending from the state downwards into civil society (Dodd 1994, p. 35).

9 These include the global structural explanation, the intergovernmental bargaining explanation, the neo-functionalist explanation, the neo-federalist explanation, the transactions cost explanation and the path dependency explanation.

10 While these arguments figure prominently in the introduction and conclusion of Dyson's text, the real analysis would seem to lie elsewhere: in the argument that 'the EMS and the EMU policy process is best understood as composed of a distinct set of inter-dependent bargaining relations and rules of the game, embedded in a framework of structures that they have a limited, and fluctuating, capacity to influence'. The

strength of the analysis lies precisely in Dyson's mapping of the different sources of structural power in the international political economy and the elucidation of their nature: world currency relations, financial markets, monetary policy ideas, economic 'fundamentals' and trade interdependence – and in his unpacking of the various bargaining relations that comprise the policy sector and demonstration of how they function and how they relate to each other and the rules of the game. Dyson shows how the EMS and EMU process involves the interaction of three levels: the intrusive context of structural power, the constituent bargaining relations and the rules of the game, and the rational actors who inhabit the process. Furthermore, the power of this complex conceptual approach is demonstrated in a detailed narrative and comparison with alternative approaches.

11   Indeed, in considering the future prospects for EMU, Dyson reaches a conclusion somewhat similar to ours. While a re-nationalisation of monetary and economic policy is a possibility, it is more likely that 'the EMU policy process will be sustained by the recognition of national policy actors that collective action, and eventual union, offered a superior means of reasserting control over foreign exchange markets and the world currency relationships than a return to national action' (Dyson 1994, p. 360). The ratification of the Maastricht Treaty, the remarkable series of detailed technical and political agreements achieved between 1992 and 1998 and the continued support for political parties and governments that favour EMU in most member states, suggests to us that this recognition *exists already* and, in many cases, has existed for a considerable period of time.

8 The international role of the European Union

Introduction

At many points in this book, it has become apparent that the internal development and the international role of the EU are intimately connected. In Chapter 2, the discussion of states and nations in Europe revealed that the changing authority and identity structures of Europe, and particularly in the countries of the EU, had both international origins and international resonances. Likewise, in Chapter 3, the relationship between change in the international political structure and the developing institutions and policies of the EU could clearly be discerned. The discussion of international political economy in Chapter 4 only served to reinforce this impression by illustrating the interconnectedness not only of the economic, the social and the political, but also by showing the ways in which these interacted to contribute to the evolution of authority and legitimacy structures as well as specific policies and activities.

In this part of the book we are concerned to identify and explore the specific position occupied by, and the roles played by, the EU in the context of the 1990s. In Chapter 5, the focus on governance served not only to demonstrate the complexity of the EU's evolving activities and roles but also to reinforce again the impression of linkage between the internal and the international – between the local, the national, the regional and the global arenas. Chapters 6 and 7, by focusing on the political economy of the Single Market and Economic and Monetary Union, underlined the ways in which the interconnectedness of the world political economy gives the EU an unavoidably weighty global presence. This chapter builds upon these foundations, to explore the ways in which the EU's international presence and role raises important questions about participation in world politics and the global political economy, and about the relationship between the EU, states and other actors in the global arena.

In this way, it could be said, the chapter focuses on all of the 'ties and tensions' around which the second half of the book is built. We have already seen that the complex interplay between the EU as a union of states and the EU as a market has an inextricably international dimension. There is also an inevitable focus on the tension between the EU as a problem-solving arena and a polity, since this is integral to many notions of 'European foreign policy'. In a world of 'complex interdependence', the international arena also sees tensions between EU policy-making and multilevel policy-making. However, it is clear that the central focus is on one set of ties and tensions above all: that between the EU 'universe' and its global environment. Through this focus are filtered the other ties and tensions; as will be seen in the course of the chapter, each of these areas is given special meaning and impact by the explicit consideration of the international dimension.

This chapter focuses on three central issues. First, there is the concept of 'actorness' in relation both to the EU and to changing conceptions of statehood: how 'statelike' is the EU in the world arena, and is statehood the standard to which the EU should be aspiring? Second, there is the structure and process of EU external policy-making, and in particular the relationship between policy-making processes and the coherence and impact of the EU's external actions. Does the complexity and messiness of the process represent a failure to achieve policy consistency, or is it a creative adjustment to the conditions of the 1990s? Finally, there is the nature of the EU as an interlocutor or protagonist in the world arena, and the extent to which the EU can be said to have developed a 'real' foreign policy. By what criteria should the EU's role be judged, and on what principles and values should it be based?

As noted in Chapter 3, these issues are central to the broader study of international relations, but they also link very closely with the areas of governance and the international political economy outlined above. They have been focused in the 1990s by a number of processes and events: some of these, such as the Maastricht Treaty of 1991 and the Amsterdam Treaty of 1997, can be seen as 'constitutive' events, in which the underlying nature of the EU's international role has been open to negotiation and renegotiation; others, such as the EU's involvement in the conflicts in former Yugoslavia or its relations with global economic institutions, have an equally profound yet more gradual evolutionary effect on the ways in which the EU is perceived and the ways in which other international actors respond to it. As in other areas of EU activity, the coincidence of the 'constitutive' and the 'evolutionary' processes contributes to the essentially unsettled nature of the EU's role and impact.

The European Union as an international actor

One of the central contested areas in the study of international relations is that of 'actorness' (Young 1972; Mansbach 1994). As noted in Chapter 2, it is possible to define the notion so as to exclude all participants other than recognised sovereign states, and for many this remains the key component of world politics. Statehood is not only the qualification for entry on to the world stage, it is also the quality that enables its possessors to act effectively in the world political process. But there are powerful challenges to this notion, and alternative conceptualisations that focus on less formal and restrictive qualifications for 'actorness'. As outlined in Chapter 3, these broader notions focus on 'softer' qualifications for participation in world politics: autonomy rather than sovereignty, representation rather than recognition, influence rather than control. They also allow for the consideration of actors not linked to specific territories, and for the central role of processes of communication and access in determining who participates, when and how (Hocking and Smith 1995, Chapter 5).

The overall image of the world arena produced by these modified approaches is what Oran Young has called a 'mixed actor system' in which there are few set conditions for participation and no settled hierarchy of participants (Young 1972, p. 136). Others have pointed to the growth of 'complex interdependence' as an essential property of the world arena, stressing the interconnectedness between actors and the multiplicity of issues on which significant interaction can occur (Keohane and Nye 1987). One clear conclusion to be drawn from such discussion might be that it is much easier to become an international actor in conditions of complex interdependence; but the corollary of such a conclusion is that there is a vital need to distinguish between actors in terms of their extent and level of participation, and the effectiveness of their actions (Hocking and Smith 1995, Chapter 5).

From this general conclusion, some important distinctions flow. They can be expressed in what might seem to be rather traditional or conventional terms – those of power. In the first place, it is important when examining international actors, including the EU, to be aware of two broad types of 'foundational power': resource power, derived from the possession of specific assets, and structural power, derived from the position an actor occupies in the international system or in major institutions (Strange 1988; Galtung 1989). A second relevant dimension of power concerns the ways in which either resource or structural power is translated into specific outcomes. Three components of this process can be observed: the power to act, the power to interact and the power to achieve results (Puchala 1971; Hocking and Smith 1995, Chapter 11). It is entirely possible for a given international actor in a specific situation to possess the power to act, but not to possess either the power to interact or the capacity to obtain results. It is also possible for an actor to claim the power to interact, but not to be able to justify or muster the resources for action itself. These resources can be essentially tangible (economic, administrative and others), but there are other equally important intangible elements, such as legitimacy and the expectations or demands of other participants in the global arena.

The fundamental point here, and it is an essential one in evaluating the EU's role as an international actor, is that 'actorness' is a variable conditioned by circumstances as well as by formal grants of authority or legitimacy. In this sense, 'actorness' occupies the same role in relation to statehood as does the concept and process of governance (see Chapter 5). It is thus possible to observe a wide range of variations or qualifications to the notion of international actorness, and these can be highly significant in conditioning international outcomes. For the EU, as will be seen, these go some way towards explaining the 'capability–expectations gap' identified by Christopher Hill as a fundamental problem in explaining the Union's international role (Hill 1993, 1998).

Seen in this light, it seems clear that the European Union is a partially formed international actor, but one of potentially great significance and impact. From the point of view of resource power (assuming for the moment that it can be mobilised) the EU ranks alongside the most powerful economic and political groupings in the world arena (Piening 1997, Chapter 1). Crucially, though, it does not have any fully autonomous defence or military capacity, and this has been seen by many commentators as a fundamental deficiency in its actorness (Bull 1982; Hill 1990; Menon *et al.* 1992). In terms of structural power, the EU is centrally placed not only in the new Europe but also in many global institutions and organisations. In many of these contexts, though, it operates alongside the continuing activities of member states (Hill 1996; Howorth and Menon 1997); this is even the case for example in the World Trade Organisation and other economic bodies, where it might be argued that the EU's actorness is at its most highly-developed. Thus, as in the area of resource power, the EU has the properties of a significant but conjoint or contingent actor, depending on temporary or permanent grants of authority from its members. But this must not be allowed to detract too much from the fact that the Union really does have immense international economic weight, nor from the crucial fact that this is observed and taken into consideration by other international actors (Smith 1994b; Piening 1997, Chapter 1).

The EU becomes, if anything, more challenging and intriguing when examined in terms of its capacity to act, interact and get results. There is, as many have observed, a substantial disparity in many areas between the EU's resources, its international position and its capacity to exert effective influence in a coherent way (Allen and Smith 1990, 1998; Hill 1993, 1998; Noorgaard *et al.* 1993). This failure to 'punch its weight' means that, for some, the EU can only ever be a failure. As will shortly be seen, though, this rather depends on what the standards for success are taken to be. For the moment, it must be observed that the EU's capacity to act internationally is fundamentally limited. On the one hand, only certain grants of competence are made to Union institutions (particularly the European Community) by the treaties on which the EU rests (Macleod *et al.* 1996; Smith 1997c). On the other hand, in areas such as foreign and security policy and justice and home affairs, the ability of the Union to act is effectively limited by the ability of its members to agree; that is to say, it is based on intergovernmental agreement and convention rather than a permanent or long-term grant of competence (Nuttall 1992, 1997; Hill 1996). Thus, although the EC has built up a complex and sophisticated network of international channels for action, and has a number of important instruments at its disposal, they are still limited and largely confined to areas of political economy. Not only this, but there is an inherent problem of 'consistency' for the Union, in the sense that actions taken under the 'first pillar' of the EC treaties may overlap with, or clash with actions taken in the 'second pillar' of Common Foreign and Security Policy (CFSP).

Much the same can be said of the Union's capacity to interact and, by extension, of its capacity to get results. Where there is an explicit grant of competence, the EC in particular can establish linkages and interactions with states, with international organisations and with significant non-state groupings in the business and related spheres. Even here, though, there can be uncertainties and apparent reversals (see below). Where there is no explicit or formal grant of competence, the EU, the EC or the Commission as the representative of the Community have what often appears to be a contingent presence: almost literally, in some contexts, the ghost at the feast being enjoyed by heads of state or government. The capacity to interact is thus often limited, leading to disappointed expectations and apparent failures to get results; for example, in global economic management. This limitation also implies that there is a form of continuous negotiation and renegotiation of the 'boundaries' between EC competence and the actions or interests of the member states (Smith 1994b).

At this point, it is important to recall the debate about 'actorness' outlined above. By what might be called the 'positive' test of actorness, the EU and its various organs are clearly deficient, although certainly not impotent. Ironically, the strength of the EU as a treaty- and law-based entity is precisely what can limit it most, by erecting institutional and legal boundaries to an expansive view of its international role. But this implies that the standard for comparison is classical statehood of the kind outlined above and in Chapter 3. It could plausibly be argued that many of the states in the international system of the 1990s, despite their claims to sovereignty, recognition and control of territory and activity, are strictly limited in their capacities to act, interact and get results. The EU, in this light, begins to appear a much more substantial presence on the world stage, especially when one recalls the impact the development of the Union has had on the perceptions of political leaders and economic groupings worldwide (Allen and Smith 1990, 1998; Piening 1997).

The argument here, as elsewhere in this book, is that the standard of classical statehood is inappropriate in judging the international role and impact of the EU. The transformation of the world arena, both politically and economically, has only served to underline the ways in which the EU forms the centrepiece of significant and effective international action. Not only this, but by its resource and structural power, the Union forms a highly significant presence in the perceptions and actions both of its members and of outsiders (Allen and Smith 1990, 1998). It is not what James Caporaso has termed a 'Westphalian protostate' (Caporaso 1996), although in some areas of international negotiation and diplomacy it certainly has statelike powers and roles. It is more than a simple 'league of states' after the model derived from classical scholarship, although it is based on a central and continuing bargain between its member states and European-level institutions. It has many properties of what has been called a 'regulatory state' (Majone 1996a, 1996b), and these properties are increasingly salient in the world arena of the 1990s. It also has some of the flexibility and the multidimensional nature of the 'post-modern state', in which the emphasis is on the political and regulatory use of space and the generation of identity (see Chapters 5–6 above, and Laffan 1996b).

It would be tempting to conclude from this that the EU is the perfect vehicle for the expression of the social, political and economic needs of its citizens in the world arena of the 1990s. No such teleology is implied here. What is argued is that the EU should be judged by criteria of actorness and international efficacy which are appropriate not only to the EU itself but also to the conditions of the 1990s. If this is done, it is inevitable that a complex and multifaceted image of the EU emerges: part autonomous agent, part channel for the actions and interactions of others, part 'systemic modifier' shaping actions and imposing more or less tangible constraints on actions by a wide variety of groupings. The rest of this chapter attempts to explore some of the ways in which this set of coexisting and potentially competing tendencies makes itself felt.

Structure and process in EU external policy

Since the 1950s, the EC and then the EU have developed a complex and sophisticated set of external policies, based on two essential components: first, the grant of competences under successive treaties and their exploitation by Community/Union institutions, and second, the demands of increasing involvement in the world arena. Whilst the Treaty of Paris (1951) had limited external policy provisions, the nature of coal and steel as internationally traded commodities meant that it also had some important resonances, for example among US steel producers who feared a super-competitive cartel in Europe. The Treaty of Rome contained a much more highly-developed external policy dimension, since by its very nature the Common Market and the Customs Union were entangled with the world trading system. Indeed, the establishment of the EEC was only possible under Article 24 of the GATT, which makes provision for customs unions under certain conditions (Macleod *et al.* 1996).

During the early development of the Community, one crucial distinction lay at the centre of external policy. The international actions of the Community were strictly limited by the treaties (and for that matter by the attitudes of member states) to commercial policy. The Customs Union and the Common External Tariff gave the Community a potentially strong but essentially narrow international role. What developed was thus a Community external policy based upon, and organised in terms of, commercial diplomacy. What might be described as 'real' foreign policy, dealing with political and security matters, was not part of the Community's remit, and there were very good reasons for a number of key members to resist any development in this direction. For the French, the priority placed on national independence, and the demands of involvement in their former colonies played a central role; for the (West) Germans, the need to present themselves as 'good Atlanticists' in NATO loomed large; for other, smaller EEC members, the conflicting demands of involvements at the European and the Atlantic level were strongly felt (Calleo 1970, 1987; Smith 1984).

Throughout the subsequent history of the Community and then the Union, this potential or actual tension between commercial and foreign policy activity has been a consistent thread. In the early 1970s, the establishment of European Political Cooperation (EPC) seemed to some to presage the emergence of a Community 'foreign policy', but this was explicitly on an intergovernmental basis. As it became formalised through the London Report of 1981, and then through the Single European Act, EPC relied upon the conceptual and practical distinctions between Community policy and policy-making and the essentially intergovernmental coordination of diplomatic positions and initiatives (Allen *et al.* 1982; Pijpers *et al.* 1988; Holland 1991; Nuttall 1992).

Such a process of development raises important questions not only of a conceptual kind but also at the level of practical organisation. Conceptually, given the increasing linkage discerned during the 1970s and 1980s between economic, political and security matters, it appeared to some commentators that the Community position was untenable: the notion of a 'civilian power' basing its international actions on commercial and related considerations could not last given the need to bring together the commercial with the political in an interdependent world (Bull 1982). The increasing use of economic weapons for political ends, for example through sanctions and boycotts and the emerging concept of economic security, militated against the rather cosy idea that the Community was 'different' (Allen and Smith 1983; Holland 1988).

At the level of practical policy and organisation, such broad concerns could find quite specific expression. During the 1960s, 1970s and 1980s, the Community built up an elaborate quasi-diplomatic network based on the international implementation of the treaties. Although the Common Commercial Policy was the core of this organisation, it must not be forgotten that almost every area of Community activity (industrial, agricultural, technological, etc.) has an inescapable international component. To put it simply, during the 1970s and 1980s the Community came up against the logic of interconnectedness both between different sectors of activity and between the 'domestic' and the international, in such a way that its organisation and structures had to be reassessed. Thus, the Commission – as the implementing arm of the Common Commercial Policy – had also to consider the ways in which this came into contact with a wide range of other international activities. In areas such as economic sanctions or economic diplomacy, the tensions between the Commission and the Council of Ministers could be discerned: although the Council was adamant that EPC for example should not become part of Community policy-making, there were circumstances in which the Community alone possessed the effective instruments of policy (for example sanctions against Argentina in 1982, against South Africa later in the 1980s) (Edwards 1984; Holland 1988).

Such considerations are important to the evaluation of the international role of the Community during the 1970s and 1980s. There is a lot of force in the argument that the position was steadily becoming unsustainable, both because of developments in the broader world arena and because of specific developments within the Community and between its members. This in turn could not fail to have an impact upon the ways in which international observers and the Community's international partners perceived the status and role of the Community and its institutions. Such tensions were exacerbated after the mid-1980s by the acceleration of political change in Europe itself, and by the conflicting expectations and images held of the Community in the wider Europe (see Chapter 3).

It is in this light that one should view the two seminal episodes of the Community's development between the mid-1980s and the early 1990s: the Single Market Programme (SMP) and the Maastricht Treaty. The SMP encapsulated the sense of linkage between sectors of activity in the Community's political economy, but it also had deep linkages to the status and role of the Community in the world arena, through the emphasis on competitiveness and on the challenges from the United States and Japan. As such, it posed important structural and procedural challenges for the Community itself, since it coincided with the Uruguay Round of trade negotiations under the GATT, and also with sensitivities, particularly in the United States, about the maintenance of economic security (Hufbauer 1990; Ishikawa 1990; Harrison 1994; Hocking and Smith 1997, Chapter 2). In broad terms, it could be argued that the SMP required the Community to develop a more sophisticated and wide-ranging international economic policy, and that this was fed by the external perceptions of a 'fortress Europe' in the making. In this context, it is significant that the Community, through the Commission, was able to develop and sustain a wide-ranging process of international negotiation, often about issues of great concern to member states, to regions or to important pressure groups in the Community (Calingaert 1988, 1996; Mayes 1993; Smith and Woolcock 1993; Smith, M. 1994b).

More explicitly linked to the development of a 'European foreign policy', though, was the process of negotiation for the Treaty of European Union which led to the Maastricht agreements. Whilst it must not be forgotten that the agreement on economic and monetary union had an inescapable international component (see Chapter 7), the centrepiece of the foreign policy debate was the so-called 'second pillar' or the provisions on a common foreign and security policy. These provisions can be viewed in two ways. In the first case, it is possible to see them as essentially a continuation of the EPC process. The procedures remained intergovernmental, with mechanisms designed to give member states a good deal of control over positions taken and actions contemplated. Although there were innovations such as the notion of 'joint actions', these were hedged around with constraints in such a way as to reduce their effect and to perpetuate the impression of a purely diplomatic and intergovernmental framework (Holland 1991, 1996; Hill 1993, 1996; Nuttall and Edwards 1994).

It is possible, though, to see the CFSP provisions in another way: as a further step in the development of a 'real' European foreign policy. The infrastructure of policy was strengthened, the procedures introduced bore at least some resemblance to those in use under the Community umbrella (for example, qualified majority voting), and the commitment, at least in general terms, to the development of defence policies was made. Whilst during the two or three years after the entering into force of the TEU there was only modest progress towards the taking of foreign policy actions, the commitment to strengthen the procedures again in the process of the 1996 IGC was taken seriously by at least some major member states and European institutions. This added up to what Forster and Wallace have characterised as an 'unstable compromise' on CFSP: whilst there had been no great leap forward, the position could not properly be sustained in the longer term without consideration of fundamental changes (Nuttall and Edwards 1994; Forster and Wallace 1996).

This in effect raises a major conceptual point about the development of Community and then Union policy-making. How far can this be seen as a 'constitutive' process dependent upon major events such as the Maastricht summit and the creation of new 'constitutional' frameworks, and how far as an evolutionary institutional process reflecting the development of policy on a more incremental and short-term basis, but none the less creating powerful institutional incentives to further integration?

To take the second possibility first, it is clear that in Community/Union external policy there has been a major and continuing process of institutional growth and change. This has been driven partly by internal needs, to clarify the allocation of competences, resources and responsibilities between institutions and elements of the organisational framework, and partly by external demands for participation in processes of negotiation or economic and political interaction. Thus, the entanglement of the EC and the EU in global institutions such as the GATT and its successor, the World Trade Organisation, has engendered powerful forces of policy development in the EC particularly (Smith 1997c, 1997d). At the same time, the process of change in the wider Europe has also made for inescapable pressures leading to innovation and changes in the balance between member states and Union (Smith 1996a; Preston 1997). Such a judgement is appropriate both to Community policy-making strictly defined – what is given to the Community by the treaties, the Common Commercial Policy and other instruments – and to the more intergovernmental processes of EPC/CFSP. It is essentially an incrementalist version of the development of policy-making structures and processes, driven by pressures and the need to provide services.

On the other hand, there is the 'constitutive' version of the development of Community/Union external policies. Here, the stakes are those of formal grants or withholdings of competence, and of the longer-term balance between institutions. Although this may reflect short-term pressures, there is an awareness among those involved that large issues are to be decided. There is thus also a higher level of politicisation and of symbolism, which is reflected in both the bargaining process and in the strategies of the participants. The intergovernmental conferences leading to the SEA, the TEU and the Amsterdam Treaty of 1997 are the prime exemplars of such 'constitutive' processes, with widespread perceptions that they were aimed at addressing foundational issues in a number of areas (Moravcsik 1991b, 1993; Laursen and Vanhoonacker 1992).

As was seen in Chapter 7, the distinction between incrementalist and constitutive versions of policy development is crucial to the 'internal' evolution of the Community/Union. But it is no less vital when it comes to the international actions and role of the EU. It is also clear that the 'fit' between incremental and constitutive processes of development can be vital to the effectiveness of EU policies, not least because it has an effect on the perceptions of outsiders. The ways in which the EU's partners view and react to its external policies are a vital component of its international role. When the day-to-day or month-to-month business of the EU has to coexist with major attempts at constitution-building, it is not surprising that outsiders can become confused, that expectations can be raised and dashed.

Examples of this tension and its potential for generating confusion are not difficult to find. Perhaps the most dramatic example during the 1990s are furnished by the EU's entanglement in the affairs of former Yugoslavia. During 1990 and 1991, the issues surrounding recognition of Croatia, Slovenia and eventually Bosnia-Herzegovina became inextricably bound up with the process of negotiation in the IGC; not only this, but relations between the EU and the United States were complicated by the American perception that the issue was a test-case for EPC and then the CFSP. The eagerness of many in the EU to prove the credentials of the CFSP came up against the realities of involvement in a zone not simply of civil war but also of anarchic inter-ethnic conflict, to such an extent that, as the conflict proceeded, serious questions were raised about the capacity of the Union to play any constructive role (Nuttall 1995; Zucconi 1996; Gow 1997). The 'end-game' as it evolved through the Dayton Accords and their implementation during 1996 and after gave the EU an essentially 'civilian' role, fittingly as some might have argued, in which it focused on the provision of international aid for reconstruction and development.

Another complication for those concerned both to analyse and to respond to the international activities of the EU is the coexistence of different modes of policy and different policy instruments. In a sense, this is a problem with any analysis of foreign policy; states and their governments will display more or less strategic or incremental modes of policy development. In the case of the EU, however, it is given additional force by the ways in which policies and instruments can be shared at different levels in the EU system, creating problems of policy coherence and policy legitimacy (Richardson 1996).

There are four main areas in which these problems of coherence and legitimacy can be discerned. First, there is the area of policy mechanisms. As already noted, the EU demonstrates a complex division of powers and responsibilities, both in its internal and in its external policies. Who has the 'voice' on a specific area of policy, even in such areas as the Common Commercial Policy, where apparently there is an exclusive Community competence, is never a closed issue. In 1994, in the aftermath of the GATT Uruguay Round Agreement, the ECJ held that on areas such as trade in financial services, which are new on the international agenda, the EC shares competence with the member states (Macleod *et al.* 1996; Smith 1997c), and despite Commission attempts to extend its exclusive competence in the 1996/97 IGC, the Amsterdam Treaty registered no real change. On areas such as transport policy, which have become increasingly internationalised if not globalised, the issue of competence is particularly taxing, since the fluidity of the policy context demands almost continuous renegotiation of the allocation of powers and responsibilities (Macleod *et al.* 1996, Chapter 11; see also Chapter 4 above).

Second, and allied to the issue of the division of powers, there is the problem of policy instruments. At the broadest level, the Common Market and the Customs

Union themselves constitute an international policy instrument, since they enable the Community to act in terms of market access and the regulation of trade. In many sectors of the Community's core activities, the ability to regulate, to establish standards or to enforce rules is an international fact of life. This partly explains why outsiders became sensitive to the completion of the internal market in the late 1980s, when it appeared that this was to be undertaken in such a way as to disadvantage non-EC firms and other groupings (Hufbauer 1990; Ishikawa 1990; Harrison 1994; Hocking and Smith 1997). Again though, many of the policy instruments are shared between the EC and member states, and they can operate at a number of internationally significant levels. For example, despite many years of Community activity, there remain important potential variations between investment regimes in different EU member states, or in the enforcement of regulatory policies (Kassim and Menon 1996; Majone 1996a, 1996b).

In many ways, the international activities of the EU can be seen as constituting a multilevel and continuous negotiation. On a wide range of issues, the member states and the European institutions have to negotiate not only before they 'go international' but also whilst international negotiations or policy-making processes are taking place. This was one of the predominant features of the negotiations in the Uruguay Round (Paemen and Bensch 1995; Woolcock and Hodges 1996), but it is also characteristic for example of negotiations for the accession of new members, which inevitably entail complex trade-offs among existing member states (Cameron, F. 1995; Preston 1995, 1997). It would be a mistake to see the EU as uniquely complicated in this respect, since US foreign economic and security policies are also subject to a process of continuous and often disabling internal negotiations (Destler 1980; Kegley and Wittkopf 1996). With the EU, though, there is a distinctive flavour, imparted by the fact that in the international arena it has few of the conventional instruments of coercion. It has thus been, in foreign policy as elsewhere, almost exclusively a diplomatic actor operating through a variety of technical and other specialised channels.

The burden of the discussion above is that, in effect, it is possible to discern at least three distinct modes of external policy-making in the EU (Smith 1996b, pp. 256–59). First, there is 'Community policy-making': the Community-based methods rooted in the treaties and in the grant of competences to European institutions. Second, there is 'Union policy-making': the mode of policy-making reflecting the coexistence of Community and intergovernmental mechanisms, and typical of CFSP, where the Community and the Commission are associated with the process but not in any position of assured competence. Finally, there is what might be called 'negotiated order': the amalgam of short- and long-term negotiation and bargaining processes which characterises a great deal of EU activity on a day-to-day basis, and which intersects with the explosion of negotiated frameworks at the international level.

The result of this sometimes uneasy coexistence can be uncertainty about the international role and status of the EU, as already noted. Because of the need for complex policy bargains, and because of the interconnectedness between the internal affairs of the Union and the world arena, policy cannot easily be insulated or approached in a rational and technical manner. This is true not only in what might be described as the core functions of the Community, but also in the area of CFSP. But to state this invites the response: such difficulties are often character-istic of policy made at the national level – or of international policy-making by national governments – and the EU is by no means unique in suffering from problems of coherence and coordination. The expanding scope and scale of external policy, and linkages not only between policy sectors but also across levels from the local to the global, have created problems of management and effectiveness for all would-be authoritative policy-makers. As noted in Chapter 5, the characteristics of policy outcomes have effects on the processes generated. Whilst this argument was originally made for domestic policy settings, it is difficult in the 1990s to draw the sharp distinction between the domestic and the international which was a foundation of the traditional state-centric approach to external policy-making.

If these are some of the problems attending the structure and process of EU policy-making, what are the results of policy itself? At the broadest level, it is clear that action in the world arena entails operating within an often overlapping set of markets, hierarchies and networks (see Chapters 3–4). In this situation, as indicated earlier, there is very often no set order of precedence between participants: the keys to effectiveness are the ability to gain access, to represent interests and to communicate wishes and needs as well as to reward or to punish those whose behaviour you wish to affect (Young 1972; Hanrieder 1978; Hocking and Smith 1995, Chapter 5). Here, the EU acts almost as a metaphor for the 1990s, since it seems both to reflect but also to contain and to channel many of these complex influences. The message, as before, is that it would be wrong to look for judgements on the EU's international role(s) in the shape of some ideal type of statehood: even statehood is much more complicated than that.

The EU as interlocutor and protagonist

Enough has been said about policy processes and structures to indicate that the EU suffers from distinctive but not, in principle, unique problems. It is important at this stage to extend the argument, by examining the ways in which the EU operates as an international interlocutor or protagonist, and to identify characteristic modes of action. This has been a concern of many analysts, not only of the EU itself, but also of the world political economy and security arena, in which the EU has loomed increasingly large (*Daedalus* 1991; Sandholtz and Zysman 1992; Rosecrance 1993).

If one takes as a starting point the conclusions of the previous section, then three broad points can be made about the problem of international action for the EU. First, the EU experiences problems arising from the internalisation and the externalisation of policy concerns (Noorgaard *et al.* 1993; Smith 1994b). The process of internalisation means that issues arising in the world arena can easily spill over into the domestic process of the EU and its member states. When this happens, it can produce the phenomenon of 'double-edged diplomacy' (Evans *et al.* 1993) in which bargains have to be made, justified and ratified in two different and often competing settings at one and the same time. In fact, with the EU, it is possible to discern a 'three-dimensional diplomacy', in which bargains reached at the international level have to be sold at EU level and then again at the level of the member states. This is true, for example, of negotiations about the enlargement of the Union, or of the interconnected arguments about regulatory policies in such areas as telecommunications and information technology (Freeman *et al.* 1991, Part II; Sandholtz 1992; Preston 1995, 1997). The process of externalisation entails the spilling over of internal EU issues in the form of international policy or action. This may be a way of diffusing conflict at the EU level, but it may also severely limit the effectiveness and adaptability of EU policies because they are hostage to internal forces. One particularly contentious example of such processes – already noted – was the debate about whether to negotiate with the breakaway Yugoslav states of Croatia and Slovenia during 1991 and early 1992; a process in which the assertiveness of German policies played a central if contested role (Owen 1995; Crawford 1996; Gow 1997).

Second, the EU experiences difficulties of policy sharing and policy control, which arise out of, and also feed into, the nature of multilevel diplomacy. Within the EU, there are problems of policy sharing when the member states are unwilling or unable to sign up to specific actions, but also when they are willing to sign up but unwilling to dedicate the necessary resources. This is particularly problematic in the CFSP area, where before the Amsterdam Treaty of 1997 there were no settled budgetary arrangements for joint actions carried out in the name of the Union (Pappas and Vanhoonacker 1996; Duff 1997). There are also problems of policy sharing between the EU and its international partners, given the persistence of member state autonomy in important areas, and the temptation for outsiders to exploit potential internal divisions within the EU. A particularly sharp example was provided during the mid-1990s by the problem of 'open skies agreements', which the United States negotiated with individual EU member states despite the Commission's efforts to establish Community competence in the area (Staniland 1995). However, in many ways, both of these forms of the problem are characteristic not only of the EU but also of the 1990s: the emphasis on international cooperation and the building of institutions for policy sharing or coordination runs alongside the desire for national autonomy and the satisfaction of national demands.

Such problems demonstrate the difficulties of policy consistency in a highly interdependent world arena, where political and economic systems are penetrated and where domestic institutional and other constraints intersect with global forces (Smith and Woolcock 1993, Chapter 1). From the perspective of the EU, it could as easily be argued that the Union is a creative adaptation to this set of conditions as it could that the Union is on the way to becoming a unique form of international actor or a European superstate (see Chapter 3). This is a rather more complex and messy way of looking at the international role of the Union, but it is arguably more in line with the awkward reality of the 1990s.

If this accounts for the imperfections and limitations of much of the EU's international action, what does it tell us about the kind of interlocutor or protagonist the EU has been or is likely to be? In Chapter 3, it was noted that the EU is both very attractive as an international partner but also a source of considerable uncertainty and ambiguity in the international and European arenas. It appears from what has already been said above that part of this ambiguity arises from the complexity and messiness of the processes by which the EU's international action is generated, and a parallel complexity in the European and world arenas.

It is thus not surprising that a number of scholars have attempted to deal with what Chris Hill (1993, 1998) has termed the 'capability-expectations gap' in exploring the international role of the EU. From this underlying mismatch between, on the one hand, an implicit statist model of foreign policy and international action, and, on the other hand, the multidimensional nature of EU international involvement, it is possible to deduce a plurality of possible international roles for the Union. One way of doing this is to stress the international demands to which the EC initially had to respond, and the functions it came to fulfil because of its resource and structural power: the stabilisation of western Europe, the management of world trade, the reshaping of north–south relations, the provision of a second 'western voice' in the Cold War system (Hill 1993). As was seen in Chapter 3, none of these was without its problems.

In the post-Cold War era, Hill discerns a number of possible future roles or functions for the EU: replacement of the Soviet Union in a new order, regional pacifier, global intervenor, mediator, bridge between rich and poor, joint supervisor of the world economy (Hill 1993, 1998). It is thus possible to identify, partly by deduction from the changes taking place in the world arena, the need for functions to be performed by the EU. The question is, though, in the light of the previous discussion in this chapter, to what extent will the EU be capable of, or willing to provide, these services for the broader international order? Hill himself noted that the system of international involvement and action generated by the EU has a number of intersecting axes: national foreign policies as against collective action, political as against military and economic concerns. What these produce is a set of subsystems of action and concern among EU members (and, it might be added, in the case of international economic policy, amongst both public and private actors). There is thus both a danger of over-extension of the EU's role from what is a shifting base of legitimacy and authority, and over-simplification of both the challenges and the potential lines of action confronting the Union.

A further question should be asked though: to what extent does the ambiguity of the EU's international role arise from matters of values or identity, as opposed to the mechanisms of policy and policy-making or the capacity to convert potential into action? The establishment of the original Communities was implanted firmly into the Cold War system, and thus could be assumed to express a set of international values in line with those of the 'west' and the 'free world'. Not only this, but the Communities were embedded into the 'multilateral system' of international economy for which the shorthand term 'Bretton Woods system' is most often used. In crucial ways, though, the Communities were a challenge to the multilateral system and indirectly to the concept of the 'free world' as a unified US-led entity. General de Gaulle saw this as clearly as anyone, and it was the basis of his challenge to US hegemony during the 1960s, particularly the Americans' dominance of the world trading and monetary systems (Calleo 1970, 1987). But the Gaullist challenge was also to the European Communities. On the one hand, de Gaulle resisted the idea that a divided Europe (a key foundation of the Communities) was a permanent fact of international life. On the other hand, he also resisted the notion that the Communities had a duty to enter fully into the freeing up of world trade, if necessary against their short-term interests. Inasmuch as the Communities constituted one of the key parts in the Cold War jigsaw, the Gaullist challenge was implicitly to them as well as to Washington.

The issue of values took another form as the 1970s and 1980s unfolded. Increasingly, it appeared to Americans and others that the Community was prepared to let commerce drive its international orientation rather than political imperatives. Three episodes in particular underlined this divergence of values. First, the Middle East War of 1973 and its aftermath, when it appeared that the European desire for oil and economic links with Arab countries took priority over the US desire for commitment to Israel and opposition to 'oil power'. These frictions coincided with the US initiative through the so-called 'Year of Europe' to reinvigorate the EC–US partnership, and with the earliest of EC attempts to define a distinctive international role (Smith 1978; Allen and Smith 1983). Partly on this basis, it became an article of faith for some EC enthusiasts that almost any distinct EC role would be in opposition to major elements of US international policy.

The onset of the 'second cold war' in the late 1970s, when on several occasions the Community and its members resisted demands for economic sanctions against Iran, the Soviet Union and others, provides a second case in point. As before, the accusation was made that the commercial priorities of EC member states and companies took precedence over western solidarity and resistance to aggression. Not only this, but it was argued more broadly that the Communities could no longer escape from the responsibilities implied by their growing international profile; in effect, that there was a moral imperative for the EC to take a more active role in international political and security issues as well as in the management of the world economy (Kolodziej 1980–81; Freedman 1983; Allen and Smith 1990). The Reaganite offensive against the Soviet Union in the early 1980s thus saw fiercer European resistance to US demands for support than even in the late 1970s. The US imposition of an embargo on strategic exports to the Soviet Union and other countries, particularly in relation to the Soviet–west European natural gas pipeline project, entailed the extra-territorial extension of US legislation in ways that were bound to evoke opposition both from the EC and from member governments.

In addition, Americans in particular suspected the Communities of a form of neo-colonialism in their relations with Third World countries, particularly through the Lomé Conventions. The building of a complex set of preferential trading agreements, accompanied by continuing attempts to maintain a presence in Africa and parts of Asia, represented not only a commercial threat to US interests but also in some cases the pursuit of an openly political or cultural agenda. The image of an economic entity based on introspective, potentially protectionist and possible neo-colonial values can be overstated, but there is no doubt that it is not simply a caricature. At the same time, the Europeans themselves were assiduously propagating the notion of 'civilian power', which at times became extended into the idea of 'civilising power': the inescapable implication being that the Communities were less threatening and better partners than the superpowers (Hill 1990).

This issue of values – what to make of the Cold War and of Europe's role in it, and what priority to give to commerce as opposed to security – had a profound shaping influence on the role played by the EC in the Cold War and in the development of the global economy. As its capacity to act and to interact grew, the Community found itself unavoidably coming into contact if not into collision with some rather difficult questions of principle and ideology. It is not surprising in this context that almost the first episode in which the EPC mechanism produced a coordinated and effective EC diplomatic position was the Helsinki Conference on Security and Cooperation in Europe, of 1975: a conference that was in many ways vital to the reshaping of conceptions of Europe that eventually contributed to the landslide of 1989 and thereafter (von Goll 1982).

The problems of the 1990s are no simpler in this respect. The Single Market Programme raised for some the spectre of 'fortress Europe', but the outcome of the Uruguay Round restored at least some faith in 'world partner Europe', the Commission's favoured version. At least in this respect, the role and position of the EU seemed to have stabilised by the mid-1990s (Piening 1997, Chapter 1). Far more taxing were the problems of the 'new Europe', in which the EU was a central focus of both attraction and uncertainty. Did the demands of a new European order dictate a whole-hearted commitment to extension of the EU's benefits, or did they on the other hand demand a hard-headed attention to the preservation of the EU's assets (Smith 1996a)? The negotiation of the 'Europe Agreements' with the countries of central and eastern Europe manifested all of the contradictions, with the political desire to stabilise and to encourage being offset by the economic desire to protect EU employment in a time of recession. This then fed through into the larger debate about the widening and deepening of the EU: was strengthening of the Union's institutions a prerequisite of further enlargement, or an obstacle to it because it made the gradient between member-ship and non-membership ever more difficult to scale (Preston 1995, 1997; Smith 1997a)?

It is at this point that the structure and process of policy come together with issues of values and the orientation of policy. There has been a historical ambiguity in the development of the EU relating to the balance between different modes of policy-making and implementation. Equally, there has been a tension between different images of the EU both in the broader international arena and in the European context: is it a 'fortress', a 'partner' or at least a potential 'superpower'? There is no doubt that on the basis of its resource and structural power, the EU has a central position in the world arena, but there are several important limitations built into that position, as well as a number of significant tensions. Many of these resolve themselves into a simple question, to which there is no simple answer: is the EU developing a 'real' foreign policy, and if it is, what should the organising principles of that policy be?

Towards a European Union foreign policy?

The European Communities and the EU have always been a foreign policy project. One way of assessing the progress made with this project is to judge it against the standard of a 'real' foreign policy, and effectively to check off the areas in which the Union has done well or could do better. Perhaps the clearest such attempt is that made by Chris Hill (1993) and reproduced in Table 8.1. As presented here, this could appear to be a crudely positivist view of the issues, and it must be remembered that Hill surrounds it with a sophisticated argument about the capacities and impact of the EU. It does, though, suggest ways in which not

Table 8.1 The conditions of a single foreign policy

If the EC were to acquire its own foreign policy it would need to possess the following:

(i) Basic constitutional powers over:

(a)	War and peace	(N)
(b)	Raising armed forces	(N)
(c)	Treaty-making	(N/Y – EC?)
(d)	Regulation of commerce (sanctions)	(Y?)
(e)	External borders (immigration)	(N?)
(f)	Cession or acquisition of territory (but for	(N)
	'enlargement')	(Y)

subject to:

(g)	Democratic accountability at the union level (cf. states)	(N?)
(h)	Judicial scrutiny	(N/Y – EC)

(ii) Mechanisms and policies

(a)	A single Ministry of Foreign Affairs and diplomatic service, with common missions aboard	(N)
(b)	A single intelligence service	(N)
(c)	A single set of armed services	(N)
(d)	A single development policy	(?50%)
(e)	A single cultural policy (?)	(?5%)

Source: Hill (1993). © Basil Blackwell Ltd 1993.

Note
'Y' = broadly possesses these powers/mechanisms; 'N' = not yet near; figures in brackets suggest how far down the road the EC has gone in creating a common policy. The judgements – inevitably provocative – assume observation of the CFSP provisions of Maastricht, which leaves the three European Communities intact but changes the title of the 'EEC' to 'EC'.)

only the conformity of the EU's foreign policy with the model, but also the distinctiveness of the EU's trajectory can be evaluated.

Beyond this broadly positivist approach to evaluation, it is important to pose another question. If the EC and the EU have always been a foreign policy project, by whom and to whom has the project been directed, and with what effect? In the early years of European construction, the dominant foreign policy aims were associated with core member states, particularly France and Germany. Often, these aims could have the effect of jeopardising or alternatively stimulating the development of the European integration project. In its turn, there has never been a time when the integration project was not seen as having resonances for foreign policy, either through the undermining of national foreign policies or through the strengthening of national policies as the benefits of economic recovery were appropriated for foreign policy purposes. The almost continuous debate since 1960 about this element of the European construction means that a focus simply on the 1980s and 1990s can be profoundly misleading (Allen *et al.* 1982; Pijpers *et al.* 1988).

The question 'whose foreign policy project?' has, though, become more insistent since 1980, and especially since 1989. One of the key factors in promoting its salience has undoubtedly been the perception in major EU member states that the scale and scope of foreign policy demands now outstrip the capacities of any single member state. Not only this, but the growing awareness of the linkages between the economic and security aspects of foreign policy has driven national leaders, however unwillingly, towards the recognition that they are doomed to collaborate, and to do so on an increasingly continuous and institutionalised basis. Roy Ginsberg has termed this search for a spreading of the costs and risks the 'politics of scale' (Ginsberg 1989). On the basis of national self-interest, there are thus compelling arguments for attempting to capture the economies of scale contained in an EU foreign policy, not only for the smaller and more apparently vulnerable EU member states, but also for the core states. In a paradoxical way, it could be argued that these national incentives are more powerful than the traditional argument that the development of European economic integration has reached a stage at which it needs to be supported with a conventional foreign policy.

This is not to argue that there are no obstacles to the development either of international economic policy or of foreign and security policy in the EU. As has been noted, the interconnectedness and globalisation of the world economy has created severe problems of policy control and implementation. It has also created a situation of multilayered diplomacy in which international negotiation comes to resemble a game of three-dimensional chess, and in which security issues have come to occupy more than an isolated corner of the chessboard. The EU, it could be argued, has been used to dealing with such issues for longer than any national policy machine, and thus it should be eminently well-suited to playing a central role through international economic policies in the late 1990s and the new millennium. Indeed, a best-selling treatment of the rivalry between the EU, the USA and Japan in the early 1990s argued precisely that the EU would be in a position to 'write the rulebook' for the international political economy of the new millennium (Thurow 1992, Chapter 10). But there are issues both of a practical and of a principled nature, as pointed out here, in the taking of a proactive role.

With CFSP, at least on the surface, the problems are rather different. One central question is still the one posed above: whose foreign policy project is this? The tensions, failings and disasters of policy towards the former Yugoslavia revealed the ways in which foreign and security policy can on the one hand be captured and, on the other hand, be disowned by those who should, in principle, be its closest adherents (Owen 1995; Crawford 1996; Gow 1997). There were numerous practical problems to be confronted, concerning budgetary provision, organisation and coordination of joint actions, and the infrastructure of CFSP (Pappas and Vanhoonacker 1996; Duff 1997). Not surprisingly, such considerations formed a major part of the discussions in the Reflection Group set up to prepare for the 1996–97 Intergovernmental Conference, and then of the IGC itself.

As the debate on CFSP developed during the Intergovernmental Conference, it became clear that, as in other areas of EU development, there was a basic tension between the 'evolutionary' and the 'constitutive' perspectives on the negotiations. On the one side, the French and the Germans (for example) argued that there was a need for a decisive step forward, to give new resources and institutional impetus to the CFSP. On the other hand, the British position in particular held that no such qualitative step was needed; in fact, that the brief experience with the Maastricht mechanisms mean that no major new initiative would be justified. A third dimension was added by the Nordic members, particularly Sweden: that in addition to the procedural and institutional measures debated by the 'great powers' among the EU membership, there should also be a more explicit definition of what the EU stood for, in the form of statements about human rights and related issues. As it turned out, the Amsterdam Treaty of 1997 was seen by many as a rather feeble attempt to move towards a 'real' foreign policy, but none the less it did address a number of these more practical issues, by allocating budgetary responsibility more clearly, by creating firmer administrative systems and by extending the range of tasks envisaged within the CFSP framework to include those of peace-keeping and humanitarian support (Duff 1997). In addition, however, it also allowed for the possibility of 'enhanced integration' between member states wishing to go further along the road to foreign policy action.

It is not by any means self-evident that the practical deficiencies so frequently debated have prevented the member states from doing anything that they wanted to do, or that dealing with them would produce a higher quality of policy output or policy principle. A 'maximalist' solution to the problem of CFSP in the 1996/97 IGC would have called for an immediate merging of CFSP with 'pillar 1', and for a rapid move towards incorporation of the WEU into the EU structure as the defence arm of the Union. A 'minimalist' outcome would have stressed the evolutionary nature of CFSP, and the incremental progress that has been made, quite apart from any 'constitutive' acts. The history of the SEA, however, should remind us that apparently evolutionary outcomes can have profound and far-reaching effects on institutions and behaviour in the EU context.

Conclusions

The international role of the EU tells us as much about the changing nature of statehood in the world arena as about the development of the EU itself. It also reveals that the history of the EU as an international actor is a history of ties and tensions, not only at the level of practice but also at the level of principles, and that this has not gone away in the 1990s. The EU has always, and inescapably, been a foreign policy project, but that does not mean that it is cast in the constraining mould of the statist version of foreign policy. Indeed, the Union's status as a kind of 'great experiment' has clearly had an impact on the wider Europe and on the international arena through processes of emulation and diffusion. At the same time, the features of the EU which give it the characteristics of a governance system or a 'regulatory state' have equally been 'exportable' not simply as a model for others but also through forms of international action. The debates surrounding the Amsterdam Treaty and its provisions for an 'area of peace, justice and freedom' may prove as important in this respect as those surrounding the Common Foreign and Security Policy.

In this way, the EU finds itself operating internationally on the frontier between several possible ways of international life. For some, it might appear that the Union has the 'strength of weakness', whilst for others it can never truly act internationally without the support of a full legal and political personality. For some, the EU functions as a vital part of the European security arena, both by providing a model for peace and stability and by furnishing a form of 'deep' societal security for its peoples. For others, the Union is a symptom of division and exclusion, symbolising new fault-lines in the new Europe. By occupying this ambiguous position, the international role of the EU tells us a great deal about the continuing contradictions between state and market, between polity and problem-solving, and between levels of policy-making. Above all, it demonstrates the inescapable ties and tensions between the EU 'universe' and its global environment. To return to a theme raised throughout this book, the project is unsettled, both in the sense that it has dynamism and fluidity and in the sense that it lacks a definitive outcome. As such, it is a metaphor for much international action in the global arena of the late 1990s.

Conclusions

9 A new model of internationalisation

Introduction

The aim of this volume has been to explore the dynamics of European integration since the 1980s, and to relate them to the changes that have taken place in the context of the European project. We began with a perspective on 'Unsettled Europe' which highlighted complex and interactive processes of change characterised by the renewed salience of market creation and fundamental shifts in the geopolitics of the continent. We also adopted a threefold analytical framework, based on the recognition of interconnectedness and contingency, on awareness of complex relationships between territory, identity and function, and sensitivity to the ties and tensions emerging from the process of integration itself. In this concluding chapter, the aim is to review our initial perspective and framework, and to propose what we have described as a 'European model of internationalisation'.

European integration interacts and intersects with wider processes of change in the contemporary nation state, international political economy and world politics. While at first view, 'unsettled Europe' and its many 'unsettled issues' appear as a weakness of capacity, confusion, multiple arenas, and ambiguity of form and function, the system is more settled and more robust than is assumed in conventional academic writings on integration. We need to take seriously the notion that it is the experimental and innovative nature of the European Union that enables it to respond to multiple agendas and Europe's diversity in a flexible manner. The EU is a harbinger of trends in political and economic order, locked as it is between modernity and post-modernity. The EU represents a form of deep regionalism in contrast to other regionalisms in the world.

Territory, identity and function

Part 1 of this volume explored the contexts, both conceptual and empirical, for evaluation of the European integration project. In doing so, it demonstrated that territory, identity and function are separating out and are no longer contained within the boundaries of the nation state. The role and salience of national borders are changing because of the pressures of market integration, social exchange, cross-border issues such as those of crime and environmental quality, and new conceptions of security. This in turn generates institutionalised problem-solving to facilitate market creation, and institution building for cross-border cooperation on a whole series of common problems. To national territory must be added an emerging European territoriality reflected in the trans-European networks, new approaches to spatial planning, the external borders of the Union, inter-regional cooperation, and policies on access to the territory of the Union. The emerging European territoriality is contested on many grounds. Some states, particularly the Union's island states, cling to the maintenance of boundaries and control. Even on continental Europe, where controls have been eliminated or much reduced, opposition to porous borders can easily be mobilised by raising sensitive issues concerning immigration, transnational crime or the domestic drug policies of neighbouring states. That said, the pressures for collective action all point to the growing salience of the collective Union space and not just national territory. Just how extensive this territory will become depends on how far south and east the Union extends. This in turn will impact on conceptions of Europe and the EU. The salience of territory, in contemporary Europe, may begin at the national level but does not end there.

Changes to boundaries are accompanied by changes in the bonding capacity of national identity. Identity politics play a significant role in this phase of European integration. This arises because of attempts by Europe to develop an international identity, the deliberate effort to fashion a European identity by deploying traditional state-building strategies in the EU, the fit between state identities and integration, European regionalism, and the growing challenge of immigration in most EU societies. The collapse of communism and the process of state-building that ensued highlight the existence of significant minorities in many European states, particularly in east central Europe and the former Soviet Union. Identity issues are salient in domestic politics, to the enlargement of the Union, the continental management of minority problems and the international role of the Union. The European Union has varied effects on different identity questions in different parts of Europe, but its intersection with the more general reshaping of the identities of individuals, states, cities and regions is unquestionable.

Our analysis of European states and nations highlighted the functional pressures on contemporary governance with a reduction in the steering capacity of national governments and their search for new patterns and modes of governance. Governments have reallocated policy responsibilities to lower levels of government, to collective problem solving in the EU, to international regimes and to the market. Our analysis did not fully accept the 'hollowing out' thesis, which argues that contemporary states are in crisis and are being consistently undermined. Whilst we accept that the move from organised to disorganised capital, and the processes of economic internationalisation outlined in the chapter on the international political economy, have significantly undermined the capacity of states for macroeconomic management, a number of caveats are in order. Even in economic policy, governments continue to have a range of instruments, particularly supply side policies, which have a major impact on the competitiveness of their economies. Notwithstanding fiscal constraints, governments continue to have a large capacity to tax, to employ and to regulate significant areas of the public and private lives of their citizens. Furthermore, national welfare states continue to be the main arena of solidarity. There is still considerable vigour in the nexus between economy, society and polity at national level, albeit with intensifying international and domestic pressures. In areas of 'hard security' and world politics, there is not unexpectedly a continuing and central role for governments, but even here there is pressure for collective action and for increased attention to the kind of 'soft power' exemplified by the EU.

The ties and tensions of European integration

The ties and tensions outlined in the Introduction between states and markets, between the EU as a polity and a problem solving arena, between different levels of policy-making and between the EU universe and its wider global environment are clearly visible in the collective arena of the Union. How these ties and tensions are being played out affects the characteristics of the emerging European system, not only at the EU level but also at the broader level of European order. Part 2 of the volume, in its analysis of governance, market, money and the international role of the Union, was designed to explore the different ties and tensions that fashion the dynamic of integration.

Our analysis of governance in Chapter 5 was primarily focused on the ties and tensions between different levels of policy-making – the regional, national and European – which are central to decision-making in the Union and the process of constitution-building. A central theme of the chapter was that governance in the Union rests largely on embedding the national in the European and the European in the national by a complex process of Europeanisation, particularly of public policy-making; this is accomplished by a system of what might be termed 'thick' rather than 'thin' institutionalisation. The second focus of the chapter was on the ties and tensions between the Union as a problem-solving arena and as a polity. While the Union has been a problem-solving arena par excellence, the current phase of integration is characterised by the emergence of polity issues on the European Union agenda.

The chapter on the market dealt primarily with the relationship between the EU as a union of states and as an international market area. While it has elements of a union of states, the substance of union, cross-border market activity, is something over which states have limited control. Indeed, the development of the union of states has been prompted by changing relations between member states and the market which, in turn, is unsettling them further. The governance of the market is characterised by a technocratic problem-solving approach, often in segmented sectoral networks, but which depends on the EU being a nascent polity. The various elements of economic integration – the internal market, the social dimension, cohesion, competitiveness and employment – illustrate the diverse and tense relation between EU-level policy and multilevel policy. The complexity of this enmeshing defies any neat division between EU and national competencies. Finally, the tension between the EU's internal concerns and its global role pervades many aspects of economic integration, in both policy and commercial spheres. Corporate responses to the SEM indicate that wherever European firms are emerging in European industries to serve European markets, a significant global dimension is usually found.

Our chapter on money also illustrated the significance of all four ties and tensions. The origin and motivation of the EMU project is frequently considered to reveal a tension, or even contradiction, between the political and the economic. A widespread view is that the economic logic of EMU is weak and the project must be understood as essentially political. We dispute this view, showing that there is a strong, long-standing, widely-held, diverse and increasing economic motivation for EMU. Where motivation is concerned, there are more ties than tensions between the political and the economic. But the effects of EMU undoubtedly reveal tensions between the EU as a union of states and a market. The arrangements for technocratic management of exchange rates, with ECOFIN and the various monetary institutions increasingly providing a problem-solving arena, stand in definite tension with the feeling that a European economic and monetary union requires more of a polity, in which institutions are accountable and reflect values and identity. The tension between EU and national policy-making has been 'resolved' in a quite novel, and unproven, way. This involves centralisation of monetary policy, decentralisation of fiscal policy and a complex system of EU-level economic policy guidelines and rules. Finally, EMU is a classic illustration of the ties and tensions between the EU's internal concerns and its role in the global environment. Changes in the international monetary system played a major role in driving, but also constraining, European monetary union. EMU, in turn, constitutes a profound change in the global environment, with effects that have yet to be discovered.

In considering the international role of the Union, we highlighted the ties and tensions between the EU universe and the wider global system. Our analysis focused on the concept of actorness in relation both to the EU and changing conceptions of statehood by asking how 'statelike' is the EU in the world arena, and whether statehood is the standard to which the EU should be aspiring. In addition, the chapter draws attention to multilevel policy-making by analysing the complexity and messiness of the Union foreign policy processes. The analysis concluded that the Union is a partially formed international actor but one of potentially great significance and impact. There is, however, a substantial disparity between the Union's resources, its international role and its capacity to exert effective influence in the global system.

The emerging system: towards a model of internationalisation

As indicated above, the analysis in this volume points to the emergence in Europe of a form of deep regionalism in terms of the scope of collective action, the level of institutionalisation and the normative underpinnings of the European project. European regionalism was and remains highly contingent on the political, economic and geopolitical context within which it develops. The distinct configuration of Europe after the Second World War led to a search for order and welfare, neither of which could be given primacy. Questions of political order (both internal and continental), political economy and security combined in the European project in a distinctive manner. The search for order and welfare are no less compelling in contemporary Europe following the collapse of the Soviet empire and the demands of an internationalising and globalising economy. Our investigation indicates that, to the imperatives of order and welfare, must now be added crucial issues of polity.

Betweenness and becoming

A central objective of the volume was to begin to characterise the emerging European system by asking just what kind of economic and political order might be emerging from the process of integration in changing circumstances. In this regard, the volume clearly identifies the 'betweenness' of the European Union, it hovers between politics and diplomacy, between the international and the domestic, between states and markets and between government and governance. We are faced with a form of political and economic order that is characterised by considerable ambiguity and incompleteness, at least when analysed from the perspective of national political order. Viewed from this perspective, the Union appears weak in terms of political authority, capacity, resources and legitimacy, whereas viewed from the perspective of global governance the Union is both vigorous and robust. Viewed from the perspective of representative democratic government, the Union is remote and undemocratic. Yet from the perspective of traditional diplomacy and 'balance of power' systems, the Union is based on law, regularised procedures, and openness. Put simply, recognition of 'betweenness' as well as interconnectedness and contingency is central to understanding the character of the Union. The European Union does not conform to the practices and patterns of a domestic economy or polity. Nor does it conform to traditional international diplomacy or multilateral trade liberalisation. This in turn leads to a sense that it might be better to abandon the notion that the Union is *something* and to consider it always in the *process of becoming*. Moreover, we need to abandon the notion that the Union is evolving towards traditional forms of political order. The characteristics of 'betweenness' and the process of becoming highlight the problem of how we should judge the Union. The analysis in this volume suggests that statehood is not the standard against which the EU should be judged, nor is it the standard to which it should aspire, because statehood itself is the subject of change and challenge.

Constitutive agreement and evolutionary transformation

Running through Part 2 of the volume is an appreciation that, in seeking to characterise the nature of the system, we need to appreciate the complex relationship between 'constitutive' events, such as treaty change and the framing of the foundation rules, and the evolutionary effect of market creation, involvement in external events and the establishment of policy regimes. Should the Union be understood as the result of an initial, over-arching, constitutive agreement or the product of an ongoing negotiated process? The duality between plan and evolution is paralleled by a number of other dualities: between wholeness and fragmentation; between incremental change and radical transformation; between continuous advance and the see-saw of progress and regress; between the pull of a supranational engine and the push of government agreement; between the internal market as one substantive piece of learning and the new Europe as a learning machine.

The development of the EU can be seen as dependent on initial, over-arching, constitutive agreement – not only on the re-establishment of a democratic and liberal order in Europe but, more specifically, on the creation of an ever-deepening and enlarging common market in a context of widespread welfare. The progress achieved is hard to understand without reference to the 'avowed aim' of the founding treaty, a 'community of values' and 'over-arching principles of good government'. Against this holist view has to be placed the prevalence of gradualism, evolution, fragmentation and the uneven development of EU policies. Clearly, progress on some things can be made without progress on others, and certainly without progress on all.

Each perspective has significant weaknesses. The holist view risks seeing deeper and wider agreement at the outset, than was really there. Its emphasis on the over-arching agreement can rob events since 1957 of all real life, being no more than the implementation of a plan. In over-emphasising ideas, and under-doing interests and material factors, it can be seen as a kind of 'upward reductionism'. But the incrementalist perspective can be characterised as a kind of 'downward reductionism'. The development of the EU is hard to understand if we see the EU only working *up* from day-to-day interaction, or even from package deals between key governments.

Our emphasis on the experimental aspect of the EU recognises the element of over-arching agreement, but in a way that allows for subsequent development. The initial constitutive agreement reflected an avowed aim of 'an ever closer union'. The substantive goals were stated in general terms and, as we discussed in Chapter 6 on market integration, their implementation was made conditional on subsequent negotiation. It aimed to reassure national concerns precisely by constraining the effect of one nationality on another. As Weiler says:

> the substance of membership is in a commitment to the shared values of the Union as expressed in its constituent documents, inter alia, to the duties and rights of a civic society covering discrete areas of public life, a commitment to membership in a polity which privileges exactly the opposite of nationalism – those human features which transcend the differences of organic ethnoculturalism.

(Weiler 1996)

Whereas the national is organic, the European is reflective, deliberative and rational.

The constitutive agreement can be seen as essential, but its significance lies in *agreement to ongoing negotiation*, more than an elaborated model of a European economy, society and polity. The over-arching agreement was thick enough to get the ball rolling, but thin enough to accommodate the diversity of situations, interests and cultures. Most importantly, it was sufficient to create a new set of collective institutions. The formation of the Community involves member states creating a deliberate mutual vulnerability, in which, as Sbragia says, 'they submit to one another' (Sbragia 1992). This would be an enormous leap in the dark, if it occurred without a 'constitutional order', which establishes institutional arrangements 'that encourage the parties to make themselves mutually vulnerable by limiting the dangers of vulnerability' (Sabel 1995, p. 101). It is the institutional arrangements that provide the crucial link between the constitutive agreement and the ongoing evolution of the Union. Their key features are outlined in our discussion of governance, in the next section.

The process is one in which ongoing and intense collaboration and deliberation between member states can redefine their shared understanding, their interests and their identities. However, the change in identities does not yield a uniform European identity and does not yield blind loyalty. The socialisation – like socialisation generally – is not complete, not determining. Indeed, even the over-arching 'agreement', which started and informs the process, is itself subject to re-examination, as evidenced in the major treaty revisions. Yet those re-examinations have particular features – preservation of the *acquis* being a condition for re-opening discussions of goals and means. In the reformulation of the treaties the EU re-assigns functions, taking account of the nature and limits of its own peculiar competence (reflected in high levels of decentralisation and delegation). Indeed, involvement in deliberation, analysis, interaction and monitoring extends beyond the member states. In recent years, this has yielded genuinely innovative approaches to governance – marked by high levels of delegation.

Analytically, our approach is one that is sufficiently flexible to encompass the undoubted *continuity* of integration, the dramatic *deepening* of interpenetration (of both markets and policy) and the *qualitative shift* in patterns of governance. Indeed, there was not just development, but *transformation*. But that transformation need not be seen as peculiar to the EU or a product of European integration *per se*. The global context changed, the political economy of the member states changed and ideas about public policy changed – to such an extent that they forced something of a re-definition of the over-arching agreement of the European project in the 1980s.

The dynamic of European integration is replete with tensions – between initial agreement and ongoing negotiation, between continuous evolution and radical shift, between incremental change and transformation, between fragmented policy domains and general principles – which shape and mould the EU system. Our analysis leads us to a sense that a grand European settlement is neither feasible nor in many ways desirable. Rather, it is the capacity of the Union for experimentation of all kinds – institutions, policies, patterns of governance, modes of representation – that allows it to manage issues in a flexible and contingent manner; no dossier is ever closed, no final constitutional settlement is in sight. Our emphasis on experimentation, pragmatism and incrementalism does not blind us to processes of deep change in Europe. We are led to conclude that there is a reconfiguration of territory, identity and function occurring in Europe that is remoulding Europe's nation states in fundamental ways.

Interpreting European public policy

It is clear that European public policy differs significantly from the economic theory of federalism, from the policy pattern in existing continental federations, from the economic instruments of a classic unitary state and from the policy scope of the post-war European welfare state. Policies that involve large expenditure or a high level of state authority – such as welfare, health, and education – remain resolutely at member state level. Taxation, even on activities or assets that are mobile, remains predominantly at member state level. Indeed, major policies with continental level, or even global, relevance – such as macroeconomic management, strategic trade policy and security – have been the subject of very limited purposive action at EU level. At the same time, the EU is involved in many local policies, pursuing economic and social regeneration and environmental protection. EU policy has an unusual constitutional status. The treaties list policies and define their goals and instruments in considerable detail. Consequently, economic and social policy is a treaty/constitutional matter in the EU, in a way in which it is not in most states. The result is that the pattern of EU policies in any area can look strange – not conforming to any coherent economic, political or diplomatic doctrine, nor to any traditional notion of the policy competencies normally found in a unitary state or federation.

Europe's unusual pattern of policy has been explained in various ways. First, it used commonly be said that the EU is *sui generis*. Second, Pelkmans says that the 'The political logic of ever more ambitious economic integration among otherwise independent countries is radically different from the logic of (economic) decentralisation in a mature federation' (Pelkmans 1997, p. 47). Third, for many, the EU's unusual policy portfolio is explained by the resistance of nation states and the predominance of intergovernmental bargaining. A fourth suggestion is that the EU policy portfolio is explained by the fact that the EU is a neo-liberal project that is re-balancing economic and social policy in the interests of capital (Steeck and Schmitter 1991; Streeck 1996). Fifth, Hirst has observed that the EU is not 'a scaled up version of the nation state'. It can do some things nation states cannot do, but cannot do other things that remain the province of the states and regions. While the EU could sustain an expansionary macroeconomic policy, it cannot create 'either the legitimacy for the specific policies of public spending or credit creation necessary to sustain such a policy or the forms of co-operation of the social interests necessary to implement it' (Hirst 1994, pp. 139–40). Each of these explanations has some force. Yet each seems to underestimate the significance of the emerging EU policy, both procedurally and substantively.

The view that the EU is *sui generis* is no longer considered an adequate explanation. While there is certainly a difference between the *integration* of states into a federal-type organisation and the *decentralisation* or *disintegration* of a large political and territorial unit, it is not clear that 'the political logic . . . is radically different'. Indeed, there is a definite parallel between the development of the EU and historical emergence of federations (Armstrong and Bulmer 1998, p. 46). The similarities and difference can only be seen if we allow for the diversity of federal arrangements, and the possibility for considerable originality in institutional design (Sbragia 1992, p. 260).

Is the absence of certain functions at European level – such as macroeconomic policy or foreign policy in a state sense – still adequately explained by member states' jealous guarding of sovereignty, or because they are 'sensitive in domestic politics'? (Pelkmans 1997, p. 30). This explanation only retains its force if there is some evidence of member states' will or ability to follow their own road. For example, in the past decade, the absence of macroeconomic policy at EU level is less a result of national wilfulness, than of a loss of faith in macroeconomic remedies, national passivity and the absence of clear principles that might inform an EU-level macroeconomic policy.

Can the pattern of European policy be explained as the victory of neo-liberalism? The evidence – on working conditions and welfare – is complex. European social policy is not unambiguously a 'floor' or a 'ceiling', but a mixture of both. In the European periphery, the integration process has involved a significant raising of the rights and expectations of many workers. This has to be weighed in the scales with the pressure on rights and standards in the northern European core. It cannot be said that there has been an unambiguous lowering of labour standard, rights and norms in Europe. While there has undoubtedly been a worldwide re-balancing in favour of capital, existing class-based analyses do not do justice to European or international developments (Grahl and Teague 1990; Schmitter and Streeck 1991; Scott 1995; Marks and McAdam 1996). Patterns of economic and social organisation and solidarity are changing too fast, and in unprecedented ways, to predict which macro-social class interest at European level gains and which loses from the different elements of the European integration project.

The final explanation, which compares the capacity of member states and the Union in both economic and political spheres, is more promising. Hirst's distinction between functional effectiveness, legitimacy and cooperation is an important corrective to both federalist and nationalist perspectives. In economic and other matters, the Union lacks a centre of political authority, capable of achieving some of the functions exercised by the nation state. However, it is no longer clear that legitimacy is generated entirely within the political sphere, and transferred to the economy and economic policy. Consequently, it is no longer clear that legitimacy can only be generated at national level. This is not to assert the emergence of popular politics at European level. Legitimacy is generated, in part, by effectiveness and can flow from the economy to politics. Firms can be repositories of legitimacy, through their ability to generate employment. Consequently, the neat coincidence – or even hierarchy – of territory, identity and function has been disturbed. Again, macroeconomic policy provides a good example. In several member states, such as Italy and Ireland, the legitimacy of national policy is closely tied to EU monetary and fiscal principles and deep involvement in the EU policy process.

The key to a more satisfactory explanation of Europe's unusual pattern of policy lies in adopting a wide conception of governance and exploring, rather than assuming, the traditional relationships between function, territory and identity. The conventional approach is to focus on the *amount* of policy competence at EU level, and *amount* of policy autonomy remaining at national level. As member states have discovered, it is equally relevant to consider the *pattern* of policy-making and implementation. Even where the EU has a role, this can range from expenditure of EU own-resources, through legally binding directives, coordination of national policy approaches, to analysis and discussion of European issues. Even where member states' sovereignty is protected by the treaties, states experience a decline in their ability to design, direct, administer and monitor public programmes. Even where member state autonomy is limited, there are certain patterns of deliberation, policy formation and imple-mentation that are more effective. Consequently, in any given policy area, the existence/non-existence of an EU role is less interesting than the nature of that involvement, its interaction with national approaches and the pattern of national response to Europeanisation. We see the emerging European pattern as a new model of internationalisation. It is internationalisation of public policy occurring in a new context. The new context is one of autonomous globalisation of many aspects of business and culture and new forms of governance in many spheres.

The characteristics of the emerging system

Governance and polity

The European Union represents a form of international governance that includes processes and practices that are normally confined within a national context. From the outset, the EU involved a search for a more vigorous governance capacity than found in traditional international organisations. The aim was to re-connect diplomacy and politics, to transform nation states into member states. By becoming member states, Europe's nation states opened themselves to a deliberate and highly conscious mutual vulnerability, as outlined in Chapter 5. An agreed constitutional order, in treaty form, provided the safeguards and protections that enabled national political leaders to take a leap in the dark towards a shared future. However, the original treaties were transformed into a constitutional charter for the Union by the European Court of Justice and the Union's legal order assumed a federal character. In this way, law became the main source of public power in the system and central to the Union's regulatory capacity.

The Union's system of collective governance has produced what we defined in Chapter 5 as a 'prismatic political system', in which rays of activity and authority are scattered or focused more or less effectively through institutions and social forces. Rather than amassing extensive and autonomous political authority, the Union gradually altered the exercise of national political authority by enmeshing the member states in a web of collaboration and cooperation. This is defined in this volume as embedding the national in the European and the European in the national. The member states became locked into the system and were exposed to varied processes of Europeanisation. The implications of integration were taken inside each national system not just as an issue in domestic politics but as a source of regime change and institutional adaptation. Europeanisation exposes the member states to the impact of supranational influences on their national systems of policy-making and on the content of public policy. The Union is not just a new level of governance but has fostered innovative approaches to governance. The openness to Europeanisaton and adaptation to growing internationalisation varies from member state to member state and within states among different social groups and institutions. In some states and among some social forces, a nostalgia for the grand era of the west European state is still evident. The balance between national and shared European competence is thus highly complex and contested in the Union. In some fields the fit between legally granted powers and actual policy activity is close, but in others the Union exercises a significant policy role without a strong legal mandate. In yet other areas, the granting of authority to the Union does not fit with fast moving technological developments or international regulation.

EU public policy-making is non-hierarchical, characterised by ongoing negotiations, and segmented in different institutional settings and policy networks. Collective institutions bind the fragmented system of European governance and have given it much of its durability and flexibility. New problems have led to the creation of new procedures and institutional mechanisms. From the outset, the Union's institutional system displayed considerable dynamism – additional voting procedures, comitology, direct elections, the establishment of the European Council, new legislative procedures, additional channels of representation and new institutions. Informal institutional procedures have been equally important – stopping the clock, conversations in corners, multiple bilaterals, tours of capitals, letters from the heads of government, informal council meetings and so on. The institutional density of the system has had powerful socialisation effects on national actors. Senior office holders, officials and even their families are drawn into a web of business and social meetings. The interests and even the identities of national actors, who are involved in the iterative process of European negotiations, are shaped by European institutions and by the unending process of collective governance. The pursuit of the national interest and the collective European interest becomes blurred. National interests are redefined and refocused, where possible, on the European or collective interest. Actors' interests, preferences and even identities are reshaped in subtle ways, not only in areas of economic and administrative activity but also in areas of 'soft security' and even some limited aspects of defence policy.

European institutions, particularly the Commission, produce analyses of possibilities, ongoing deliberation and continuous interaction. The institutions – like others in certain economic or political spheres – 'transform transactions into discussions, for discussion is precisely the process by which parties come to reinterpret themselves and their relations to each other by elaborating a common understanding of the world' (Sabel 1994). Shared principles and innovative approaches to governance, such as mutual recognition or partnership, contribute new ideas that assist in the search for a shared understanding of the problems to be dealt with. The EU system, when working effectively, moves actors from a 'bargaining mode' to a 'problem-solving mode' of governance (Majone 1996b). Problem-solving governance is characterised by an openness to deliberation, experimentation, learning-by-doing and evaluation. In the Union this is aided by the delegation of discussion to a level at which the participants know what they are talking about. Hence, in the EU, the detailed technical negotiations are undertaken by Commission advisory groups and Council working parties. The process is animated by the politics of the pragmatist, the expert and the myriad of committees in the system. The Court, prompted by member states, citizens or firms, produces a form of monitoring of member states' performance and a degree of reason-giving. This helps not only by enforcing EC laws, but also by allowing member states to make non-conditional agreements.

The growing intensity of the Union's policy process and the expansion in the policy remit of the Union has greatly enhanced the salience of the Brussels arena of politics. The extension of political space from the domestic to the European created additional channels of representation and voice. Mobilisation has been a distinct feature of the dynamic of integration since the mid-1980s and has contributed to internationalisation and transnationalism in Europe. The mobilisation of interest organisations, pressure groups, regions, cities, even the churches, in the Brussels space takes national actors out of their member state containers, provides them with new strategic opportunities but also a more complex and diffuse political environment. The nested games within each state/society nexus are augmented by transnational connected games. In viewing the EU as a novel form of governance, we need to extend our conceptual framework – not only from a 'state centric' approach to a 'multilevel' one, but also to the emergence in the Union of non-state, associative forms of governance.

The 'betweenness' of the Union, the relationship between the over-arching framework and its day-to-day evolution, its contested nature and the degree of diversity that it must accommodate, all serve to enhance the patchy and partial nature of European integration. The Union's system of loosely coupled collective governance, which works on the basis of considerable decentralisation and delegation, faces a continuous challenge of effectiveness both in systemic terms and in relation to its policy regimes. The politics of integration are replete with instances of lowest common denominator bargaining and national obstruction, as the member states grapple with the impact of internationalisation on their domestic systems or national preferences. A key dossier may be held hostage to national party competition and domestic electoral cycles. Member states can and do extract costly side payments in return for agreement on systematic change. Moreover, the need to accommodate diverse interests and preferences produces tortuous and tardy negotiations. The absence of agreement on an over-arching constitutional framework leads to iterative processes of treaty change that result in an extremely complex constitutional order and a myriad of decision-rules across the pillars. It is not difficult to find evidence of weakness and limited capacity in the EU. In fact, the pervasive media portrayal of the Union inevitably high-lights weakness and conflict. The Union faces limits to its authority, limits to the carrying capacity of its institutions, and limits to the level of agreement possible among the member states. It seeks to overcome these limits by innovation, experimentation, socialisation, institution-building, patience and flexibility. The evidence in this volume suggests that there is considerable strength and capacity in the EU system. Crafted in the crucible of global and national change, the Union has demonstrated a capacity for deep integration, innovative policy-making and a responsiveness to changing geopolitics. A cursory look at its achievements since the mid-1980s confirms its ability to engage in significant strategic initiatives, notably the single market project and EMU, while enlarging and altering the Union's financial system and expanding cooperation in justice and home affairs. During periods when neither the economic or political environment is conducive to a deepening of integration, the strategy is to maintain the existing *acquis communautaire*, avoid big initiatives and concentrate on changes in discrete areas of policy.

Whereas effectiveness was a constant challenge to the Union in the past, it was assumed that the system could rest on the authority and legitimacy of the member states consenting, in the form of treaties ratified by national constitutional provisions, to the creation of the system. Legitimacy was also bound up with the Union as a source of order and welfare. In the 1990s, democracy and legitimacy emerged as key themes in the contemporary discourse on European integration. This distinctive arena of governance raises old and fundamental questions of political theory, whereas no such discourse is apparent in relation to the World Trade Organisation or the UN. This in itself highlights the distinctive nature of internationalisation in the Union. The debate stems from strong normative concerns about contemporary governance at the national and European levels. The challenge of democracy in the Union is a challenge to theory because demo-cratic institutions and practice, as we know them, evolved within the sovereign nation state. Hence, the EU is a challenge to how we conceptualise democracy, legitimacy and authority in contemporary politics.

The intensification of treaty change, big projects such as EMU and enlargement, brought polity issues – rather than just the 'politics of policy' – to the fore in the Union. Whereas previously, the EU could rest on the 'shadow of the past' and the instrumental benefits it afforded the member states and their peoples, this appears insufficient as the Union begins to go beyond regulation and market creation into core attributes of statehood, money, borders and security. A marked feature of both political and scholarly writing on the EU in the 1990s was a focus on the so-called 'democratic deficit' in the Union. In discussing this, we begin by identifying conventional views on the democratic deficit and existing measures taken to address the perceived problem. We then outline our perspective on the emergence of politics and democracy in the EU.

The democratic deficit is commonly seen as a result of the Union's institutional design, decision rules, the dominance of delegated expert knowledge, a weakness of accountability, hostile public opinion in some member states, and the absence of a political community in the Union. The debate on democratising the Union's decision-making process has been dominated by a discussion of the powers of the European Parliament. Armed with enhanced democratic credentials following the first direct elections in 1979, and unhappy with its place in the Union's institutional order, the European Parliament has persistently argued for more power. It engaged in advocacy politics and co-opted friendly national governments to its cause. The process of treaty revision provided an opportunity for the parliament, and its advocates secured additional powers for it in the Single Act, the Treaty on European Union and the Treaty of Amsterdam. Like all relatively young institutions in a radically changing institutional landscape, the EP has had to struggle to establish its influence and presence in the EU system. It has managed to insert itself in the Union's 'politics of policy' by using its legislative powers and through the work of its committees. The Parliament's links to its electorate are less secure than its place in the 'politics of policy'. Turnout in European elections is low (56 per cent in 1994) and EP elections are manifestly less relevant to national electorates than national general elections.

A second strand of thinking on the democratic deficit reflects the fear that the consent of the people may be become a constraint on the future development of the system. Political leaders in Europe feel this to be the case. Shocked by the Danish 'No' in June 1992, EU institutions and the member state governments are beginning to confront the need to enhance accountability and address issues of democracy. Speech after speech and communiqué after communiqué resonate with references to the citizens of Europe and the need to bring the system closer to its peoples. This stems from a belief that political integration was intrinsic to the European project and that a political community, however nascent, required the development of a 'sense of community' and of the 'we feeling'. Moreover, it was motivated by the belief that economic integration needed a measure of political integration. The citizens of the member states may need to feel more at home with its institutions so that they will not deny their consent to future treaty change. The Union may also need a reservoir of goodwill from the people to enable the system to weather the inevitable storms of enlargement and EMU.

A third element of thinking on the democratic deficit concerns the relation between the Union and democracy in the member states. This begins from the fundamental fact that the democratic nature of the EU derives, first and foremost, from it being a system of democratic states. There are concerns in many of the member states, not just in Scandinavia, about the impact of integration on their national democracies. This has generated measures to enhance the role of national parliaments in the EU system, for example the Treaty of Amsterdam's protocol on the role of national parliaments. The Conference of European Affairs Committees (COSAC) provides an important transnational link for national parliamentarians and the domestic European committees provide an arena of deliberation on the national dimension of integration.

Another significant element of European democracy is the inclusion in the Treaty of Amsterdam (1997) of the founding values of the EU system. Article F(6) stated that 'the Union is founded on the principles of liberty, democracy, respect for human rights and fundamental freedoms, and the rule of law, principles which are common to the Member States'. Hence, these universal values, which were rooted in the particular contexts of the member states, are to be given a wider European context. European states that respect these principles may become members of the Union and all member states face sanctions if there are serious breaches of these values. The treaty underlines the historic mission of the Union to extend a liberal order, based on democracy and the rule of law, throughout western Europe and the wider continent.

Indeed, it should not be forgotten that, prior to the widespread discussion of the democratic deficit, the rights of individual Europeans were enhanced significantly by the EU. Since the 1950s, EC provisions on the free movement of workers has gradually increased the rights of workers and their families as they move from one member state to another. Advocacy by the Commission and activism by the European Court of Justice established the principle of non-discrimination on the basis on nationality in the EU system. The thickness of these rights was greatly enhanced over time. Then, in 1992, the Treaty on European Union made provision for citizenship of the Union, which entailed – in addition to pre-existing free movements rights – additional political rights. The development of citizenship as an additional layer was highly contentious in the member states, notably in Denmark, where the electorate was fundamentally opposed to the whole concept of European citizenship. Since Maastricht, it has not proved possible to add to the citizenship provisions in any substantial way because of the opposition of some member states and their peoples, which remain wedded to citizenship rooted in the nation state.

What are we to make of these diverse diagnoses and remedies for the democratic deficit? Do they provide a vision of an emerging European polity? The term 'deficit' implies an inadequacy or insufficiency, but what is the appropriate benchmark against which to test the Union? In our view the question of European democracy requires careful consideration of the elements of democracy and the context in which the EU is developing. Democracy has, at least, three components that need to be distinguished: the rule of law, deliberation and governance, and participation and consent. The EU is seeking to develop a democratic system of governance in a context that differs from that in which democratic nation states emerged. First, it is developing at a time when traditional forms of democratic deliberation, participation, consent and administration are under severe strain within nation states. This is evident in widespread uncertainty about the effectiveness of government, the emergence of anti-party parties, declining memberships of collective organisations and low levels of participation. Second, the EU is developing without the binding force of nationality, which played a major role in creating and sustaining many, if not all, democratic systems. Third, the EU is developing in a context of autonomous globalisation of much economic activity and culture. Fourth, the EU is seeking to develop a democratic system in a context of strong internal diversity between its member states. In our view, these distinctions and contextual factors imply that European democracy cannot be measured against the template of the post-war European nation state.

As regards the first component of democracy, the rule of law, the EU cannot be said to have a democratic deficit. It has been argued that 'with all its imperfections the Community domesticates the balance of power into something which, if not as "democratic" as domestic norms, has made the international system in Europe take a huge step in their direction' (Duchêne 1994, p. 405). The analysis in this volume leads us to the conclusion that the EU has indeed democratised interstate relations by embedding these relations in a strong legal framework, by establishing a model of civic statehood and by underpinning and enlarging fundamental rights and freedoms in Europe. In fact, as stated above, the Union is central to the spread of a liberal order throughout the continent. Embedding these values in the continental order adds another layer to their protection.

Overall, it seems that democratisation of the EU is following the well-worn Union path of incremental change and pragmatic adaptation, not unlike the process of market creation identified in Chapter 6. This has progressed further on the first component of democracy, the rule of law, than on the other two, deliberation/policy-making and consent/participation. While there is a strong case for the progressively enhanced role of the EP in the legislative process, there is significant scepticism, among non-parliamentarians and scholars, that the standard recipe for institutional reform offers a solution in itself to the democratic deficit. This scepticism derives from the absence of party political competition at European level, to which we would add the widely-felt limitations of parliamentary representation as an adequate form of democratic participation.

While government leaders often speak of the need to bring the Union closer to its citizens, there are limits to what can be achieved by this rhetoric and the associated symbolism. The same political leaders show a marked reluctance to communicate the realities of power in contemporary Europe to their electorates. They persist with an old language of national interest, when in reality, Janus-like, they serve both the national government and the collective European government. National politicians, to a far greater degree than hitherto, need to engage their electorates in a dialogue about internationalisation and its consequences for political order. Multilevel democracy will also crucially rest on channels of participation within states for regions and localities. For governments, individuals and interest groups, democratic participation, channels of influence, identity and rights may begin within their national polities but they do not end there.

So far, we have seen that the process of enhancing and reinforcing the democratic element in the Union is based on making explicit the values on which it is founded, on enhancing individual rights, on strengthening the powers of the directly elected parliament, in supporting a European civil society, and by rendering its decision-making processes more open and transparent. Together, these add basic democratic ideals, processes and accountability to the EU system, which can contribute to the emergence of a transnational democratic polity at EU level. However, they are not sufficient in themselves. The decision-making and administrative systems remain inadequately democratic and suffer from an ineffectiveness that erodes legitimacy. The overall system provides a legal citizenship of great value, but little sense of political community. In our view, the key challenge is to fill out these two components of democracy – policy-making and consent/participation – and the context in which Europe is being constructed provides a guide to what is possible.

In a context of ineffective government, no bonding nationalism, globalisation and internal diversity, it is utterly irrelevant to envisage a European democratic state of a conventional kind. While these contextual factors have been described in negative terms, there is a positive side to the new environment. While old systems of representation, participation and administration are being sidelined, new forms are emerging, in Europe and elsewhere. Indeed, there are reasons why the EU is a particularly fertile source. Side by side with the development of the powers of the EP, the Commission has worked to create political space and channels of representation for national groups in the Brussels arena. Its strategy is in tune with, and enhances, the development of associative democracy within the member states and at an EU level. These channels involve moves from traditional government roles – allocating, directing, administering and underwriting monopoly representation – to new central roles – policy entrepreneurship, monitoring of decentralised policy experiments, facilitation of deliberation, protection of non-statutory organisations and supporting interest group formation. Because the Commission does not have traditional state instruments and power, it is forced to invent and nurture these new forms of governance. In this way, the Union contributes to the development of a European civil society that is at the forefront of new modes of democracy worldwide. We are confident that the new forms of governance play a crucial part in the emerging European democracy. In Europe, as elsewhere, the relationship between new forms of decentralised and associative governance and traditional representative democracy is unresolved and constitutes a central challenge to contemporary democracy.

Beyond associative democracy, there remains the challenge of political community in the Union. The borders of nation states are not just territorial borders but define national societies and political communities based on the bonding capacity of nationalism. The national polity is constituted by the demos. Within national borders, political communities operate on the basis of majority rule through competitive elections. Mass democracy and nationalism are central to the European model of the nation state. The key question for the Union is how a political community can be forged without a demos. Scholars are deeply divided about the consequences of this for political community and democracy in the EU. According to Weiler *et al.*, the rigorous implication of the no demos thesis is that, in the absence of a demos there cannot be a democracy or democratisation at EU level. Weiler himself and others are far less pessimistic (Weiler *et al.* 1995; Chryssochoou 1996; Hix 1998).

In analysing the development of political community at the EU level, it is useful to distinguish between identity, on the one hand, and democratic participation, on the other. The Union is engaged in creating symbols of belonging that are increasingly visible throughout Europe. Added to this is the expansion of rights that rest on Europe's tradition of civic nationalism. The purpose of these policies is gradually to alter peoples' consciousness of cultural and political space. These strategies will not lead to the supercession of national, regional and local identities, which is neither feasible nor desirable, but offer the possibility of multiple identities with a European identity acting as a roof or shelter for other identities. Already in Europe, those actively involved in the Union's governance structures feel part of a collective project and there are many Europeans who adopt multiple identities with ease. However, there are other Europeans who wish to maintain exclusive national identities. These tensions between singular and multiple identities, between exclusive and inclusive identities, are to be expected in an internationalising world. A relatively weak European identity is all that is required in the Union because it does not represent 'big government', nor is it a war-making political order.

The question of political participation by citizens in the Union should also be addressed. Because of the lack of salience associated with EP elections, individuals participate in the Union as consumers, workers or members of associative groups rather than as individual voters. A number of scholars argue for the need to inject some traditional majoritarian competitive politics into the system while rejecting standard recipes of institutional reform, in terms of the European Parliament. The devices usually cited in the literature are Europe-wide referendums and the direct election of the President of the Commission (Hix 1998). The idea of Europe-wide referendums as a means of injecting an element of direct democracy into the system may have some merit. The direct election of the Commission President would further represent a competitive election on a Europe-wide basis and would alter the opportunity structures for political parties at the European level. Europe's traditional political families have been strengthening their traditional ties in the 1990s and, as a result, have established the basis for policy agendas that could be put to the European electorates. Traditional political competition would help construct new democratic identities in Europe and hence would contribute to transcending the no-demos problem.

The EU is the only regionalism in the international system where there is pressure to democratise politics above the level of the state, to mark a decisive shift from diplomacy to politics. The process of democratisation is following the well-worn Union path of incremental change, but unlike market creation there is no over-arching goal or big idea. Europe's leaders lack any sense of where the system is going or the kind of system that is desirable. They even lack a language to describe adequately and explain to their electorates the essence of the collective project and their involvement in it. In fact, national political leaders are extremely cautious in relation to the politics of integration. They are far happier to launch big projects in the economic sphere which greatly disturb economic actors than to disturb the balance or logic of domestic politics. European citizenship, the enhanced role of the European Parliament, growing transnationalism, the Union as a community of values and the debate on transparency have injected more politics into the EU system, but Europe's political leaders could be more innovative in the use of new means of communication and additional political contests with a European dimension. This would make the Union more polity like, without pre-ordaining a transition to a form of conventional statehood.

The Union as an economic space and currency region

The EU economic system lies between international liberalisation and a domestic economy, sharing certain characteristics of each. In comparison with inter-national liberalisation, the EU's supranational institutions, constitutional order and norms greatly qualify the purely diplomatic and territorial element. Yet, in comparison with a domestic economy, these and other provisions offer an element of protection or reassurance to member states' national and territorial interests. This 'protection' of member states is not necessarily achieved by the *absence* of EC rules or the *minimisation* of Community competence. Indeed, over time, this aspect of reassurance to member states has evolved into the novel European doctrine of the 'level playing field'. The level playing field doctrine might be seen as a European compensation for the lack of fiscal federalism.

The European model of internationalisation involves freeing of trade and significant deregulation, combined with new rule setting, the development of common policies, the transfer of power to central institutions and the development of redistributive mechanisms. This contrasts with the freeing of trade under a hegemonic power (the establishment of an imperial market), and with multilateral trade liberalisation. It also contrasts with the economic union in the United States which has less emphasis on a 'level playing field' between states, but a much greater inter-state distributive mechanism. Each of the major bargains or agreements in the history of post-war European integration have conformed to this European model of internationalisation. The Treaty of Rome agreement combined the common market with the CAP, the Coal and Steel Community and new institutions. The Single European Act combined the completion of the internal market and the reform of the CAP with the Delors I package and institutional development. Indeed, it was the SEA which led to the explicit statement of the 'level playing field' doctrine that encapsulates the European model. The Maastricht agreement combined EMU and the Uruguay GATT agreement with the Delors II package.

It can be argued that the European model of internationalisation has a particular relevance at the end of the twentieth century. To foreign trade have been added very significant international investment, a globalisation of some technology, transnational information flows and networks, and global financial markets. These developments have greatly increased the economic inter-dependence of countries and, it can be argued, call for an international regulatory framework that extends well beyond trade. The European Union is *the* model for the regulation of economic internationalisation that extends beyond trade. The European model of integration seems more conducive to sustainable, stable and the desirable internationalisation of economic activity. It is arguably a more effective, as well as a more equitable, approach than that occurring in some other parts of the world. Indeed, the WTO is now having to address the fact that internationalisation goes well beyond trade, and is discovering that this involves the need for complex regulatory frameworks. The EU is an important model of how such deep internationalisation can be achieved and managed without conflict (O'Donnell and Murphy 1994). European monetary union also represents a new model of internationalisation. It establishes a currency area without a centralisation of political authority and without the hegemonic power that characterised other international currencies.

The European model of internationalisation has produced a distinctive and unusual pattern of economic policy with five main elements: macroeconomic policy, the internal market, cohesion, competitiveness policy and labour market policy. The experimentation and innovation so evident in institution building in the Union, are also evident in the development of the Union's panoply of economic instruments.

The single market is by far the most important strand of EU economic policy. Given the failure of the harmonisation drive in the 1960s and 1970s, the Union built on ECJ judgements to discover a new regulatory strategy, centred on mutual recognition where possible and minimal harmonisation where necessary. The balance between mutual recognition and harmonisation determines the balance between deregulation and re-regulation in the internal market. That balance varies across sectors and, given their diverse starting points, across member states and professional groups. There is an element of competition among regimes, driven by different regulatory cultures, whose interaction has resulted in a regulatory patchwork (Héritier 1996, pp. 149–67). But the 'level playing field' doctrine sets limits to regulatory competition, reflected in new regulation and harmonisation in the social and environmental areas. Governments and public opinion in high standards countries are unwilling to countenance 'social dumping' or a 'race to the bottom' in health, safety or consumer protection. While national welfare states remain the primary institutions of European social policy, they do so in the context of an increasingly constraining multi-tiered polity.

The scope and content of economic union is uncertain and contested because there is no undisputed functional or technical definition of economic and monetary union. It has long been recognised that the harmonisation necessary to create a functioning internal market could be achieved in a number of ways – ranging from deregulation of national interventions to re-regulation and the conduct of policy by a supra-national institution. Different groups, and perhaps nations, have different views on the desirable 'economic order'. Bhagwati, for example, challenges what he sees as the growing belief that harmonisation of policies and institutions is necessary, on the grounds that 'economic analysis can readily confirm that this is a false notion' (Bhagwati 1994, p. 240). By contrast, Pelkmans and Robson argue that an undiluted application of the principles of free movement would, through its impact on the 'effective jurisdiction' of member states, 'drastically undermine the delicately balanced packages of public policy regulation, market intervention, income redistribution measures and macro-economic policies that are at present determined at the level of national politics' (Pelkmans and Robson 1987). It follows that the necessary scope and content of economic union, the balance of negative and positive integration, will be contested by various interest groups.

Given the fragmentation of the national models and the attenuation of ideological conflict between left and right, it is now clear that the play of this contest is only partly determined by conflicting national views on the balance of deregulation and re-regulation – and still less by conflicting ideological perspectives on the desirable 'economic order'. To a significant extent, the indeterminacy in the market integration process is resolved by particular conjunctures – including enlargement, global pressures and changing ideas.

Numerous examples of the contingent nature of integration could be cited. Periodic enlargement, by bringing in countries at different levels of economic development, prevented the system settling down. Global competitive pressures made fine-grained national differences on the 'economic order' seem less relevant. Changes in ideas about the organisation of enterprises, inflation and public finance reduced the significance of finding elaborate compromises between the post-war economic 'models' of the leading west European nations. In this sense, the relative merits of the doctrines outlined by Bhagwati and Pelkmans/Robson is an empirical and historical question, rather than an analytic or ideological one.

The incremental, political and contested nature of economic union also reflects the powerful role of ideas and interaction in shaping the EU. There is clear evidence that the presence or absence of a shared perspective on the direction of the union materially influences behaviour in the Council and other institutions. However, as our discussion of the evolution of the internal market in Chapter 6 shows, it would be wrong to say that this shared perspective or understanding involves a rigid, all-encompassing, model of what European Union must look like. In other words, the powerful role of ideas is not inconsistent with our emphasis on the pragmatic elements of the system. This is so because of the importance of interaction in the policy process. Pragmatism consists precisely of a collective, practical, experimental approach to problem-solving, which rejects the strong distinction between immediate, material goals and ultimate goals and which thereby recognises the significance of ideas, and a plurality of ideas.

While the Union influences business and economic performance through a wide range of policies – on competition and mergers, state-aids, agriculture, transport, energy, external trade, SMEs, regional development, trans-European networks, research and technological development, harmonisation and standard setting – it faces difficulty in combining these policies in a coherent and strategic way. However, the Union's relative incapacity should not be exaggerated, since national efforts to use these diverse instruments for strategic goals have been undermined by technical and organisational change, including globalisation and the fragmentation of national ensembles of economic governance. Indeed, a particular example of EU innovation is the approach taken to what Pelkmans calls the 'standards/certification/quality nexus' (Pelkmans 1997).

The internal market process was, and continues to be, evolutionary. Additional areas, such as energy, have been brought within its remit, the capacity of European standards bodies has been strengthened and new European-level agencies established. It is, by definition, an unfinished project, and a key illustration of our contention that the EU is in a permanent state of becoming. The idea of the EU as a 'regulatory state' undoubtedly captures a key aspect, and confirms the view that the EU should not be read against the template of the classical post-war European nation state. However, the emerging European regulatory agencies have not acquired the power of rule-making, rule enforcement and adjudication granted to many of the American regulatory bodies.

The quantitative accumulation of market-opening measures produced a qualitative shift in the degree of integration, the pattern of market governance in Europe and, it seems, in the nature of the integration process. It redefined the original treaty goal of a common market, since the Treaty of Rome made the implementation of free movement of services, capital and labour dependent on subsequent agreement on harmonisation. By the time the EU got around to making real these elements of the over-arching agreement, the context had changed sufficiently to change ideas about market regulation. While the internal market can be seen as reflecting a worldwide strengthening of capital relative to labour, it also allows new combinations of economies of scale and scope, which are giving rise to new, less hierarchical and more participative, patterns of economic organisation. In addition, the Union encourages member states to run with the grain of new forms of public governance, as evidenced in its sponsoring of partnership projects in many spheres. Indeed, this deliberate strategy, which made space for a focus on important new economic and organisational realities, was reinforced by the Union's peculiar economic policy – particularly EMS and the transition to EMU – which had the effect of suspending conflict between member states (and, in most cases, within them) on macroeconomic policy.

The significance of EU economic policy was enhanced by changes in its context – the political economy of the member states and the international environment. The deepening of the Union has both reflected and reinforced a weakening of the domestic ensembles of macroeconomic management, wage bargaining, enterprise organisation, industrial relations, welfare provision, sector regulation, state intervention and legitimisation. It has also been prompted by radical changes in the international context. Thus, the EU has changed, but so has the world in which it resides, everything to which it might be compared, including the bricks and mortar of which it is made.

From the beginning, the Union has had to take the distributional consequences of its policies into account. Different sectors and regions have been aided in the process of adjustment to market forces, through the Coal and Steel Community, the CAP and the European Social Fund (ESF). However, the major past and future evolution of EU cohesion policy must be viewed in the context of enlargement. Enlargement greatly widened the disparities in income and development within the Union. In the context of the internal market programme, it involved a massive regime exportation to Europe's poorer periphery – which was forced to dismantle its statist form of capitalism, confront severe competition and meet new rules. The regime exportation includes not only new approaches to market governance, but also the influence of the Commission on national governments and regional actors. This regime exportation is more important than the resource-transfer that accompanied it. In addition, it has unsettled not only the periphery, but also the core. In response to the claims of the periphery, it was reiterated that the EU model has, from the start, been more about rules than money, about competition not transfers – a message that was underlined by the fact that the EMU will not be supported by the type of fiscal federalism found in other monetary unions. With little nostalgia for its stultifying past, the relatively young populations of the periphery have begun to compete – as is reflected in the relatively high growth rates in the 1990s. In contrast, much of the core is ambivalent about the new patterns of economic organisation – as is reflected in low growth and anxiety about the periphery's ability to attract competitive enterprises. The upshot is a remarkable inversion of the analysis and fears articulated at the time of the Werner Report. In the late 1960s it was feared that the growth of peripheral regions/countries, used to high inflation and currency devaluation, could be curtailed by EMU. In the late 1990s, it is feared that monetary policy, set for a slow-growth European core, may be somewhat loose for the high-growth periphery. In like manner, while eastern enlargement will put pressure on the cohesion resources of the Union, the more interesting and profound effects may come from a further unsettling of existing economic and social arrangements.

On the issues of competitiveness and employment, the Union has recently become involved in what might be termed *thin* policy integration. The fact that the EU is drawn – by the limits of its competence and resources, its Europe-wide perspective, the bargained nature of its policies and the continuing relevance of national and regional determinants of competitive advantage – into policy approaches and areas that differ from that which nation states have traditionally undertaken, may be an advantage. It is, thereby, drawn to experimental policy approaches, in which it must rely on national governments, agencies, firms and trade unions for implementation and evaluation. The ultimate test of its recent employment initiative is whether the EU uses its limited, but influential, role to develop innovative approaches to employment, and whether its freedom from the mainstream, large-scale and administratively complex, labour market policy responsibilities of member states is seen as an opportunity rather than a constraint.

An intriguing aspect is that the recent initiatives on competitiveness and employment might be seen bring the EU (in these areas at least) towards a loose international forum, such as the OECD and the ILO. Nevertheless, there remains a connection between EU initiatives in these areas and the deep level of political and legal integration in many other areas. Furthermore, while the EU might be drawn in the direction of international organisations, these international organisations are also being drawn in the direction of the EU. This is evident in the increasing complexity of the issues addressed by the WTO and the deepening content of liberalisation and regulatory agreements. Over time, this increasing complexity and depth may require the elaboration of richer over-arching agreements and principles, within which negotiated governance and problem solving in diverse areas can proceed.

The completion of the internal market is of historic significance. With it, the EU signalled that it did not intend to be bypassed by the dynamic change occurring in the world economy, it did not intend to live off its past wealth, becoming a *rentier* continent. The ultimate success of the new European project depends on whether advancing integration also advances 'good' governance of markets, industries and the macroeconomy. In the circumstances prevailing in the 1980s and 1990s, prioritising European integration (without a Fortress Europe) cut with the grain of fundamental changes in economic organisation, public administration, social life and technology. A significant part of that movement was the liberalisation and internationalisation of markets. It is, of course, too early to say whether the economic measures are sufficient to lay the basis for sustained prosperity on the European continent. A lot depends on whether the system's tendency to fragmentation and capture continues to be counterbalanced by its ability to reorient sectors and rules in a transformative way. While the experiments in new forms of public governance are recent and diverse, there is a strong possibility that they constitute the seeds of an enduring new system that can be generalised.

While the absence of a macroeconomic policy has been a key feature of the system since the foundation of the Community, the launch of the euro marks a definite change. With the transfer of monetary policy to the ECB, the Union acquires a major instrument of both internal and international economic management. There is every reason to believe that the ECB will have sufficient independence and technical expertise to establish the credibility of the euro. The more interesting, and difficult, questions concern economic policy. Two aspects are particularly important: policy on the external value of the euro and the balance between monetary and fiscal policy. Given the low levels of economic policy coordination in the first three decades, there has long been fears that the system will be unbalanced, with greater authority, coherence and effectiveness in monetary policy than economic policy. These fears were enhanced by the design of EMU, set out in the Maastricht Treaty, which accorded a greater role to the Council, and a smaller role to the Commission, than is normal in Pillar 1. In this regard, it is important to note the remarkable, if low-key, progress made in 'multilateral surveillance' in recent years. Although large parts of economic policy remain in the hands of national authorities, it is now clear that they are exposed to strong supranational influences.

Indeed, there are a number of reasons why the single currency will, in time, create political pressures for an enhanced economic management capacity at the Union level. One is the long-term impact of the Stability and Growth Pact regime on domestic policy and regulatory structures, wage bargaining and distributional settlements. Another is the fact that the European monetary union does not contain the fiscal instruments at EU level to cushion member states and regions from the full effects of asymmetric shocks. While interesting technical arguments have been advanced in recent years concerning the likelihood of asymmetric shocks (Krugman 1990, 1993; CEC 1993), the real constraint is clearly a political reluctance to countenance significant distributive instruments, the small scale of the Union's budget and the improbability of significant new EU-level spending programmes. Given the pressure for reform of domestic structures, the further unsettling of national wage bargaining and the enhanced EU focus on employment, pressure for development of economic policy is likely. The interesting issue is what form that policy should take. Existing proposals for such development, and critiques of EMU, are based on theoretical formulae of little relevance or on various successful national models. We do not believe that they offer a blueprint for European policy, given the distinctive form of economic policy in the Union. While the Union's unusual structure constrains it from exercising economic policy in a traditional manner, we believe that this equally creates the possibility for discovery of policy approaches more consistent with current technological and organisational realities.

Much discussion of Europeanisation focuses on convergence and divergence. There is a tendency to resist any convergence hypothesis – for example, in industrial relations studies – on the grounds that there are clearly divergent *trends* in different member states (Ferner and Hyman 1998; Roche and Geary 1998). Given the different starting points of the many national models, divergent *trends* are, of course, consistent with some convergence in *patterns* of governance. What seems certain, is that, while the dominant continental European models – German, French, Scandinavian – are under severe strain, remarkable innovations are emerging in unlikely places and coming from diverse directions. Inside the space of a decade and a half the EU has created both the new internal market and a new macroeconomic and monetary landscape. It is thus providing the European economy with regulatory and macroeconomic instruments made in and for the radically new economic and political environment that has emerged. By means of the EU, the countries of Europe can modernise, modify – and in some cases discard – policies and institutions made for the post-war world. Responding to the demand of internationalisation, small member states, such as the Netherlands and Ireland, are inventing post-corporatist forms of macroeconomic concertation and structural reform which sustain strong economic growth (O'Donnell and O'Reardon 1997; Visser and Hemerijck 1997). Under the pressure of integration, Italy is beginning to achieve a new combination of macroeconomic control and microeconomic invention that might achieve not only competitive success but also social stabilisation. Regional governments and agencies in various large and small member states are using their relative freedom from the macroeconomic and administrative headaches of national governments, to explore new approaches to economic regeneration. The peripheral countries, so hungry for integration and modernisation, are adopting the organisational innovations that were invented in Asia but subsequently underpinned the economic regeneration of the US (Sabel 1996). Furthermore, wherever these innovations in social and economic organisation are occurring, the European Commission is to be found, as either a catalyst, a partner or a keen observer of new governance (O'Donnell 1993, 1997).

A significant presence in the international system

No less distinctive is the role of the Union in international relations, a role that has been forged in the context of changing geopolitics and the shifting ability of the member states to act collectively in the international system. The development of the international role of the Union has mirrored the internal development of the Union in many respects, notably, the disjuncture between deep economic integration and weaker political integration. In a highly pragmatic and incremental process, the Union has gradually built up a significant presence in the international system based on its legal powers and a range of policy instruments that can be deployed externally.

The establishment of the Community of Six in the 1950s had immediate consequences for other European states, regional organisations and the wider international system. In the same way, the establishment and growth of the Communities was conditioned by the impact of international factors; most importantly, the United States played and continues to play a central role in the evolution of the Union's foreign policy as hegemon, brake but also *demandeur*. The Union's development as a trading block endowed it with a considerable presence in the international political economy and led it to develop an impressive array of external policy instruments, particularly in trade and aid. The Union built up a panoply of association agreements and trade arrangements with its immediate neighbours and former colonies. It gradually became the dominant force in the west European political economy, absorbing most of the EFTA states as members. From the 1970s onwards, the Union began the more difficult task of cooperating on foreign policy in European Political Cooperation (EPC). The development of EPC displayed all of the characteristics of the evolution of the EU – an incremental process of institution-building, establishing standard operating procedures, speaking with one voice in international fora and developing a collective view on some of the major issues of international politics. The process was codified in the Single Act and became more ambitious in the Treaty on European Union as a common foreign and security policy.

Although there is often a tendency to separate 'foreign policy' from 'internal politics' in analysis of the EU, the way in which the Union's internal order has evolved has had major implications for the Union as an international actor. The Union's prismatic mode of governance manifests itself starkly in its external capacity and reach. Competence is fragmented between external relations in Pillar 1 and the CFSP in Pillar 2. Its capacity in international politics rests largely on 'soft power', aid, trade and its internal policy regimes. It lacks the attributes of 'hard power', most obviously defence. Moreover, in the exercise of 'soft power', the Union is constantly running up against the limits of internal agreement. Important external agreements are frequently undermined by the political pressure of EU producers. EU external policy emerges from multiple and complex decision-making procedures. There are constant wrangles about external representation and who is competent to speak on behalf of the Union. There is an unsettled and uneven distribution of responsibility for external policy in the Commission and the Council. Outside actors are confronted with hydra-headed representation and multiple channels, and national foreign policies continue to have considerable salience given the varying interests and historical trajectories of the member states.

Yet despite these caveats, the Union has a presence in the international system and is of immense importance in its continental environment (Allen and Smith 1991/92; Hill 1993; Smith 1996a). It contributes to global governance as it aggregates the views of the member states and reduces the transaction costs of international negotiations. The Union is most effective when it can use 'soft power' – market access, the Union budget, its attraction as a community of values, and its ability to impose conditions for membership. It is weakest when external events demand that it react quickly, when faced with military conflict, when the USA has a major interest in a particular region or issue and when there is a divergence of interests and views among the member states. The USA, once the champion of European integration, is deeply ambivalent about the emergence of a European external identity, especially in security and perhaps in the financial markets as well.

Whither the Union?

Adequate understanding of the emerging system in the EU is not just of academic interest but is bound up with consideration of how Europe governs itself as it enters the twenty-first century. Debate about the form of political and economic governance that is evolving in the EU stems from strong normative concerns about the nature and purpose of the Union. The analysis in this volume, with its emphasis on contingency, innovation and experimentation, leads us to the conclusion that the EU does not follow textbook forms of either political or economic order and that a 'United States of Europe', a federal superstate, is the least likely outcome and should be ruled out of political discourse on integration. While mindful of the potential in any system to disintegrate, the analysis in this volume leads us to the conclusion that European integration is part of the landscape of politics in Europe and intrinsic to how the small- and medium-sized states that populate the continent govern themselves. They are locked in to the system either as members, aspiring members or states that are loosely coupled with the system. If neither a federal superstate nor a return to a classical national state is likely, what then is the likely shape of the Union in future? What does the evolution of the Union's distinctive model of internationalisation tell us about its future trajectory? Given the 'unsettled' nature of the Union and Europe more generally, what would a more settled system look like?

The Union's evolution will be shaped by the following. First, the Union is in the process of establishing a single currency that will further deepen the level of economic integration and will have implications for the Union as a polity. Second, this development takes place in the context of changing patterns of governance and politics in the member states, coupled with shifts in technology and in the international political economy. Hence, developments in the EU will continue to interact and intersect with other processes of change, much as they have done in the past. Third, enlargement will have a major impact on conceptions of Europe, on the Union's institutional and policy balance and on the nature of the EU as a polity.

EMU is the last large-scale economic project in the Union and the accession of countries to the east and south will eventually bring to an end the dynamic of enlargement in the development of the Union. It could well be that, notwithstanding the processes of deep change identified in this volume, the Union is entering a period of consolidation over the next twenty-five years. However, this process of consolidation will not lead to the re-emergence of a high degree of congruence between territory, identity and function at the EU level as found in the classical nation state. Rather these characteristics will combine in novel and distinctive ways with echoes of Europe's universalist past. The dominance of the nation state in global politics and in the politics of continental order has blinded us to other traditions – such as empire and Christianity – which are so deeply rooted in Europe's past. The EU represents an attempt to embed and enmesh Europe's national tradition in a wider universalist tradition, to tame the worst excesses of one tradition by embedding it in another European tradition. The EU can only succeed by mobilising the institutions, actors and resources of the member states and therefore by reaffirming them.

Inevitably, however, there are tensions between the national and the European and these tensions are likely to continue in the system. Already these tensions are leading to demands for a clearer delineation of competencies at the EU and national levels. The politics of subsidiarity are crucial to the system during this phase of its evolution. However, the EU does not, in general, represent a process of zero-sum bargaining between the national and the European. Rather, states trade formal sovereignty and control for representation, voice and influence. This should be seen as a positive sum game, although not to all states and all national groups at any one time. The salience of the Brussels arena will continue to grow as more and more areas of public policy become matters of common concern. The system is likely to see a greater concentration on making the existing regulatory regimes work. This process depends on peer pressure, advocacy coalitions and on norms of collective governance. It will operate through research, learning by doing, evaluation and expert working parties. The system must evolve within the warp and weave of national politics and electoral cycles, although states will find it more difficult to hold the system to ransom. Disagreement and diversity will be managed by 'variable geometry', flexibility and transition periods.

The Union has embarked on an enlargement process to its east and south with no clear strategic thinking and direction about the consequences of this process for the existing model of integration. On the one hand, there are those who argue that the west European model of integration designed for six states, and stretched to fifteen, cannot be extended to embrace another ten or fifteen states. From this perspective, the Union is at a critical juncture in its development and is in need of fundamental reform. For some, this would need a wider and looser Europe and for others an enhanced central capacity and authority. On the other hand, there are those who argue that incrementalism will suffice; that the Union has engaged in pragmatic incremental adjustment in the past and will continue to do so. The multidimensional character of integration makes it difficult to see which of these approaches will prevail. The establishment of the single currency and the debate on defence could well demand an enhanced capacity at the centre, whereas other areas will continue to be characterised by a high degree of decentralisation. The institutional consequences of enlargement are likely to be profound in that difficult issues of representation and effectiveness will have to be addressed. In addition, if the new members are to embrace the challenge of collective action, the system will have to develop beyond its character as a west European club and ways will have to be found to ameliorate the deep asymmetry between east and west.

The prismatic nature of the Union is set to continue with segmented bargaining and problem-solving in different policy arenas. The system will rely largely on its ability to co-opt national actors into collective decision-making and collective governance. Arising from EMU, the system will begin to take on a less diplomatic and more domestic appearance. This is already manifest in the growing importance of the ECOFIN Council in the system and the decline in the General Affairs Council of Foreign Ministers. The latter will retain responsibility for the Union's relations with the outside world, new policy areas and formal constitutional change but will play second fiddle to the ECOFIN as collective economic governance become central to the management of the single currency. Both these Councils will feed into the European Council – a growing centre of political authority in the system. The supranational institutions will continue to exercise a pivotal role in the system in the search for collective solutions to European-wide problems. The Commission, in particular, will have to focus not just on policy entrepreneurship but on management as well. It will be aided in this by the establishment of more European-level agencies.

The trajectory of the Union as a polity is very difficult to plot, as the politicisation of the EU system is novel and the emphasis on bringing Europe closer to its citizens is a relatively recent concern for Europe's political leaders. Democratising the EU is a challenge in two senses. First, there is no road map for democratising political space above the level of the state. Second, national representative democracies are themselves challenged by the prevalence of social exclusion, on the one hand, and new forms of associative democracy, on the other.

There is an increase in individualism and a weakening of the collective institutions that animated European politics in the past. There is also a weakening level of public trust in domestic institutions. It could be argued that the EU as an arena of politics is in tune with the new politics of associative democracy and negotiated order found in the member states and may not need political innovation in the traditional sense. Put simply, this view would argue that the EU can be democratised in bits and pieces in line with the way the EU has done things in the past. However, the disquiet in a number of member states about the impact of the EU on their national democracies, in addition to the growing stakes in integration itself, may force Europe's political leaders to be more innovative in their approach to the political character of integration. The likely avenues identified in this chapter are the introduction of political contests with a European dimension, a further deepening of European citizenship, which would allow for multiple identities and multiple citizenships, and an extension of associative democracy.

Conclusions

Our analysis demonstrates that European integration has evolved and continues to evolve within a distinctive configuration which, in turn, has produced a distinctive model of internationalisation. While it may or may not be possible to identify a European model of society, economy or polity, it is undoubtedly the case that there is now a European model of economic and political internationalisation. It involves the member states and all other states that aspire to membership or are part of the internal market. The Union is characterised by 'variable geometry' internally and fuzzy edges externally as its remit extends beyond its borders. The EU, from the outset, implied a model of internationalisation that combined a search for order (west European and internal political order), welfare through managed liberalisation, and modernisation. At the end of the 1990s the European model of internationalisation is characterised by a continuing stress on the Union as a market space, in addition to a new emphasis on the Union as a polity and a 'community of values'. The EU developed in an incremental, pragmatic and experimental manner by building a dense institutional fabric, an organic system of law and an advanced level of economic integration. Although the EU has not transcended the nation state, it has transformed the exercise of political authority in Europe by embedding the national in the European and the European in the national. Europe's deep regionalism represents a break with Europe's past – the Europe of imperialism, war and balance of power. The present system rests on a delicate balance among the large states and between the large and small. It represents a diffusion of state power, a taming of power and a domestication of conflict.

The European Union cannot be adequately understood using either a template of national policy or a model of international relations. We believe that Europe's context has, by the sort of strange coincidence of which history is full, facilitated disclosure of policy approaches and possibilities that may become more general. Patterns of economic and social governance are changing and this is reflected more quickly and more visibly in the EU, since it is new, always part-formed, and unburdened by the large-scale expenditure programmes of the post-war nation state. The transfer of policy competence to the EU has also produced a transformation of national approaches. The member states (and societies) differ such that there is no simple way to 'scale them up' and, in any case, the leading national post-war models are under severe strain. The international sphere differs from the national, and the EU represents a particular model of internationalisation. Ideas are a factor, but ideas about Europe and European integration have evolved in tandem with ideas about economic policy and governance. This complex set of constraints has also turned out to create opportunities. The evolving European policy system contains important elements that are of general relevance and may, indeed, provide clues to the patterns of governance that will be common in an increasingly interdependent world. A pragmatic approach, forced on the EU by the need to achieve consensus in diversity, has given rise to a system that uses experimentalism and decentralisation as ongoing principles of policy-making and implementation. The policy portfolio of the EU tells us as much about the nature of policy and governance at the end of the twentieth century as about the development of the EU itself. The possibility of a treble transition – from constraint to opportunity, from transfer to transformation, and from the particular to the general – is an important part of our overall interpretation of European integration.

References

Allen, D. and Smith, M. (1983) 'Europe, the United States and the Middle East: a case study in comparative policy-making'. *Journal of Common Market Studies*, 22(2), December: 125–46.

Allen, D. and Smith, M. (1989) 'Western Europe in the Atlantic system of the 1980s: towards a new identity?'. In Gill, S. (ed.) *Atlantic Relations: the Reagan Era and Beyond*. London: Harvester-Wheatsheaf, 88–110.

Allen, D. and Smith, M. (1990) 'Western Europe's presence in the contemporary international arena'. *Review of International Studies*, 16(1), January: 19–37.

Allen, D. and Smith, M. (1991–92) 'The European Community in the New Europe: bearing the burden of change'. *International Journal*, XLVII(1), Winter: 1–28.

Allen, D. and Smith, M. (1996) 'External policy developments'. In Nugent, N. (ed.) *The European Union 1995: Annual Review of Activities*. Oxford: Blackwell, 63–84.

Allen, D. and Smith, M. (1997) 'External policy developments'. In Nugent, N. (ed.) *The European Union 1996: Annual Review of Activities*. Oxford: Blackwell, 73–93.

Allen, D. and Smith, M. (1998) 'The European Union's presence in the New European Security Order: barrier, facilitator or manager?'. In Rhodes, C. (ed.) *The European Union in the Global Community*. Boulder: Lynne Rienner.

Allen, D., Rummel, R. and Wessels, W. (eds) (1982) *European Political Cooperation: Towards a Foreign Policy for Western Europe?* London: Butterworth.

Allesina, A. and Grilli, V. (1994) 'On the feasibility of a one-speed or multi-speed European Monetary Union'. In Eichengreen, B. and Frieden, J. (eds) *The Political Economy of European Monetary Unification*. Boulder: Westview Press.

Alting von Geusau, F.A.M. (1993) *Beyond Containment and Division; Western Cooperation from a Post-totalitarian Perspective*. Dordrecht: Nijhoff.

Andersen, S. and Eliassen, K. (eds) (1993) *Making Policy in Europe: the Europeification of National Policy-making*. London: Sage.

Anderson, B. (1991) *Imagined Communities*. London: Verso.

Anderson, P. (1996) 'The Europe to come'. *London Review of Books*, 25 January.

Andreasen, L.E., Coriat, B., den Hertog, F. and Kaplinsky, R. (1995) 'Flexible organisations: European industry and services in transition'. In Andreasen, L.E., Coriat, B., den Hertog, F. and Kaplinsky, R. (eds) *Europe's Next Step: Organisational Innovation, Competition and Employment*. London: Frank Cass.

Andrews, D.M. and Willet, T.D. (1997) 'Financial interdependence and the state: international monetary relations at century's end'. *International Organization*, 51(3): 479–511.

Armstrong, K. and Bulmer, S. (1998) *The Governance of the Single European Market*. Manchester: Manchester University Press.

Artis, M. and Ostry, S. (1986) *International Economic Policy Coordination*. London: Routledge, for the Royal Institute of International Affairs.

Asmus, R. (1991) 'Germany and America: partners in leadership'. *Survival*, 33(6), November–December: 546–66.

Bailey, A.R. and Bailey, M.C. (1997) *The EU Directive Handbook*. Boca Raton: St Lucie Press.

Bailey, J. (ed.) (1992) *Social Europe*. Harlow: Longman.

Balassa, R. (1961) *The Theory of Economic Integration*. Homewood: Irwin.

Baldwin, R. (1994) *Towards an Integrated Europe*. London: Centre for Economic Policy Research.

Barrell, R. (1990) 'Has the EMS changed wage and price behaviour in Europe?' *National Institute Economic Review*, November: 64–72.

Beer, S.H. (1973) 'The modernisation of American federalism'. *Publius*, 3(Fall): 49–95.

Berghahn, V. (1986) *The Americanisation of West German Industry 1945–1973*. Leamington Spa: Berg.

Bergsten, C.F. (1981) 'The costs of Reaganomics'. *Foreign Policy*, 44(Fall): 24–37.

Bergsten, C.F. (1997a) 'The Dollar and the Euro'. *Foreign Affairs*, 76(4), July: 83–95.

Bergsten, C.F. (1997b) 'American politics, global trade'. *The Economist*, 27 September: 25–28.

Bhagwati, J. (1994) 'Free trade: old and new challenges'. *Economic Journal*, 104: 231–46.

Bieback, K.J (1991) 'Harmonisation of social policy in the European Community'. *Les Cahiers de Droit*, 32(4): 913–38.

Boltho, A. (ed.) (1982) *The European Economy: Growth and Crisis*. Oxford: Oxford University Press.

Booth, K. and Smith, S. (eds) (1997) *The Globalisation of World Politics*. Oxford: Oxford University Press.

Brett, E.A. (1985) *The World Economy Since the War: the Politics of Uneven Development*. London: Macmillan.

Breuilly, J. (1985) 'Reflections on Nationalism'. *Journal of Philosophy and Social Science*, 15: 65–75.

Brown, L. and Rosati, J. (1987) 'The Reagan administration and economic interdependence: turbulent relations with the EC'. *International Journal*, XLII(3): 438–72.

Bücker A., Joerges, C., Neyer, J. and Schlacke, S. (1996) 'Social regulation through European Committees; an interdisciplinary agenda and two fields of research'. In Pedler, R.H. and Schaefer, G. (eds) *Shaping European Law and Policy: The Role of Committees and Comitology in the Political Process*. Maastricht: European Institute of Public Administration.

Buiter, W., Corsetti, G. and Roubini, N. (1993) 'Excessive deficits: sense and nonsense in the Treaty of Maastricht'. *Economic Policy*, 16: 57–100.

Bull, H. (1977) *The Anarchical Society: a Study of Order in World Politics*. London: Macmillan.

Bull, H. (1982) 'Civilian power Europe: a contradiction in terms?' *Journal of Common Market Studies*, 21(2), December: 149–64.

Bullmann, U. (1997) 'The politics of the third level'. In Jeffery, C. (ed.) *The Regional Dimension of the European Union: Towards a Third Level in Europe?* London: Frank Cass.

Bulmer, S. and Wessels, W. (1987) *The European Council: Decision-Making in European Politics*. London: Macmillan.

Bulmer, S., Jeffery, C. and Paterson, W.E. (1996) *Germany's European Diplomacy: Shaping the Regional Milieu*. Forschungsgruppe Europa, Zentrum Für Angewandte Politikforschung: Munich.

Buzan, B. (1991) *People, States and Fear: an Agenda for Security Studies in the Post-Cold War Era* 2nd edn. Hemel Hempstead: Harvester-Wheatsheaf.

Calingaert, M. (1988) *The 1992 Challenge from Europe*. Washington, DC: National Planning Association.

Calingaert, M. (1996) *European Integration Revisited: Progress, Prospects, and US Interests*. Boulder: Westview Press.

Calleo, D. (1970) *The Atlantic Fantasy: the US, NATO and Europe*. Baltimore: Johns Hopkins University Press.

Calleo, D. (1987) *Beyond American Hegemony: the Future of the Western Alliance*. New York: Basic Books.

Calleo, D. and Rowland, B. (1973) *America and the World Political Economy: Atlantic Dreams and National Realities*. Bloomington: Indiana State University Press.

Cameron, D. (1992) 'The 1992 initiative: causes and consequences'. In Sbragia, A. (ed.) *Euro-Politics: Institutions and Policy-making in the 'New' European Community*. Washington, DC: The Brookings Institute.

Cameron, D. (1993) 'British exit, German voice, French loyalty: defection, domination and cooperation in the 1992–3 ERM crisis'. Paper delivered at the Third International Conference of the European Community Studies Association, Washington, DC.

Cameron, D. (1995) 'Transnational relations and the development of European economic and monetary union'. In Risse-Kappen, T. (ed.) *Bringing Transnational Relations Back In: Non-state Actors, Domestic Structures and International Institutions*. Cambridge: Cambridge University Press.

Cameron, F. (1995) 'The European Union and the fourth enlargement'. In Nugent, N. (ed.) *The European Union 1994: Annual Review of Activities*. Oxford: Blackwell, 17–34.

Caporaso, J. (1996) 'The European Union and forms of state: Westphalian, regulatory and post-modern'. *Journal of Common Market Studies*, 34(1): 29–52.

Caporaso, J. and Keeler, J.T.S. (1993) 'The European community and regional integration theory'. Paper prepared for delivery at the Third Biennial International Conference, 27–29 May, Washington, DC.

CEC (1988) *The Economics of 1992*. Luxembourg: Office for Official Publications of the European Communities.

CEC (1989) 'Horizontal mergers and competition policy in the European Community'. *European Economy*, No. 40. Luxembourg: Office for Official Publications of the European Communities.

CEC (1990) 'One market, one money'. *European Economy*, Luxembourg: Office for Official Publications of the European Communities.

CEC (1993) 'Stable money – sound finances community public finance in the perspective of EMU'. *European Economy*, 53. Luxembourg: Office for Official Publications of the European Communities.

CEC (1994) *Growth, Competitiveness, Employment – the Challenges and Ways Forward into the 21st Century*. Luxembourg: Office for Official Publications of the European Communities.

CEC (1996) 'Economic evaluation of the internal market: reports and studies'. *European Economy*, No. 46. Luxembourg: Office for Official Publications of the European Communities.

CEC (1997) *Twenty-Sixth report on Competition Policy*. Luxembourg: Office for Official Publications of the European Communities.

Christiansen, T. (1994) 'European integration between political science and international relations theory: the end of sovereignty'. Florence: EUI Working Paper RSC No. 94.4.

Christiansen, T. (1996a) 'European governance in the 21st century: dilemmas and opportunities'. Paper presented to the Royal Irish Academy, Dublin, 22 November.

Christiansen, T. (1996b) 'A maturing bureaucracy? The role of the Commission in the policy process'. In Richardson, J. (ed.) *European Union: Power and Policy Making*. London: Routledge, 77–95.

Chryssochoou, N.D. (1996) 'Europe's could-be demos: recasting the debate'. *West European Politics*, 19: 788–801.

Coen, D. (1997) 'The evolution of the large firm as a political actor in the European Union.' *Journal of European Public Policy*, 4(1), 91–108.

Cohen, B. (1977) *Organising the World's Money: the Political Economy of International Monetary Relations*. New York: Basic Books.

Cohen, B. (1994) 'Beyond EMU: the problem of sustainability'. In Eichengreen, B. and Frieden, J. (eds) *The Political Economy of European Monetary Unification*. Boulder: Westview Press, 149–65.

Cohen, B. (1997) 'The political economy of currency regions'. In Mansfield, E. and Milner, H. (eds) *The Political Economy of Regionalism*. New York: Columbia University Press.

Commission Sec (1992) 2272 final. 'An open and structured dialogue between the Commission and interest groups'. Brussels: European Commission, 2 December.

Coriat, B. (1995) 'Organisational innovations: the missing link in European competitiveness'. In Andreasen, L.E., Coriat, B., den Hertog, F. and Kaplinsky, R. (eds) *Europe's Next Step: Organisational Innovation, Competition and Employment*. London: Frank Cass.

Cox, A. and Watson, G. (1995) 'The European Community and the restructuring of Europe's national champions'. In Hayward, J. (ed.) *Industrial Enterprise and European Integration: From National to International Champions in Western Europe*. Oxford: Oxford University Press.

Cram, L. (1994) 'The European Commission as a multi-organization: social policy and IT policy in the EU'. *Journal of European Public Policy*, 2: 195–218.

Crawford, B. (1996) 'Explaining defection from international cooperation: Germany's unilateral recognition of Croatia'. *World Politics*, 48(4), July: 482–521.

Daedalus (1991) 'Searching for security in a global economy'. 120(4), Fall.

Dahl, R. (1994) 'A democratic dilemma'. *Political Science Quarterly*, 109(1): 23–34.

Dahrendorf, R. (1986) 'The Europeanization of Europe'. In Dahrendorf, R., Sorensen, T.C. and Pierre, A.J. *A Widening Atlantic? Domestic Change and Foreign Policy*. New York: New York University Press.

Dai, X., Cawson, A. and Holmes, P. (1995) 'The rise and fall of high definition television: the impact of European technology policy'. *Journal of Common Market Studies*, 34(2), June: 149–66.

De Grauwe, P. (1997) *The Economic of Monetary Integration*, 3rd edn. Oxford: Oxford University Press.

Delors, J. *et al.* (1989) *Report on Economic and Monetary Union in the European Community*. Luxembourg: Office for Official Publications of the European Communities.

Dent, C. (1997) *The European Economy: the Global Context*. London: Routledge.

DePorte, A.W. (1986) *Europe Between the Superpowers: the Enduring Balance*, 2nd edn. New Haven: Yale University Press.

Destler, I.M. (1980) *Making Foreign Economic Policy*. Washington, DC: The Brookings Institute.

Dicken, P. (1992) *Global Shift: the Internationalisation of Economic Activity*, 2nd edn. London: Paul Chapman.

Diebold, W. (1972) *America and the Industrial World: United States Foreign Economic Policy in the 1970s*. New York: Praeger.

Dobson, W. (1991) *Economic Policy Coordination: Requiem or Prologue?* Policy Analysis in International Economics, 30. Washington, DC: Institute for International Economics.

Dodd, N. (1994) *The Sociology of Money: Economics, Reason and Contemporary Society*. Cambridge: Polity.

Dogan, M. (1994) 'The decline of nationalisms within Western Europe'. *Comparative Politics*, 26: 281–305.

Dorf, M.C. and Sabel, C. (1998) 'A constitution of democratic experimentalism', *Columbia Law Review*, 98(2): 267–473.

Duchêne, F. (1994) *Jean Monnet: The First Statesman of Interdependence*. London: Northon and Company.

Duff, A. (1997) *The Treaty of Amsterdam: Text and Commentary*. London: Sweet and Maxwell.

Dunn, J. (1993) 'Political theory, political science and policy-making in an interdependent world'. *Government and Opposition*, 28: 242–60.

Dunn, J. (ed.) (1995) *Contemporary Crisis of the Nation State?* Oxford: Blackwell.

Dyson, K. (1994) *Elusive Union: the Process of Economic and Monetary Union in Europe*. London: Longman.

Edwards, G. (1984) 'Europe and the Falklands crisis'. *Journal of Common Market Studies*, 22(4), June: 295–313.

Eichener, V. (1993) 'Social dumping or innovative regulation? Processes and outcomes of European decision-making in the sector of health and safety at work harmonisation'. EUI Working papers, No. 92/28. Florence: European University Institute.

Eichener, V. (1997) 'Effective European problem-solving: lessons from the regulation of occupational safety and environmental protection'. *Journal of European Public Policy*, 4(4), December: 591–608.

Eichengreen, B. (1993) 'European Monetary Unification'. *Journal of Economic Literature*, 31: 1321–57.

Eichengreen, B. (1994a) 'Fiscal policy in EMU'. In Eichengreen, B. and Frieden, J. (eds) *The Political Economy of European Monetary Unification*. Boulder: Westview Press.

Eichengreen, B. (1994b) *International Monetary Arrangements for the 21st Century*. Washington, DC: The Brookings Institute.

Eichengreen, B. (1996) *Globalizing Capital: A History of the International Monetary System*. Princeton: Princeton University Press.

Eichengreen, B. and Frieden, J. (1994) 'The political economy of monetary unification: an analytical introduction'. In Eichengreen, B. and Frieden, J. (eds) *The Political Economy of European Monetary Unification*. Boulder: Westview Press.

Elazar, D.J. (1987) *Exploring Federalism*. Alabama: University of Alabama Press.

Ellwood, D. (1992) *Rebuilding Europe: Western Europe, America and Postwar Reconstruction*. London: Longman.

Ergas, H. (1984) 'Corporate strategies in transition'. In Jacquemin A. (ed.) *European Industry: Public and Corporate Strategies*. Oxford: Clarendon Press.

Esping-Anderson, G. (1990) *The Three Worlds of Welfare Capitalism*. Cambridge: Polity Press.

European Commission (1995) 'Commission's work programme for 1995'. OJ C225, 30, August, pp. 1–58.

European Community (1995) Report of the Council of Ministers on the Functioning of the Treaty on European Union. 12 April.

European Union (1996) *Commission Annual Report 1995*. Official Publications: Luxembourg.

Evans, P., Jacobson, H. and Putnam, R. (eds) (1993) *Double-Edged Diplomacy: International Bargaining and Domestic Politics*. Berkeley: University of California Press.

Fawcett, L. and Hurrell, A. (eds) (1995) *Regionalism in World Politics: Regional Organisation and International Order*. Oxford: Oxford University Press.

Ferner, A. and Hyman, R. (1998) *Changing Industrial Relations in Europe*. Oxford: Basil Blackwell Publishers.

Flora, P. and Heidenheimer, A.J. (1982) *The Development of Welfare States in Europe and America*. London: Transaction Publishers.

Forster, A. and Wallace, W. (1996) 'Common foreign and security policy: a new policy or just a new name?'. In Wallace, H. and Wallace, W. (eds) *Policy-Making in the European Union*. Oxford: Oxford University Press: 412–35.

Franklin, M., Marsh, M. and McLaren, L. (1994) 'Uncorking the bottle: popular opposition to European unification in the wake of Maastricht'. *Journal of Common Market Studies*, 32(4), December: 455–72.

Freedman, L. (ed.) (1983) *The Troubled Alliance: Atlantic Relations in the 1980s*. London: Heinemann.

Freeman, C., Sharp, M. and Walker, W. (eds) (1991) *Technology and the Future of Europe*. London: Pinter.

Frieden, J. (1991) 'Inverted interests: the politics of national economic policy in a world of global finance'. *International Organization*, 45: 425–51.

Frieden, J. (1992) 'Comments on Alberto Giovannini "What Happened? Exploring the political dimension of optimum currency areas" '. In de la Dehesa, G., Giovannini, A., Guitan, M. and Portes, R. (eds) *The Monetary Future of Europe*. London: Centre for Economic Policy Research.

Frieden, J. (1994) 'Making commitments: France and Italy in the European Monetary System'. In Eichengreen, B. and Frieden, J. (eds) *The Political Economy of European Monetary Unification*. Boulder: Westview Press.

Frieden, J. (1996) 'The impact of goods and capital market integration on European monetary politics'. *Comparative Political Studies*, 29(2): 193–222.

Gaddis, J.L. (1992) *The United States and the End of the Cold War*. New York: Oxford University Press.

Galtung, J. (1989) *Europe in the Making*. New York: Crane Russak.

Garcia, S. (ed.) (1993) *European Identity and the Search for Legitimacy*. London: Pinter.

Garrett, G. (1994) 'The politics of Maastricht'. In Eichengreen, B. and Frieden, J. (eds) *The Political Economy of European Monetary Unification*. Boulder: Westview Press, 47–65.

Garrett, G. and Weingast, B. (1993) 'Ideas, interests and institutions: constructing the European Community's internal market'. In Goldstein, J. and Keohane, R. (eds) *Ideas and Foreign Policy: Beliefs, Institutions and Political Change*. Ithaca: Cornell University Press.

Garvin, T. (1990) 'The Return of History: Collective Myths and Modern Nationalisms'. *Irish Review*. No. 9: 16–29.

Geroski, P. (1989) 'The choice between diversity and scale'. In Davis, E. (ed.) *1992: Myths and Realities*. London: Centre for Business Strategy.

Geroski, P. and Jacquemin, A. (1985) 'Industrial change, barriers to mobility and European industrial policy'. *Economic Policy*, 1: 169–218.

Giavazzi, F. and Giovannini, A. (1989) *Limiting Exchange Rate Flexibility: the European Monetary System*. Cambridge, MA: MIT Press.

Gibb, R. and Michalak, W. (eds) (1994) *Continental Trading Blocs: the Growth of Regionalism in the World Economy*. Chichester: Wiley.

Gilpin, R. (1987) *The Political Economy of International Relations*. Princeton: Princeton University Press.

Ginsberg, R. (1989) *Foreign Policy Actions of the European Community: the Politics of Scale*. Boulder: Lynne Rienner.

Giovannini, A. (1992) 'Economic and Monetary Union: what happened? Exploring the political dimension of optimum currency areas'. In de la Dehesa, G., Giovannini, A., Guitan, M. and Portes, R. (eds) *The Monetary Future of Europe*. London: Centre for Economic Policy Research.

Goodhart, C. (1989) *Money, Information and Uncertainty*. London: Macmillan.

Gourevitch, P. (1978) 'The second image reversed: the international sources of domestic politics'. *International Organization*, 32(4): 881–911.

Gourevitch, P. (1984) 'Breaking with orthodoxy: the politics of economic policy responses to the Depression of the 1930s'. *International Organization*, 38(1): 95–128.

Gow, J. (1997) *Triumph of the Lack of Will: International Diplomacy and the Yugoslav War*. London: Hurst.

Grahl, J. and Teague, P. (1990) *1992 – The Big Market: The Future of the European Community*. London: Lawrence & Wishart.

Grande, E. (1996) 'The new role of the state in telecommunications: an international comparison'. *West European Politics*, 17(3), July: 138–57.

Gros, D. and Thygesen, N. (1992) *European Monetary Integration: From the European Monetary Sysytem to European Monetary Union*. London: Longman.

Haas, E.B. (1990) 'The limits of liberal nationalism in Western Europe'. In Crawford, B. and Schulze, P. (eds) *The New Europe Asserts Itself*. Berkeley: University of California Press.

Habermas, J. (1991) 'Citizenship and national identity: some reflections on the future of Europe'. Paper presented at the University of Louvain.

Haftendorn, H. and Tuschhoff, C. (eds) (1993) *America and Europe in an Era of Change*. Boulder: Westview Press.

Halliday, F. (1986) *The Making of the Second Cold War*. London: Verso.

Hamm, B. (1992) 'Europe: a challenge to the social sciences'. *International Social Science Journal*, 131, February: 3–22.

Hanrieder, W.F. (1978) 'Dissolving international politics: reflections on the nation-state'. *American Political Science Review*, 72(4): 1276–87.

Harden, I. (1990) 'EuroFed or monster bank'. *National Westminster Bank Quarterly Review*, August: 2–13.

Harrison, G. (ed.) (1994) *Europe and the United States: Competition and Cooperation in the 1990s*. Armonk: Sharpe.

Harvey, B. (1992) *Networking in Europe: A Guide for European Voluntary Organisations*. London: Bedford Square Press.

Hayes-Renshaw, F. and Wallace, H. (1997) *The Council of Ministers*. London: Macmillan.

Held, D. (1987) *Models of Democracy*. Cambridge: Blacksell.

Held, D. (1989) *Political Theory and the Democratic State*. Cambridge: Polity Press.

Held, D. (1996) *Models of Democracy*. Cambridge: Polity Press.

Helleiner, E. (1994) *States and the Reemergence of Global Finance: from Bretton Woods to the 1990s*. Ithaca: Cornell University Press.

Henderson, D. (1992) 'International economic integration: progress, prospects and implications'. *International Affairs*, 68(4), October: 633–53.

Héritier, A. (1996) 'The accommodation of diversity in European policy-making and its outcomes: regulatory policing as a patchwork', *Journal of European Public Policy*, 3(2): 149.

Héritier, A., Knill, C. and Mingers, S. (1996) *Ringing the Changes in Europe: Regulatory Competition and Redefinition of the State.* Berlin: Walter de Gruyter.

Hill, C. (1990) 'European foreign policy: power bloc, civilian model – or flop?'. In Rummel, R. (ed.) *The Evolution of an International Actor: Western Europe's New Self-assertiveness.* Boulder: Westview Press: 31–55.

Hill, C. (1993) 'The capability–expectations gap, or conceptualising Europe's international role'. *Journal of Common Market Studies,* 31(3), September: 305–28.

Hill, C. (ed.) (1996) *The Actors in Europe's Foreign Policy.* London: Routledge.

Hill, C. (1998) 'Closing the capability–expectations gap?'. In Peterson, J. and Sjursen, H. (eds) *A Common Foreign Policy for Europe? Competing Visions of the CFSP.* London: Routledge.

Hirst, P. (1994) *Associative Democracy: New Forms of Economic and Social Governance.* Cambridge: Polity Press.

Hirst, P. and Thompson, G. (1992) 'The problem of "globalisation": international economic relations, national economic management an international economic management and the formation of trading blocs'. *Economy and Society.* 21(4): 357–96.

Hirst, P. and Thompson, G. (1996) *Globalization in Question.* Cambridge: Polity Press.

Hix, S. (1998) 'The study of European Union II: the 'new governance' agenda and its rival'. *European Journal of Public Policy,* 5: 38–65.

Hocking, B. (1993) *Localizing Foreign Policy: Non-central Government and Multilayered Diplomacy.* London: Macmillan.

Hocking, B. and Smith, M. (1995) *World Politics: an Introduction to International Relations.* London: Harvester-Wheatsheaf/Prentice-Hall.

Hocking, B. and Smith, M. (1997) *Beyond Foreign Economic Policy: the United States, the Single European Market and the Changing World Economy.* London: Cassell/Pinter.

Hoekman, B. and Kostecki, M. (1995) *The Political Economy of the World Trading System: from GATT to WTO.* Oxford: Oxford University Press.

Hoffmann, S. (1992) 'Balance, concert, anarchy or none of the above'. In Treverton, G. (ed.) *The Shape of the New Europe.* New York: Council on Foreign Relations Press, 194–220.

Hogan, M. (1991) *The Marshall Plan: America, Britain, and the Reconstruction of Western Europe, 1947–1952.* Cambridge: Cambridge University Press.

Holland, M. (1988) *The European Community and South Africa: European Political Cooperation under Strain.* London: Pinter.

Holland, M. (ed.) (1991) *The Future of European Political Cooperation.* London: Macmillan.

Holland. M. (ed.) (1996) *Common Foreign and Security Policy: The Record of Reforms.* London: Pinter.

Hollis, M. and Smith, S. (1990) *Explaining and Understanding International Relations.* Oxford: Clarendon Press.

Holm, U. (1992) 'The French discourses on Maastricht'. Paper delivered to the Inaugural Pan-European Conference, Heidelberg, Germany, September.

Hooghe, L. (1996) 'Building a Europe with the regions: The changing role of the European Commission'. In Hooghe, L. (ed.) *Cohesion Policy and European Integration: Building Multi-Level Governance.* Oxford: Oxford University Press.

Hooghe, L. and Keating, M. (1994) 'The politics of European regional policy'. *Journal of European Public Policy,* 1(3): 367–93.

Howorth, J. and Menon, A. (eds) (1997) *The European Union and National Defence Policy.* London: Routledge.

Hufbauer, G. (ed.) (1990) *Europe 1992: An American Perspective.* Washington, DC: The Brookings Institute.

Hyde-Price, A. (1996) *The International Politics of East-Central Europe*. Manchester: Manchester University Press.

IAB (1995) 'The European Monetary Union: possible consequences for employment and earnings'. *IAB Labour Market Research Topics*, No. 14. Nurnberg: Institute for Employment Research.

Ikenberry, J.G. (1986) 'The state and strategies of international adjustment'. *World Politics*, 39: 53–77.

Inglehart, R. (1990) *Cultural Shift in Advanced Industrial Society*. Princeton: Princeton University Press.

Isard, P. (1995) *Exchange Rate Economics*. Cambridge: Cambridge University Press.

Ishikawa, K. (1990) *Japan and the Challenge of Europe 1992*. London: Pinter, for the Royal Institute of International Affairs.

Jachtenfuchs, M. (1995) 'Theoretical perspectives on European governance'. *European Law Journal*, 1: 115–33.

Jacobson, D. and Andreosso, B. (1996) *Industrial Economics and Organisation: A European Perspective*. London: McGraw-Hill.

Jacquemin, A. (1998) *European Competitiveness: the Reports of the Competitiveness Advisory Group*. London: Edward Elgar.

Jacquet, P. (1992) 'The politics of EMU: a selective overview'. In de la Dehesa, G., Giovannini, A., Guitan, M. and Portes, R. (eds) *The Monetary Future of Europe*. London: Centre for Economic Policy Research.

James, H. (1996) *International Monetary Cooperation Since Bretton Woods*. Washington, DC: Oxford University Press.

Jeffery, C. (1997) 'Conclusions: sub-national authorities and European domestic policy'. In Jeffery, C. (ed.) *The Regional Dimension of the European Union: Towards a Third Level in Europe?* London: Frank Cass: 204–219.

Johnston, R.J., Taylor, P.J. and Watts, M.J. (eds) (1995) *Geographies of Global Change: Remapping the World in the Late Twentieth Century*. Oxford: Blackwell.

Journal of Common Market Studies (1996) Special Issue on 'The European Union and a Changing European Order'. *Journal of Common Market Studies*, 34(1), March.

Judge, D. and Earnshaw, D. and Cowan, N. (1994) 'Ripples or waves: the European Parliament and the European Community policy process'. *Journal of European Public Policy*, 1: 27–52.

Julius, D. (1990) *Global Companies and Public Policy: the Growing Challenge of Foreign Direct Investment*. London: Pinter, for the Royal Institute of International Affairs.

Kahler, M. (1983) 'Western Europe: the diplomatic consequences of Mr Reagan'. In Oye, K., Lieber, R. and Rothchild, D. (eds) *Eagle Defiant: United States Foreign Policy in the 1980s*. Boston: Little Brown: 273–310.

Kassim, H. and Menon, A. (eds) (1996) *The European Union and National Industrial Policies*. London: Routledge.

Katzenstein, P.J. (1997) 'United Germany in an integrating Europe'. *Current History*, March: 116–23.

Kay, J. (1990) 'Identifying the strategic market'. *Business Strategy Review*, 1(1): 1–22.

Kay, N. (1991) 'Industrial collaborative activity and the completion of the internal market'. *Journal of Common Market Studies*, 29(4), June: 347–475.

Keal, P. (1983) *Unspoken Rules and Superpower Dominance*. London: Macmillan.

Keating, M. and Hooghe, L. (1996) 'By-passing the nation state? Regions and the EU policy process'. In Richardson, J. (ed.) *European Union: Power and Policy-Making*. London: Routledge.

Kegley, C.W. (ed.) (1991) *The Long Postwar Peace: Contending Explanations and Projections*. New York: HarperCollins.

Kegley, C.W. and Wittkopf, E. (1996) *American Foreign Policy: Pattern and Process*, 5th edn. New York: St Martin's Press.

Kenen, P. (1996) *Economic and Monetary Union in Europe*. Cambridge: Cambridge University Press.

Kennedy, P. (1988) *The Rise and Fall of the Great Powers: Economic Change and Military Conflict from 1500 to 2000*. London: Unwin Hyman.

Keohane, R. (1984) *After Hegemony: cooperation and Discord in the World Political Economy*. Princeton: Princeton University Press.

Keohane, R. (ed.) (1986) *Neorealism and its Critics*. New York: Columbia University Press.

Keohane, R. and Hoffmann, S. (eds) (1993) *After the Cold War: International Institutions and State Strategies in Europe, 1989–1991*. Cambridge: Harvard University Press.

Keohane, R. and Nye, J. (1987) *Power and Interdependence: World Politics in Transition*, 2nd edn. Boston: Little, Brown.

Kindleberger, C. (1973) *The World in Depression, 1929–1939*. Berkeley: University of California Press.

Knorr, K. (1973) *Power and Wealth: the Political Economy of International Power*. New York: Basic Books.

Kohler Koch, B. (1996) 'Catching up with change: the transformation of governance in the European Union'. *Journal of European Public Policy*, 3: 359–80.

Kolodziej, E. (1980–81) 'Europe: the partial partner'. *International Security*, 5(3): 104–31.

Korpi, W. (1989) 'Power, politics and state autonomy in the development of social citizenship: social rights during sickness in eighteen OECD countries since 1930'. *American Sociological Review*, 54: 309–28.

Krasner, S. (ed.) (1983) *International Regimes*. Ithaca: Cornell University Press.

Krasner, S. (1988) 'Sovereignty: an institutional perspective'. *Comparative Political Studies*, 21: 66–94.

Kratochwil, F. (1989) *Rules, Norms and Decisions: on the Conditions of Practical and Legal Reasoning in International Relations and Domestic Affairs*. Cambridge: Cambridge University Press.

Krugman, P. (1992) 'Policy problems of monetary union'. In Krugman, P. (ed.) *Currencies and Crises*. Cambridge: MIT Press.

Krugman, P. (1990) 'Policy problems of a monetary union'. In De Grauwe, P. and Papademos, L. (eds) *The European Monetary System in the 1990s*. London: Longman.

Krugman, P. (1993) 'Lessons of Massachusetts for EMU'. In Torres, F. and Giavazzi, F. (eds) *Adjustment and Growth in the European Monetary Union*. London: CEPR and Cambridge: Cambridge University Press.

Ladrech, R. (1994) 'Europeanisation of domestic politics and institutions: the case of France'. *Journal of Common Market Studies*, 32: 69–87.

Laffan, B. (1996a) 'Ireland: a region without regions – the odd man out?'. In Hooghe, L. (ed.) *Cohesion Policy and European Integration: Building Multi-Level Governance*. Oxford: Oxford University Press.

Laffan, B. (1996b) 'The politics of identity and political order in Europe'. *Journal of Common Market Studies*, 34(1), March: 81–102.

Laffan, B. (ed.) (1996c) *Constitution-Building in the European Union*. Dublin: Institute of European Affairs.

Laffan, B. (1997) 'From policy entrepreneur to policy manager: the challenge facing the European commission'. *Journal of European Public Policy*, 4(3): 422–38.

Laursen, F. and Vanhoonacker, S. (eds) (1992) *The Intergovernmental Conference on Political Union*. Maastricht: European Institute of Public Administration.

Lazonick, W. (1991) *Business Organisation and the Myth of the Market Economy*. Cambridge: Cambridge University Press.

Leibfried, S. and Pierson, P. (1995) *European Social Policy: Between Fragmentation and Integration*. Washington, DC: The Brookings Institute.

Leibfried, S. and Pierson, P. (1996) 'Social policy'. In Wallace, H. and Wallace, W. (eds) *Policy-Making in the European Union*. Oxford: Oxford University Press.

Lemke, C. and Marks, G. (eds) (1992) *The Crisis of Socialism in Europe*. Durham: Duke University Press.

Link, W. (1986) *The East–West Conflict: the Organisation of International Relations in the Twentieth Century*. Leamington Spa: Berg.

Llobera, J.R. (1993) 'The role of state and nation in Europe'. In Garcia, S. (ed.) *European Identity and the Search for Legitimacy*. London: Pinter, 64–80.

Ludlow, P. (1982) *The Making of the European Monetary System*. London: Butterworth.

Ludlow, P. (1991) 'The Commission'. In Keohane, R.O. and Hoffmann, S. (eds) *The New European Community*. Boulder: Westview Press, 85–132.

Lynch, R. (1994) *European Business Strategies: the European and Global Strategies of Europe's Top Companies*. London: Kogan Page.

MacCormick, N. (1993) 'Beyond the sovereign state'. *The Modern Law Review*, 56: 1–18.

McGowan, F. and Wallace, H. (1996) 'Towards a European regulatory state'. *European Journal of Public Policy*, 3: 560–76.

Macleod, I., Hendry, I. and Hyett, S. (1996) *The External Relations of the European Communities*. Oxford: Oxford University Press.

McNamara, K. (1997) *Consensus and Constraint: the Politics of Monetary Co-operation in Europe*. Ithaca: Cornell University Press.

Majone, G. (1993a) 'The European community between social policy and social regulation'. *Journal of Common Market Studies*, 31(2): 153–71.

Majone, G. (1993b) 'Deregulation or re-regulation? Policymaking in the European Community since the single act'. EUI Working Papers, SPS No. 93/2.

Majone, G. (1994) 'The rise of the regulatory state in Europe'. *West European Politics*, 17(3): 77–101.

Majone, G. (1996a) *Regulating Europe*. London: Routledge.

Majone, G. (1996b) 'A European regulatory state?' In Richardson, J. (ed.) *European Union: Power and Policy-Making*. London: Routledge, 263–77.

Majone, G. (1997) 'The agency model: the growth of regulation and regulatory institutions in the European Union'. *EIPASCOPE*, 3: 9–14.

Mann, M. (1993) 'Nation-states in Europe and other continents: diversifying, developing, not dying'. *Daedalus*, 3: 115–40.

Mansbach, R. (1994) *The Global Puzzle: Issues and Actors in World Politics*. Boston: Houghton Mifflin.

Marks, G. (1992) 'Structural policy in the European Community'. In Sbragia, A. (ed.) *Euro-Politics: Institutions and Policy-making in the 'New' European Community*. Washington, DC: The Brookings Institute.

Marks, G. (1996) 'Exploring and explaining variation in EU cohesion policy'. In Hooghe, L. (ed.) *Cohesion Policy and European Integration: Building Multi-Level Governance*. Oxford: Oxford University Press.

Marks, G. and McAdam, D. (1996) 'Social movements and the changing structure of political opportunity in the European Union'. In Marks, G., Scharpf, F., Schmitter, P. and Streeck, W. (eds) *Governance in the European Union*. London: Sage.

Marks, G., Hooghe, L. and Blank, K. (1996a) 'European integration from the 1980s: state-centric vs. multilevel governance'. *Journal of Common Market Studies*, 34(3), September: 341–78.

Marks, G., Scharpf, F.W., Schmitter, P.C. and Streeck, W. (1996b) *Governance in the European Union*. London: Sage.

Marsden, D. (1992) 'Incomes policy for Europe? Or will pay bargaining destroy the Single European Market?'. *British Journal of Industrial Relations*, 30(4): 587–604.

Mason, M. and Encarnation, D. (1994) *Does Ownership Matter? Japanese Multinationals in Europe*. Oxford: Oxford University Press.

Mayes, D. (ed.) (1993) The external implications of European integration. London: Harvester-Wheatsheaf.

Mazey, S. and Richardson, J. (eds) (1993) *Lobbying in the European Community*. Oxford: Oxford University Press.

Mearsheimer, J. (1990) 'Back to the future: instability in Europe after the Cold War'. *International Security*, 15(1): 5–56.

Meehan, E. (1993) 'Citizenship and the European Community'. *The Political Quarterly*, 64(2), April–June: 172–86.

Menon, A., Forster, A. and Wallace, W. (1992) 'A common European defence'. *Survival*, 34: 98–118.

Miller, J.D.B. (1981) *The World of States: Connected Essays*. London: Croom Helm.

Milward, A. (1992) *The European Rescue of the Nation State*. London: Routledge.

Milward, A., Lynch, F., Romero, F., Ranieri, R. and Sorensen, V. (1993) *The Frontier of National Sovereignty: History and Theory 1945–1992*. London: Routledge.

Mjøset, L. (1992) *The Irish Economy in a Comparative Institutional Perspective*. Dublin: National Economic and Social Council. Pl.8967.

Modelski, G. (1972) *Principles of World Politics*. New York: Free Press; London: Collier-Macmillan.

Molyneux, P. (1996) 'Banking and financial services'. In Kassim, H. and Menon, A. (eds) *The European Union and National Industrial Policy*. London: Routledge.

Monti, M. (1996) *The Single Market and Tomorrow's Europe: a Progress Report from the European Commission*. London: Kogan Page.

Moran, M. (1994) 'The state and the financial services revolution'. *West European Politics*, 17(3), July: 158–77.

Moravcsik, A. (1991a) 'Negotiating the single act'. In Keohane, R. and Hoffmann, S. (eds) *The New European Community: Decisionmaking and Institutional Change*. Boulder: Westview Press.

Moravcsik, A. (1991b) 'Negotiating the single European Act'. *International Organization*, 45(1): 19–56.

Moravcsik, A. (1993) 'Preferences and power in the European Community: a liberal intergovernmentalist approach'. *Journal of Common Market Studies*, 31(4): 473–525.

Moravcsik, A. (1994) 'Why the European Community strengthens the state: domestic politics and international cooperation'. Paper presented at the Annual Meeting of the American Political Science Association, New York, 1–4 September.

Muller, W.C. and Wright, V. (1994) 'Reshaping the state in Western Europe: the limits of retreat'. *West European Politics*, 17(3): 1–11.

Nau, H. (1984–85) 'Where Reaganomics works'. *Foreign Policy*, 57, Winter: 14–38.

Nello, S. (1991) *The New Europe: Changing Economic Relations Between East and West*. London: Harvester-Wheatsheaf.

Nelson, R. (1993) 'A retrospective'. In Nelson, R. (ed.) *National Innovation Systems: a Comparative Analysis*. Oxford: Oxford University Press.

NESC (1989) *Ireland in the European Community: performance, prospects and strategy*. NESC Report No. 88. Dublin: National Economic and Social Council.

Neven, D., Nuttall, R., and Seabright, P. (1993) *Merger in Daylight: the Economics and Politics of European Merger Control*. London: CEPR.

Noorgaard, O., Pedersen, T. and Petersen, N. (eds) (1993) *The European Community in World Politics*. London: Pinter.

Northedge, F.S. (1976) *The International Political System*. London: Faber.

Nuttall, S. (1992) *European Political Cooperation*. Oxford: Clarendon Press.

Nuttall, S. (1995) 'The European Union and former Yugoslavia: deus ex machina or machina sine deo?'. In Nugent, N. (ed.) *The European Union 1994: Annual Review of Activities*. Oxford: Blackwell.

Nuttall, S. (1997) 'The Commission and foreign policy-making'. In Edwards, G. and Spence, D. (eds) *The European Commission*, 2nd edn. London: Cartermill. 303–20.

Nuttall, S. and Edwards, G. (1994) 'Common foreign and security policy'. In Duff, A., Pinder, J. and Pryce, R. (eds) *Maastricht and Beyond*. London: Routledge, 84–107.

O'Donnell, R. (1993) *Ireland and Europe: Challenges for a New Century*. Dublin: Economic and Social Research Institute.

O'Donnell, R. (1994) 'European integration'. In Norton, D. (ed.) *Economics for an Open Economy*. Dublin: Oak Tree Press.

O'Donnell, R. (1997) 'Irish policy in a global context: from state autonomy to social partnership'. *European Planning Studies*, 5(4): 545–58.

O'Donnell, R. and Murphy, A. (1994) 'The relevance of the European Union and European integration to the world trade regime'. *International Journal*, 49(3), Summer: 536–67.

O'Donnell, R. and O'Reardon, C. (1997) 'Ireland's experiment in social partnership'. In Fajertag, G. and Pochet, P. (eds) *Social Pacts in Europe*. Brussels: European Trade Union Institute.

Obradovic, D. (1993) 'Community law and the doctrine of divisible sovereignty'. *Legal Issues of European Integration*, 1: 1–20.

Olsen, J.P. (1995) 'Europeanization and nation-state dynamics'. Arena Working Paper, No. 9.

Owen, D. (1995) *Balkan Odyssey*. New York: Harcourt and Brace.

Oxley, H. and Martin, J.P. (1991) 'Controlling government spending and deficits: trends in the 1980s and prospects of the 1990s'. *OECD Economic Studies*, 17: 145–201.

Padgett, S. and Paterson, W.E. (1991) *A History of Social Democracy in Postwar Europe*. London: Longman.

Padoa-Schioppa, F. (1987) *Efficiency, Stability and Equity: a Strategy for the Evolution of the Economic System of the European Community*. Oxford: Oxford University Press.

Paemen, H. and Bensch, A. (1995) *GATT to WTO: the European Community in the Uruguay Round*. Leuven: Leuven University Press.

Palmer, J. (1988) *Europe Without America? The Crisis in Atlantic Relations*. Oxford: Oxford University Press.

Pappas, S. and Vanhoonacker, S. (eds) (1996) *The European Union's Common Foreign and Security Policy: the Challenges of the Future*. Maastricht: European Institute of Public Administration.

Pedler, R.H. and Schaefer, G. (1996) *Shaping European Law and Policy: The Role of Committees and Comitology in the Political Process.* Maastricht: European Institute of Public Administration.

Pelkmans, J. (1994) 'Is convergence prompting fragmentation?: the EMS and National Protection in Germany France and Italy'. In Guerrieri, P. and Padoan, P. (eds) *The Political Economy of European Integration.* New York: Harvester-Wheatsheaf.

Pelkmans, J. (1997) *European Integration: Methods and Economic Analysis.* Harlow: Longman.

Pelkmans, J. and Robson, P. (1987) 'The aspirations of the White Paper', *Journal of Common Market Studies,* 25(3): 181–92.

Peters, G. (1992) 'Bureaucratic politics and the institutions of the European Community'. In Sbragia, A. (ed.) *Euro-Politics.* Washington DC: The Brookings Institute, 75–122.

Peters, T. (1995) 'European monetary union and labour markets: what to expect?' *International Labour Review,* 134(3): 315–32.

Peterson, J. (1996) *Europe and America in the 1990s: Prospects for Partnership,* 2nd edn. London: Routledge.

Piening, C. (1997) *Global Europe: the European Union in World Affairs.* Boulder: Lynne Rienner.

Pijpers, A., Regelsberger, E. and Wessels, W. (eds) (1988) *European Political Cooperation in the 1980s.* Dordrecht: Nijhoff.

Pinder, J. (1983) 'Interdependence: problem or solution'. In Freedman, L. (ed.) *The Troubled Alliance: Atlantic Relations in the 1980s.* London: Heinemann, 67–87.

Pivetti, M. (1996) 'Maastricht and the political independence of central banks: theory and facts'. *Contributions to Political Economy,* 15: 81–104.

Pollack, M. (1995) 'Regional actors in an intergovernmental play: the making and implementation of EU structural policy'. In Mazey, S. and Rhodes, C. (eds) *The State of the European Union III.* Boulder: Lynne Rienner.

Portes, R. (1994) 'The future of European monetary integration'. In Cobham, D. (ed.) *European Monetary Upheavals.* Manchester: Manchester University Press.

Preston, C. (1995) 'Obstacles to EU enlargement: the classical Community method and the prospects for a wider Europe'. *Journal of Common Market Studies,* 33(3), September: 451–63.

Preston, C. (1997) *Enlargement and Integration in the European Union.* London: Routledge.

Puchala, D. (1971) *International Politics Today.* New York: Dodd Mead.

Putnam, R. and Bayne, N. (1987) *Hanging Together: Cooperation and Conflict in the Seven-Power Summits,* 2nd edn. Cambridge: Harvard University Press.

Reich, R. (1991) *The Work of Nations: Preparing Ourselves for Twenty-First Century Capitalism.* New York: Knopf.

Reinicke, W. (1992) *Building a New Europe: the Challenge of System Change and Systemic Reform.* Washington, DC: The Brookings Institute.

Richardson, J. (ed.) (1996) *European Union: Power and Policy-Making.* London: Routledge.

Robbins, K. (1989) 'National identity and history: past, present and future'. Text of an address to the RIIA, London.

Roche, W.K. and Geary, J. (1998) 'Negotiated governance, industrial relations regimes and European integration'. In O'Donnell, R. and Larragy, J. (eds) *Negotiated Governance and European Integration.* Luxembourg: European Commission.

Rockman, B.A. (1990) 'Minding the state – or a state of mind?'. *Comparative Political Studies,* 23: 25–55.

Rometsch, D. and Wessels, W. (eds) (1996) *The European Union and Member States: Towards Institutional Fusion?* Manchester: Manchester University Press.

Rose, R. and Urwin, D. (1970) 'Persistence and change in western party systems since 1945'. *Political Studies,* 18: 287–319.

Rosecrance, R. (1993) 'Trading states in a new concert of Europe'. In Haftendorn, H. and Tuschhoff, C. (eds) *America and Europe in an Era of Change*. Boulder: Westview Press, 127–46.

Rosenau, J. and Czempiel, E.-O. (eds) (1992) *Governance without Government: Order and Change in World Politics*. Cambridge: Cambridge University Press.

Ross, G. (1995) *Jacques Delors and European Integration*. Cambridge: Polity Press.

Ruggie, J. (1982) 'International regimes, transactions, and change: embedded liberalism in the postwar economic order'. *International Organization*, 36: 379–415.

Ruggie, J.G. (1993a) 'Multilateralism: the anatomy of an institution'. In Ruggie, J.G. (ed.) *Multilateralism Matters*. New York: Columbia University Press, 3–50.

Ruggie, J.G. (1993b) 'Territoriality and beyond: problematising modernity in international relations'. *International Organization*, 47(1), Winter: 39–74.

Sabel, C. (1994) 'Learning by monitoring: the institutions of economic monitoring'. In Smelser, N. and Swedberg, R. (eds) *Handbook of Economic Sociology*. Princeton: Princeton University Press.

Sabel, C. (1995) 'Constitutional ordering in historical context'. In Rogers Hollingsworth, J. and Boyer, R. (eds) *Contemporary Capitalism, the Embeddedness of Institutions*. Cambridge: Cambridge University Press, 154–88.

Sabel, C. (1996) *Ireland: Local Partnerships and Social Innovation*. Paris: OECD.

Sandholtz, W. (1992) *High-Tech Europe: the Politics of International Cooperation*. Berkeley: University of California Press.

Sandholtz, W. (1993) 'Choosing union: monetary politics and Maastricht'. *International Organization*. 47(1): 1–41.

Sandholtz, W. (1996) 'Money troubles: Europe's rough road to monetary union'. *Journal of European Public Policy*, 3(1): 84–101.

Sandholtz, W. and Zysman, J. (1989) '1992: recasting the European bargain'. *World Politics*, 42(1): 95–128.

Sandholtz, W. and Zysman, J. (1992) 'Europe's emergence as a global protagonist'. In Sandholtz, W. *et al.* (eds) *The Highest Stakes: Economic Foundations of the Next Security System*. New York: Oxford University Press: 81–113.

Sandholtz, W., Borrus, M., Zysman, J. Conca, K., Stowsky, J., Vogel, S. and Weber, S. (1992) *The Highest Stakes: Economic Foundations of the Next Security System*. New York: Oxford University Press.

Sbragia, A. (1992) 'Thinking about the European future: the uses of comparison'. In Sbragia, A. (ed.) *Euro-Politics: Institutions and Policy-making in the 'New' European Community*. Washington, DC: The Brookings Institute.

Scharpf, F. (1991) *Crisis and Choice in European Social Democracy*. Ithaca: Cornell University Press.

Schmitter, P.C. and Streeck, W. (1991) 'Organised interests and the Europe of 1992'. In Ornstein, N.J. and Perlman, M. (eds) *Political Power and Social Change*. Washington, DC: AEI Press, 46–67.

Schneider, V., Dang-Nguyen, G. and Werle, R. (1994) 'Corporate actor networks in European policy-making: harmonising telecommunications policy'. *Journal of Common Market Studies*, 32: 473–98.

Schôpflin, G. (1993) *Politics in Eastern Europe*. Oxford: Blackwell.

Scott, J. (1995) *Development Dilemmas in the European Community: Rethinking Regional Development Policy*. Buckingham: Open University Press.

Shonfield, A. (1959) *Modern Capitalism*. London: Oxford University Press.

Smith, A. (1983) *Theories of Nationalism*, 2nd edn. London: Duckworth.

Smith, A. (1991) *National Identity*. Harmondsworth: Penguin.

Smith, A. (1992) 'National identity and the idea of European unity'. *International Affairs*, 68(1), January: 55–76.

Smith, M. (1978) 'From the "Year of Europe" to a year of Carter: continuing patterns and problems in Euro–American relations'. *Journal of Common Market Studies*, 17(1): 26–44.

Smith, M. (1984) *Western Europe and the United States: the Uncertain Alliance*. London: George Allen and Unwin.

Smith, M. (1994a) 'Beyond the stable state? Foreign policy challenges and opportunities in the New Europe'. In Carlsnaes, W. and Smith, S. (eds) *European Foreign Policy: the EC and Changing Perspectives in Europe*. London: Sage, 21–44.

Smith, M. (1994b) 'The European Union, foreign economic policy and the changing world arena'. *Journal of European Public Policy*, 1(2), Autumn: 283–302.

Smith, M. (1996a) 'The European Union and a changing Europe: establishing the boundaries of order'. *Journal of Common Market Studies*, 34(1), March: 5–28.

Smith, M. (1996b) 'The European Union as an international actor'. In Richardson, J. (ed.) *European Union: Power and Policy-making*. London: Routledge, 247–62.

Smith, M. (1997a) 'Doing unto others . . . ? The European Union and concepts of negotiated order in Europe'. Inaugural Lecture. Loughborough University, February.

Smith, M. (1997b) 'Regions and regionalism'. In White, B., Little, R. and Smith, M. (eds) *Issues in World Politics*. London: Macmillan, 69–89.

Smith, M. (1997c) 'The Commission and external relations'. In Edwards, G. and Spence, D. (eds) *The European Commission*, 2nd edn. London: Cartermill.

Smith, M. (1997d) 'Competitive Cooperation and the European Union's emergence as a strategic partner for the United States in the world political economy'. Paper presented at the 5th Biennial Conference of the European Community Studies Association, Seattle, WA, May.

Smith, M. and Woolcock, S. (1993) *The United States and the European Community in a Transformed World*. London: Pinter, for the Royal Institute of International Affairs.

Smith, S. (1994c) 'Foreign policy theory and the new Europe'. In Carlsnaes, W. and Smith, S. (eds) *European Foreign Policy: the EC and Changing Perspectives in Europe*. London: Sage, 1–20.

Smith, S., Booth, K. and Zalewski, M. (eds) (1996) *International Theory: Positivism and Beyond*. Cambridge: Cambridge University Press.

Snyder, F. (1994) 'EMU – metaphor for European Union?: Institutions, rules and types of regulation'. In Ren, G. and Dehousse, F. (eds) *Europe After Maastricht*. München: Law Books in Europe.

Soskice, D. (1990) 'Wage determination: the changing role of institutions in advanced industrialised countries'. *Oxford Review of Economic Policy*, 6(4): 36–61.

Spero, J.E. and Hart, J. (1997) *The Politics of International Economic Relations*, 5th edn. London: Routledge.

Staniland, M. (1995) 'The United States and the external aviation policy of the EU'. *Journal of European Public Policy*, 2(1): 19–40.

Steinbruner, J. (ed.) (1989) *Restructuring American Foreign Policy*. Washington, DC: The Brookings Institute.

Stopford, J. and Strange, S. (1991) *Rival States, Rival Firms: Competition for World Market Shares*. Cambridge: Cambridge University Press.

Story, J. (ed.) (1993) *The New Europe: Politics, Government and Economy Since 1945*. Oxford: Blackwell.

Strange, S. (1988) *States and Markets: an Introduction to International Political Economy*. London: Pinter.

Strange, S. (1994) 'Rethinking structural change in the international political economy: states, firms and diplomacy'. In Stubbs, R. and Underhill, G. (eds) *Political Economy and the Changing Global Order*. London: Macmillan, 103–15.

Streeck, W. (1996) 'Neo-voluntarism: a new European social policy regime'. In Marks, G., Scharpf, F., Schmitter, P. and Streeck, W. (eds) *Governance in the European Union*. London: Sage.

Streeck, W. and Schmitter, P. (1991) 'From national corporatism to transnational pluralism: organised interests in the single European market'. *Politics and Society*, 19(2): 133–64.

Stubbs, R. and Underhill, G. (eds) (1994) *Political Economy and the Changing Global Order*. London: Macmillan.

Sun, J.M. and Pelkmans, J. (1995) 'Regulatory competition in the internal market'. *Journal of Common Market Studies*, 33(1): 67–89.

Tarrow, S. (1995) 'The Europeanisation of conflict: reflections from a social movement perspective'. *West European Politics*, 18: 223–51.

Tavlas, G.S. (1993) 'The "new" theory of optimum currency areas'. *The World Economy*, 16: 663–85.

Tavlas, G.S. (1994) 'The theory of monetary integration'. *Open Economies Review*, 5: 211–30.

Taylor, P.J. (ed.) (1993) *Political Geography of the Twentieth Century: A Global Analysis*. London: Belhaven Press.

Temple-Lang, J. (1996) 'Community constitutional law'. In Laffan, B. (ed.) *Constitution-Building in the European Union*. Dublin: Institute of European Affairs, 124–40.

Thatcher, M. (1988) Address to the College of Europe, Bruges, Belgium, 15 October.

Thompson, G. (1991) 'The evolution of the managed economy in Europe'. *Economy and Society*, 21(2): 125–51.

Thomsen, S. and Woolcock, S. (1993) *Direct Investment and European Integration: Competition Among Firms and Governments*. London: Pinter, for the Royal Institute of International Affairs.

Thurow, L. (1992) *Head to Head: the Coming Economic Battle Among Japan, Europe and America*. New York: Morrow.

Tilly, C. (1992) *Coercion, Capital and the European State, AD 990–1992*. Oxford: Blackwell.

Tilly, C. (ed.) (1975) *The Formation of National States in Western Europe*. Princeton: Princeton University Press.

Tinbergen, J. (1954) *International Economic Integration*. London: Macmillan.

Treverton, G. (1992a) *Germany, America and the Future of Europe*. Princeton: Princeton University Press.

Treverton, G. (ed.) (1992b) *The Shape of the New Europe*. New York: Council on Foreign Relations Press.

Tsoukalis, L. (1991) *The New European Economy*. Oxford: Oxford University Press.

Tsoukalis, L. (1996) 'Economic and monetary union: the primacy of high politics'. In Wallace H. and Wallace, W. (eds) *Policy-Making in the European Union*. Oxford: Oxford University Press.

Tsoukalis, L. (1997) *The New European Economy Revisited*. Oxford: Oxford University Press.

Tucker, R. and Hendrickson, D. (1992) *The Imperial Temptation: the New World Order and America's Purpose*. New York: Council on Foreign Relations Press.

van Ham, P. (1994) 'Can institutions hold Europe together?'. In Miall, H. (ed.) *Redefining Europe: New Patterns of Conflict and Cooperation*. London: Pinter, for the Royal Institute of International Affairs, 186–205.

Venables, A. (1985) 'Discussion of Geroski and Jacquemin'. *Economic Policy*, 1: 212–14.

Visser, J. and Hemerijck, A. (1997) *A Dutch Miracle: Job Growth, Welfare Reform and Corporatism in The Netherlands*. Amsterdam: Amsterdam University Press.

von Goll, G. (1982) 'The nine at the conference on security and cooperation in Europe'. In Allen, D., Rummel, R. and Wessels, W. (eds) *European Political Cooperation: Towards a Foreign Policy for Western Europe?* London: Butterworth, 60–9.

Waever, O. (1990) 'Three competing Europes: German, French, Russian'. *International Affairs*, 66(3): 153–70.

Waever, O. (1996) 'European security identities'. *Journal of Common Market Studies*, 34(1), March: 103–32.

Waever, O., Buzan, B., Kelstrup, M. and Lemaitre, P. (eds) (1993) *Identity, Migration and the New Security Agenda in Europe*. London: Pinter.

Wallace, H. (1971) 'The impact of the European communities on national policy-making'. *Government and Opposition*, 6, 520–38.

Wallace, H. (1992) 'What Europe for which Europeans?'. In Treverton, G. (ed.) *The Shape of the New Europe*. New York: Council on Foreign Relations Press, 15–34.

Wallace, H. (1993) 'European governance in turbulent times'. *Journal of Common Market Studies*, 31(3), September: 293–304.

Wallace, H. (1997) 'Pan-European integration: a real or imagined community?' *Government and Opposition*, 32(2), Spring: 215–33.

Wallace, H. and Wallace, W. (1996) *Policy-Making in the European Union*. Oxford: Oxford University Press.

Wallace, H. and Young, A.R. (1996) 'The single market: a new approach to policy'. In Wallace, H. and Wallace, W. (eds) *Policy-Making in the European Union*. Oxford: Oxford University Press.

Wallace, W. (ed.) (1990) *The Dynamics of European Integration*. London: Pinter.

Wandycz, P.S. (1992) *The Price of Freedom*. London: Routledge.

Webber, M. (1996) *The International Politics of Russia and the Former Soviet Union*. Manchester: Manchester University Press.

Weiler, J.H.H. (1993) 'Fin-de-siècle Europe'. Paper presented to the Third Biennial International Conference, European Community Studies Association, Washington, May.

Weiler, J.H.H. (1996) 'European neo-constitutionalism: in search of foundations for European constitutional order? *Political Studies*, 44: 517–33.

Weiler, J.H.H., Haltern, U.R. and Mayer, F.C. (1995) 'European democracy and its critique'. *West European Politics*: 4–39.

Weiner, A. (1994) 'Citizenship policy in a non-state: implications for theory'. Paper presented to the Second ECSA World Conference, Brussels, 5–6 May.

Welford, R. and Prescott, K. (1996) *European Business*, third edition. London: Pitman Publishing.

Wessels, W. (1991) 'The EC council: the community's decision-making center'. In Keohane, R.O. and Hoffmann, S. (eds) *The New European Community*. Boulder: Westview Press, 133–54.

Wilks, S. (1996) 'Regulatory compliance and capitalist diversity in Europe'. *Journal of European Public Policy*, 3(4): 536–59.

Willet, D. (1986) 'Exchange rate volatility, international trade, and resource allocation: a perspective on recent research'. *Journal of International Money and Finance*, 5: 101–12.

Williams, A.M. (1987) *The Western European Economy*. London: Routledge.

Williamson, J. (1975) 'The implications of monetary integration for peripheral areas'. In Vaizey, J. (ed.) *Economic Sovereignty and Regional Policy*. Dublin: Gill and Macmillan.

Williamson, J. (1983) *The Open Economy and the World Economy: A Textbook in International Economics*. New York: Basic Books.

Williamson, J. (1992) 'The rise and fall of political support for EMU'. In de la Dehesa, G., Giovannini, A., Guitan, M. and Portes, R. (eds) *The Monetary Future of Europe*. London: Centre for Economic Policy Research.

Wilson, T.M. and Smith, M.E. (1993) *Cultural Change and the New Europe: Perspectives on the European Community*. Boulder: Westview Press.

Woolcock, S. and Hodges, M. (1996) 'The European Union in the Uruguay Round'. In Wallace, H. and Wallace, W. (eds) *Policy-Making in the European Union*. Oxford: Oxford University Press, 301–24.

Young, O.R. (1972) 'The actors in world politics'. In Rosenau, J., Davis, V. and East, M. (eds) *The Analysis of International Politics*. New York: Free Press; London: Collier-Macmillan, 125–44.

Young, O.R. (1982) 'Regime dynamics: the rise and fall of international regimes'. *International Organization*, 36(2), Spring: 277–97.

Zucconi, M. (1996) 'The European Union in former Yugoslavia'. In Chayes, A. and Chayes, A. (eds) *Preventing Conflict in the Post-Communist World*. Washington, DC: The Brookings Institute, 237–78.

Index